Administrative Science & Politics in the USSR & the United States

Administrative Science & Politics in the USSR & the United States

Soviet Responses to American Management Techniques 1917–Present

JAMES CLAY THOMPSON
RICHARD F. VIDMER

PRAEGER

PRAEGER SPECIAL STUDIES • PRAEGER SCIENTIFIC
BERGIN & GARVEY PUBLISHERS, INC.

Library of Congress Cataloging in Publication Data

Thompson, James Clay, 1943-
  Administrative science and politics in the United States and the Soviet Union.

  Bergin & Garvey Publishers book.
  Bibliography:
  Includes index.
  1. Management—Soviet Union—History.
  2. Management—United States—History.
  3. Comparative management. I. Vidmer, Richard F.
  II. Title.
  HD70.S63T56   1982   658'.00947   82-12977
  ISBN 0-03-059633-5

Published in 1983 by Praeger Publishers
CBS Educational and Professional Publishing
A Division of CBS, Inc.
521 Fifth Avenue, New York, New York 10175 U.S.A.

0123456789   056   987654321

Printed in the United States of America

To Pat and Nancy

Table of Contents

Acknowledgments

Intellectually, the major influence on the arguments presented in this work can be found in Zbigniew Brzezinski and Samuel Huntington's *Political Power: USA/USSR*. Presupposing that the strengths and weaknesses determine the wisdom or folly of a state's diplomacy, economic policy, science, and the like, Brzezinski and Huntington sought to compare and contrast the two superpowers along common macro-political dimensions: (1) What are the principal similarities and differences between the Soviet and American political systems? (2) What are the strengths and weaknesses of each system? (3) Are the two systems becoming more alike or less so? By contrast, our purposes are more modest. Starting from the *presumption* that the bureaucratic phenomenon exists irrespective of sociopolitical system, we seek to identify the extent to which the conceptual language and analytical tools of administrative science in the two countries have, in fact, converged. Our findings indicate that despite major efforts to emulate *select* aspects of the American discipline, Soviet approaches maintain distinctive elements that are unlikely to disappear in the foreseeable future.

Our interest in comparing Soviet and American developments in administrative science has been stimulated and advanced by analysts studying the USSR—Alfred Meyer, Erik Hoffmann, Paul Cocks, Michael Ellman, Robert Miller, Donald Schwartz, and many others. Similarly, students of contemporary organization theory in the United States—James D. Thompson, Herbert Simon, James March, Michael Cohen, Todd LaPorte, Graham T. Allison, Donald Schon, and many others—have supplied many useful ideas for this work.

There are also certain institutions to which we are deeply indebted. First and foremost, the Department of Political Science at the University of Michigan, where we both received graduate degrees, provided a firm grounding in Soviet studies as well as organization theory. There, general ideas on Soviet developments were augmented by fruitful discussions with colleagues at the Center for Russian and East European Studies, William Zimmerman, Zvi Gitelman, and William Ballis. Similarly, one of us (Vidmer) remains deeply indebted to the International Research and Exchanges Board for the opportunity to participate in a six-month exchange visit to the Soviet Union where materials invaluable for this work were gathered. The Institute for

Public Policy Studies at Michigan, with its resources of both people and research material, was also a major source for developments in organizational behavior, and we profited in untold ways from conversations with Thomas Anton, Larry Mohr, Pat Crecine and others. The Department of Def—, where Thompson spent two years on a sabbatical, was also helpful, although, of course, all the views and opinions contained herein are those of the authors.

A number of knowledgeable people in both countries, including the following, allowed us to interview them in the places and on the dates noted, either in person or by telephone, and we would like to thank them for the special insights and information they were able to provide: John Austin (21 June 1977); Murray Fishbach (Ann Arbor, Mich., 8 April 1977); Madis Khabakuk (Tallinn Polytechnical Institute, 22 April 1976); Vadim Marshev (MGU Management Center, Moscow, 28 June 1976); Vadim Ivanovich Marshev (Center of Management Problems, MGU Management Center, Moscow, 12 July 1976); G. K. Popov (MGU Management Center, Moscow, 7 June 1976); L. V. Savel'ev (Tallinn, Estonian SSR, 27 April 1976); Thomas Schreiber (University of Michigan Graduate School of Business, Ann Arbor, Mich.); and Myron Uretsky (21 June 1977).

Finally, we would like to thank Maggie Davis, Betty Brown, Jackie Hinson and Cynthia Stubbs, who helped transform scribbles into sentences. Linda Harris provided the bibliography. Polly Clark assisted with the index. Our editors—Jim Bergin and Jenna Schulman—have shown patience and tolerance as they suffered lengthy delays while one emergency or another in the bureaucracy or on Capitol Hill slowed down our progress. As a final note, much of Chapter 8 appeared in a somewhat different form in *Slavic Review*, 40 (Fall 1981), pp. 404–22, and appears here with the editors' permission. All the mistakes that remain are, of course, ours.

We dedicate this book to our wives, Pat Thompson and Nancy Vidmer, who, in the sometimes agony of trying to work together, helped keep us friends and offered their moral support and critical comments.

JCT
RFV

Author's Note

Leonid Brezhnev died shortly after this book was put into page proofs. We do not believe, however, that his death changes our conclusions. Soviet administrative science will remain to be in flux as tensions within the Soviet economy continue. The "Americanizers" in the Soviet administrative science community may, however, have more difficulty gaining access for their views, since much of that access had been provided through family and other ties with the Brezhnev-Kosygin leadership that is now gone.

JCT
RFV

1

Introduction

. . .[A] government consists of a conglomerate of semi-feudal, loosely allied organizations, each with a substantial life of its own. . . . Thus government behavior relevant to any important problem reflects the independent output of several organizations, partially coordinated by government leaders. Government leaders can substantially disturb, but not substantially control, the behaviors of these organizations.

—Graham T. Allison

The national economy of the USSR consists of a huge number of diverse and yet closely connected branches of industry. This complex system . . . is constantly expanding and developing. Qualitatively new means of labour are evolved. New technological processes are introduced. The relations between the various branches of industry change, as does the extent of their dependence on each other. All this calls for thorough scientific research into the processes of production management, as a special field of human activity.

—D. Gvishiani

The cold war's gradual tranformation, from intense confrontation between the United States and the Soviet Union in the period immediately after World War II to a period of relations known as détente and then the abrupt change back into tension following the Soviet invasion of Afghanistan, has been accompanied in each country by images of the other's society, leadership, and organization that have grown in sophistication. Despite Soviet actions in Afghanistan, senior American policy-makers no longer envision a monolithic, messianic force single mindedly bent on the destruction of capitalist nations and domination of the world international political system. Rather, the Soviet Union is seen as a society that has "structural and managerial weaknesses" and problems "emerging in many of the basic factors that have produced economic growth in the past."[1] In a like manner, Soviet leaders

1

are now finding "sober minded, realistic" leaders in the United States[2] The growing symmetry of attitudes and perceptions has led to the recognition that there are common features in the two socioeconomic systems; and this recognition of a modicum of commonality has prompted serious comparative analysis of Soviet and American society.[3] Although the notion that the two societies will eventually converge holds little appeal to scholars from either the Soviet Union or the United States, the proposition that each has attempted to learn from the other and to adapt certain ideas, techniques, practices, or procedures has considerable acceptance. Much of Soviet behavior in the 1960s, for example, has been characterized as an attempt to adopt certain American modes in order to compete more effectively.[4] In the 1970s, American specialists exchanged scientific, medical, and engineering data in a wide variety of areas with their counterparts in the Soviet Union. The highlight of the scientific data exchange undoubtedly was the link-up in space between Soviet cosmonauts and American astronauts in 1975.

Such emulation extends to more than scientific, medical, and engineering data. In the Soviet Union, administrative theorists have traditionally looked westward (primarily to the United States) for useful techniques and relevant ideas related to the management of complex bureaucracies. This looking westward began with Lenin and continues today. Indeed, bureaucratic phenomena are found in all societies and the response of modern industrial states to them has been remarkably similar—the objective of both socialist and capitalist societies in the twentieth century has been "to integrate complexity and manage changes through advances in organization and technology."[5] As bureaucracies—both governmental and industrial—have grown to become the dominant institutions of modern societies, the capacity to manage these large-scale production and public-sector organizations has become crucial to political leadership in coping with complex problems. At the core of politics in the late twentieth century is the capacity of political leaders to cope with increasing complexity. The upheavals in Poland, beginning in the summer of 1980 and continuing through 1982, and the inability of American leaders to find a solution to seemingly endless inflation and simultaneous economic stagnation in the 1970s and 1980s serve as reminders of the severe nature of the kinds of problems with which political leadership must deal. Administrative science is therefore of extreme importance. This is so because administrative science is that body of knowledge, techniques, and practices that are concerned with the structure, management, and operations of complex governmental (or public, nonmarket) and industrial (or market) systems.

The transformation of the work of politics in industrial societies in the last half of the twentieth century—from regulating conflict within society to managing the bureaucratic state (whether it be Eastern or Western, socialist or capitalist, authoritarian or pluralistic) and from channeling conflict within society to bureaucraticaly solving problems—has only recently been recognized and poses vexing problems for managers as well as politicians. In the United States, it is increasingly suggested that problems are simply too complex to manage and that solutions generated for one set of problems often create more difficulties than they relieve. Voters in the United States blame politicians rather than managers for the current situation, reflecting the fact that this transformation of politics is only dimly perceived by those most affected. In the Soviet Union, it is not acceptable to socialist ideology to admit that problems may not be solved. This doctrinal difficulty poses a severe challenge to the Soviet managers, as the Soviet Union moves into a period of labor, energy, and capital shortages.

Inseparability of Administrative Science and Politics

This study is therefore concerned with administrative science and with politics. The two are seen as inseparable, although there is a lingering (but dying) tradition that has insisted that politics and administration must be separated.[6] According to the older tradition, politics is the art of deciding who gets what and how they get it (or, in the jargon of political science, the authoritative allocation of values) and is characterized by rough-and-tumble exchanges, bargains, backscratching, logrolling, deceit, and so on. Administration, in contrast, is said to be characterized by professional managers, whose only concern is with the effective and efficient implementation of policy. It is, of course, obvious that different definitions of "effective and efficient" by the different individuals and groups affected by the implementation of programs render moot the idea that administration can be nonpartisan, especially in a plural society but also in a highly centralized one. Nevertheless, the separation of "politics" (and the connotation that politics is somehow inherently evil and to be avoided) and administration (and the connotation that it is somehow "above politics") has introduced a false dichotomy into administrative science and has befuddled much of the writing about it. If one desires to study complex, industrial, and bureaucratic societies, one must study both politics and administration. We shall elaborate on this point in Chapter 4.

We intend to compare and contrast Soviet and American approaches to administrative theory and, in particular, to identify how and where specialists in the USSR have purposively adopted U.S. ideas. We do not intend to engage in a comprehensive analysis of all the literature of administrative science, since that task is not of central concern here and, indeed, as we indicate in Chapter 2, much of the literature of administrative science is so seriously flawed that it has taken many years of research to move away from it. We are more concerned with the identification of conceptual frameworks, theoretical problems posed by those frameworks, and the process of transnational diffusion from the United States into the Soviet Union. To do that, we will identify major schools of administrative science that have developed in the United States and observe how some of the ideas of these schools have been imported into the Soviet Union without serious modification, whereas others have been subject to serious alterations and still others have not been introduced at all. Given that managing large-scale industrial and governmental systems may be the central problem of politics in the 1980s and 1990s, analysis of the organizing constructs and conceptual lenses is of major importance since those constructs and lenses shape and direct (and perhaps distort) the attention of managers in policy making, program development, and program evaluation—the three steps of the policy process. As we compare perspectives in administrative science, we will be able to increase our understanding of how managers in both countries comprehend opportunities and limitations in the situations confronting them.

In our view, each of the two countries' perspectives has certain advantages and limitations. Ideology imposes constraints on what solutions are appropriate or possible. But we do not intend to engage in a normative discussion of the alleged "superiority" of the American or Soviet approach to administrative science. That judgment is best left to the reader. We do intend, however, to point out the strengths and limitations in each approach. The Soviet approach, for example, can be said to have difficulties with the idea that there may be multiple solutions, all of which could be described as adequate, to a problem. By this we mean that the sophisticated mathematical approaches may not yield the "one best way" to solve a managerial problem—indeed, the solution yielded may be inappropriate on other grounds. At the same time, the American view that the common good is advanced in a highly plural society by millions of decisions made by millions of decision makers may be faulty. By this we mean that it is not evident that people over the long run will act in their own self-interest, since it is inherently impossible to know what long-range self-interest is. Indeed, millions of short-range decisions may lead to massive long-term problems not easily amenable to solution in a highly plural system.

MAJOR ISSUES

We do intend to focus on three major issues:[7]

1. What are the principal similarities and differences between admiinistrative science in the United States and in the Soviet Union?

2. What are the distinctive traits of theoretical analysis in each country?

3. Is administrative science in the two countries becoming more similar or is it evolving in divergent paths?

SECONDARY ISSUES

These questions lead to numerous secondary issues, which we shall also explore. Is there a relationship between doctrine and administrative science?

How and in what manner do ideological biases restrict inquiry or prescribe certain acceptable mode and languages of inquiry? Can important issues and problems be identified that are purposely ignored in either or both countries? What have been the political consequences for the Soviet Union of emulation of capitalist techniques? How have certain domestic groups within the Soviet Union reacted to American ideas? Are there identifiable schools of administrative science in each country, which compete or overlap with other schools, or remain isolated from one another? How has the diffusion of knowledge about administration influenced the capacity of specialists in the USSR to define goals and learn new approaches to their subject matter? On what basis have new ideas been outside the bounds of "acceptable" theoretical work in each country? Is there a distinctive socialist or capitalist management science or are major concepts interwoven into both?

Our choice of topics for comparative analysis is designed to help answer these questions. In the first chapters we will deal with the emergence of administrative science, first in the United States and then in the Soviet Union. Of major importance is the fact that administrative science emerged encumbered with a profound intellectual problem—it began as a search for better means of control of processes within the bureaucracy. This bias has had severe repercussions. Another major point is the fact that administrative science first emerged in the United States; this led to the importation of many capitalist ideas into the USSR. Despite ideological and doctrinal incompatibility of their respective social contexts, Frederick Taylor (with *Principles of Scientific Management*) and Henry Ford (with his assembly line) influenced Soviet administrative specialists immensely. Even Stalin's destruction of scientific inquiry in the 1930s did not end Soviet fascination with and emulation of Western, and particularly American, techniques.

Yet in the period after World War II, which will be the subject of Chapters 4–7, Soviet administrative science remained buried in its "traditional hermetic exercises" far removed from American thinking. American specialists were dealing with an explosion of new approaches, concepts, and ideas, ranging from new ways of viewing organizations to techniques that promised to deliver even better methods of control. American approaches included operations research, cybernetics, systems theories, network analysis, and a host of quantitative methods. World War II had had a profound impact on American thinking, and most leaders of American business and government from the close of the conflict to the early 1980s were profoundly influenced by it. In 1960, for example, it was widely believed that American administrative science and economics had reached the point where the central function of government was to "fine tune" the ever-growing productivity of American industry. Robert McNamara, president of Ford Motor Company in 1960, was named secretary of defense by President Kennedy. He had first distinguished himself in application of modern administrative science to military problems during World War II and attempted to bring similar techniques into government.[8]

For the Soviet Union, it would require Khruschchev's "agonizing reappraisal" of the past at the Twentieth Party Congress in 1956 before the doors to change were opened and quantitative techniques could be adapted from the American experience. In fact, after 1956, the American model became in many ways a role model and was consciously utilized to promote developments in Soviet administrative science that were similar to those in American administrative thought. "Americanization" continues to represent a strong current in Soviet thinking, despite formidable internal constraints to the adoption process and the turn of events in relations between the countries following the Soviet intervention in Afghanistan.

In the final chapters of the book, we review the state of the art as it exists in the Soviet Union with reference to principal American views and approaches. We identify and examine a jungle of competing viewpoints, which exists in both countries. This jungle is full of alternative conceptual tools, levels of analysis, and approaches. Almost by accident and certainly against the wishes of many in the Soviet Union, several specialists have recreated the disarray and acrimony extant in American administrative science, and we will review the major Soviet schools, their standard bearers, and important journals. In our conclusion, we speculate on the future paths of development in both countries and the possibility of convergence, however slight.

Interdisciplinary Nature of the Field

Before we begin, the reader needs to know that there is a massive literature in administrative science, enriched by important contributions from psychology, social psychology, economics, sociology, business administration, political science, mathematics and statistics, systems engineering, and even history. Perhaps the major characteristic of this mass is one that we have already identified: it is a jungle with no clear paths. Indeed, the theoretical angles and levels of analysis are so divergent that we make no pretense at untangling this thicket. We thus limit our study to middle-range approaches to administrative phenomena. Except to illustrate the emergence of administrative science in the early twentieth century, we will ignore microanalytical perspectives, which tend to focus on (1) the individual and the workplace; or (2) operations research and other mathematical approaches, which concentrate on such narow problems as how to efficiently organize a supply line. At the same time we will avoid macrolevel analyses of the social order, with their inherent normative biases.

By restricting our study to the middle ranges—the organizational level of analysis—we hope to accomplish several things. Doctrinal stereotypes on both sides can and will be avoided since, as already noted, we simply are not interested in confirming a view that one or the other society provides some alleged optimal framework for managing large, complex organizations. By focusing on common facets of organizational behavior and organizational structure, we intend to facilitate comparative analysis.

We begin our analysis with the observation that a similar notion of management is held in both the United States and the Soviet Union. The Russian word *upravlenie* can refer to management, administration, control, steering, cybernetic control, industrial management, public administration, or regulation, depending upon context or nuance.[9] In each case, "*upravlenie*" is the correct term, since it always refers to purposive, goal-oriented activity designed to raise the status of an object in question to a more progressive state. Western conceptions of organizations, at least until recently (with the introduction of the apurposive or garbage-can approach and the idea that organizations are in fact organized anarchies), are strikingly similar—purposiveness, goal specificity, and rationality are considered defining traits. It is from the common vantage point of the management of large, complex organizations in the United States and the Soviet Union that our study proceeds.

2

The Emergence of Administrative Science

> *Now one of the very first requirements for a man who is fit to handle pig iron is that he shall be so stupid and so phlegmatic that he more nearly resembles in his mental make-up the ox than any other type....[and] is unable to understand the real science of doing this class of work....[H]e must consequently be trained by a man more intelligent than himself into the habit of working in accordance with the laws of this science before he can be successful.*
>
> —Frederick Winslow Taylor

> *[T]he humane treatment of employees...would lead to the weakening of the authority of the "boss" and to the breaking down of discipline in the shop. To...[the men surrounding Henry, Ford] the sole end of industry was production and profits, and the one sure way of getting these things out of labor was to curse it, threaten it, drive it, insult it, humiliate it, and discharge it on the slightest provocation; in short—to use a phrase much on the lips of such men—"put the fear of God in labor." And they were always thinking of themselves as the little gods who were to be feared.*
>
> —Samuel Marquis

Introduction

In the previous chapter we defined administrative science and offered an overview of the book. In this chapter, we will trace the emergence of administrative science by examining the writings and works of major writers and industrialists. Although Karl Marx and Max Weber wrote extensively about bureaucracy, administrative science can be said to have truly begun with the writings of Frederick Winslow Taylor and the work of Henry Ford.

After a discussion of Taylor and Ford, we shall examine the work of Luther Gulick, who gave the theoretical underpinnings to the rationalization of the administrative structure. Finally, we will review the contributions to administrative science made by those who may broadly be categorized as members of the human-relations school. Between 1880 and the 1930s, administrative science emerged. Its writings and works have shaped modern management, yet much that was done was based on false assumptions and faulty beliefs. It is our view that the way in which administrative science developed is related to the serious problems of modern industrial societies.

Early Work

In the last quarter of the twentieth century, when management is in the era of automation, data and word processing, the computer, and other sophisticated devices and techniques for control, it is difficult to understand a world in which the notion of the rational control of large-scale systems did not exist. But in the middle of the nineteenth century, barely over a hundred years ago, no central body of thought existed on dealing with the new form of industrial organization that had emerged in England and spread throughout Europe, North America, and the rest of the world. Industrial bureaucracy was playing an increasingly important role in those societies; for many, that role disrupted a way of life that had hardly changed for centuries. In Europe, the writings of Karl Marx and the actions of the Luddites, who burned factories, represented the feelings of many. Marx wrote numerous tracts denouncing bureaucracy as the agent of the ruling classes. Bureaucrats, wrote Marx (foreshadowing current criticism), were incompetent and petty. It was the task of its victims—the workers and peasants—to throw off their shackles, to overthrow the existing order, and to establish a classless society in which bureaucracy would fade away.[1]

In the later part of the nineteenth century, Max Weber also was studying the new form of organization. Weber attempted to describe what was different about bureaucracy as a form of organization from organizations that preceded bureaucracy. Weber's descriptive analysis—in contrast to Karl Marx's—was not based on an antibureaucratic stance. Rather, Weber argued that bureaucracy had become the dominant form of organization because of its advantages as a form of organization. Bureaucracy differed from earlier forms (which Weber labeled "charismatic" and "traditional") in that it operated on the basis of regularized, impersonal, and legal procedures and was characterized by hierarchy, specialization, advancement by merit, a separation of official funds from the personal monies of people employed by the organization, and differential power of individuals based upon position in the hierarchy.[2]

Both Marx and Weber were concerned with the impact of industrial bureaucracy on society. For Marx, bureaucracy caused the dehumanization of workers and managers alike, and the new system therefore had to be destroyed. (As we shall see, Lenin would regard the problem in an entirely different light.) For Weber, bureaucracy was inherently effective and efficient, compared to its predecessors. And although the Weberian idea that hierarchy is efficient has come under attack (an organization may be so hierarchical and multilayered that it becomes inefficient), Weber's analysis marks him as the father of organization theory.[3]

In Europe, the relationship between industrial bureaucracy and society was questioned because bureaucracy there was displacing an earlier and well-established pattern of economic and political activity. In America, however, there was very little debate as to the appropriateness of industrial bureaucracy. Since unfettered capitalism was a "given" in the United States and would not seriously be questioned until well into the twentieth century, industrial bureaucracy was accepted and encouraged. The central problem was that as industrial organizations grew beyond the family enterprise and began to employ several hundreds or thousands of workers, instead of dozens or a few hundred, the traditional system of management—based on formal and informal ties between owners and their workers—had to give way. Personal relationships disappeared. A different kind of management, able to cope with large numbers of workers in huge industrial enterprises like steel mills, was needed. It is at this point that we come to Frederick Winslow Taylor and Henry Ford.

Frederick Winslow Taylor and Scientific Management

There is an unfortunate tendency in the literature of professional academia to dismiss social science done prior to the development of behaviorism. This has been disastrous for the understanding of modern bureaucracy. In our view, Frederick Winslow Taylor's *Principles of Scientific Management*,[4] first published in 1911, is as seminal a work as March and Simon's *Organizations* and Cyert and March's *Behavioral Theory of the Firm*.[5] As such, Taylor's *Principles* should be read carefully by contemporary students of management. Indeed, it is still used as a primer in many countries.[6] In the current debate over the problem of rebuilding the industrial base of the United States to make it more competitive with other industrial nations, it is interesting to note that many of these competitor nations are those that have taken Taylor seriously.[7]

Frederick W. Taylor was a most unusual person. Born of wealthy Philadelphia parents who were members of the establishment, Taylor went to Exeter in preparation for a Harvard education. Like other members of the

American elite, he had traveled widely in Europe and spoke both German and French.[8] But Taylor decided not to go to Harvard, and instead went to work as a pattern maker and machinist at an industrial firm. A common laborer, he was also a member of the Philadelphia Cricket Club. The latter background allowed him to explore his theories of management as he saw it at the level of the worker, since he, or members of his family, were frequently friends of the owners. Given Taylor's background, that his writings were favorable to the owners—although couched in idealistic terms of helping the average employee as well as management—is not surprising. In his introduction to *The Principles of Scientific Management*, he quoted President Theodore Roosevelt as saying that "The conservation of our national resources is only preliminary to the larger question of national efficiency."[9]

Thus Taylor presents his magnum opus in idealistic terms. The practical consequences of his work as applied by Henry Ford and other American industrialists were distinctly nonidealistic, but Taylor did not live to be concerned about this; he died in 1915, four years after *The Principles of Scientific Management* was published. Henry Ford did not have the assembly line, with all its attendant horrors for the worker, fully running until the year Taylor died. But we will quote Taylor at some length to illustrate the impact of his work. He published *Principles of Scientific Management* for the following reasons:

> *First.* To point out, through a series of simple illustrations, the great loss which the country is suffering through the inefficiency in almost all of our daily acts.
> *Second.* To try to convince the reader that the remedy for this inefficiency lies in systematic management, rather than searching for some unusual or extraordinary man.
> *Third.* To prove that the best management is a true science, resting upon clearly defined laws, rules, and principles, as a foundation. And further to show that the fundamental principles of scientific management are applicable to all kinds of human activities, from the simplest individual acts to the work of our great corporations, which call for the most elaborate cooperation. And, briefly, through a series of illustrations, to convince the reader that whenever these principles are correctly applied, results must follow which are truly outstanding.[10]

As a simple illustration of scientific management, Taylor discussed the fact that at Bethlehem Steel, where he was employed at the time, all workers used the same size of shovel regardless of the material that was being shoveled. Taylor's question—obvious to the late-twentieth-century reader—was whether workers could work more efficiently using different-sized shovels to move different materials. Taylor found that the ideal limit for a load on a shovel was 21 pounds: more weight would tire the workers out quickly and lead to lost efficiency, less weight would lead to an unnecessary number of movements. Taylor then had shovels of different sizes brought to the workplace and trained the workers to use one shovel to move one material, another shovel for a second material, still another shovel for a third material, and so on. By employing time-and-motion studies, Taylor found the optimal level at which workers could shovel material, and that optimal level was far in excess of what the workers had previously been shoveling.

This example may seem trivial to the modern reader, but it contains the core of the method Taylor used to change the workplace, the relationship of workers to their work, and the rate of work in American industry and in the industries of many countries thereafter. The first part of the core has to do with the fact that prior to Taylor and time-and-motion studies, workers had been expected to bring their own tools to the workplace or, with some exceptions, to use any tool they felt like using. Over centuries, various families or groups had developed tools that reflected personal, family, or group tastes. These tools were often elaborately decorated and passed on from generation to generation. Taylor found that these tools were not appropriate to the tasks required, and he concluded that personal tools would have to be replaced by *standardized* tools provided by management and *designed for the task*, no matter how simple the task. The second part of Taylorism involved the use of time-and-motion studies to determine the most efficient way to do a job. In a time-and-motion study, a manager timed how long it took an employee to do a job and then carefully eliminated wasted motion, by (1) changing the motions of the worker, (2) changing the tools supplied to the worker, (3) changing the positions of the supplies around the worker, or (4) dividing and specializing the task. The third part of Taylor's method involved paying the workers who could work at the new rate a bonus. Those who could not work at the new rate either were reassigned to a different task at their previous rate or were simply discharged.

Taylorism Illustrated

Perhaps the best way to illustrate the impact of Taylorism in practical terms is with a lengthy example. We shall quote the example,[11] interrupting with commentary where appropriate.

While Taylor was at Bethlehem Steel, he was confronted in 1898 with the problem of improving the rate at which a gang of men were loading pig iron into railroad cars (since there were then no magnetic cranes, the work was done by hand).

The first illustration is that of handling pig iron, and this work has been chosen because it is typical of perhaps the crudest and most elementary form of labor which is performed by man. This work is done by men with no other implements than their hands. The pig iron handler stoops down, picks up a pig weighing about 92 pounds, walks for a few feet or yards and then drops it on to the ground or upon a pile. This work is so crude and elementary in its nature that the writer firmly believes that it would be possible to train an intelligent gorilla so as to become a more efficient pig-iron handler than any man can be. Yet it will be shown that the science of handling pig iron is so great and amounts to so much that it is impossible for the man who is best suited to this type of work to understand the principles of this ......ce, or even to work in accordance with these principles without the aid of a man better educated than he is. And the further illustrations to be given will make it clear that in almost all of the mechanic arts the science which underlies each workman's act is so great and amounts to so much that the workman who is best suited actually to do the work is incapable (either through the lack of education or through insufficient mental capacity) of understanding this science. This is announced as a general principle, the truth of which will become apparent as one illustration after another is given.

Commentary: The general principle that the worker is too stupid to understand the nature of his work is firmly embedded in administrative science. In the United States, or so goes the ideology undergirding Taylor's work, management—which is better educated and is drawn from superior social classes—is the group equipped to make important decisions and, because the worker cannot know better, those decisions should not be questioned. Taylorism was imported into the Soviet Union virtually without change. The Soviet working class also cannot understand its own best interests and must be guided by the vanguard of the proletariat—the elite, who are better educated and thus better able to grasp the nature of the problem. The elitism that shaped early administrative science is readily apparent, and thus it should not be surprising that the practical applications of Taylorism, such as in Henry Ford's automobile assembly plants, was one of the primary causes of the growth of labor unions. And if the Polish labor unrest in 1980–1983 (as well as in 1956 and 1970) holds any lesson for administrative science in centrally planned economies, it is that Taylorism brings out similar resentments in both socialist and capitalist workers.

Let us return to Taylor's narrative.

One of the first pieces of work undertaken by us, when the writer started to introduce scientific management into the Bethlehem Steel Company, was to handle pig iron on task work. The opening of the Spanish War [in 1898] found some 80,000 tons of pig iron placed in small piles on an open field adjoining the works. Prices for pig iron had been so low that it could not be sold for a profit, and it had therefore been stored. With the opening of the Spanish War the price of pig iron rose, and this large accumulation of pig iron was sold. This gave us a good opportunity to show the workmen, as well as the owners and managers of the works, on a fairly large scale the advantages of task work over the old-fashioned day work and piece work, in doing a very elementary class of work.

The Bethlehem Steel Company had five blast furnaces, the product of which had been handled by a pig-iron gang for many years. This gang, at this time, consisted of about 75 men. They were good, average pig-iron handlers, were under an excellent foreman who himself had been a pig-iron handler, and the work was done, on the whole, about as fast and cheaply as it was anywhere at that time.

A railroad switch was run out into the field, right along the edge of the piles of pig iron. An inclined plank was placed against the side of a car, and each man picked up from his pile a pig of iron weighing about 92 pounds, walked up the inclined plank and dropped it on the end of the car.

We found that this gang were loading on the average about 12½ long tons per man per day. We were surprised to find, after studying the matter, that a first-class pig-iron handler ought to handle between 47 and 48 long tons per day, instead of 12½ tons. This task seemed to us so very large that we were obligated to go over our work several times before we were absolutely sure that we were right. Once we were sure, however, that 47 tons was a proper day's work for a first-class pig-iron handler, the task which faced us as managers under the modern scientific plan was clearly before us. It was our duty to see that the 80,000 tons of pig iron was loaded on to the cars at the rate of 47 tons per man per day, in place of 12½ tons, at which rate the work was then being done. And it was further our duty to see that this work was done without bringing on a strike among the men, and to see that the men were happier and better contented when loading at the new rate of 47 tons than they were when loading at the old rate of 12½ tons.

Commentary: Taylor (and Lenin) wrote and acted in the spirit of rationalism. The basic tenet of rationalism was that once the basic, irreducible "facts" of a matter were understood, it was contrary to scientific truth to do anything except that which was demanded by the "facts." Thus when Taylor found that the men could load at a rate approximately four times the rate at which they were then working, it became his absolute duty to ensure that the men under his command would work at the rate his scientific facts revealed. And furthermore, who could argue with scientific facts? The Newtonian view of the world—it is as ordered as a Swiss watch ticking away—is clearly exhibited here. This notion, that there exists a central body of rules by which the world operates and that those rules offer an ordered universe in a steady state, was central to the time of Taylor. The task was to discover and exploit those rules through the application of the scientific method. The notion of a world subject to rational control—and it is a notion at best—is the driving force of Taylorism and all of its lineal descendants such as operations research, planned-programming-budgeting-systems (PPBS), management-by-objective (MBO), zero-based budgeting (ZBB), and many of the other late twentieth century management techniques which come and go as fads. These techniques quickly pall because they suffer from a central problem, which can be traced back to Taylor's *Principles:* the notion that complex socioeconomic and political difficulties are amenable to rational (e.g., scientific) solutions. Despite this central, and fatal, problem, the popularity of these fads continues, and both American and Soviet administrative science have been strongly influenced by them. Only in the last few years have some American theorists begun to make inroads, as they develop a body of knowledge not dependent upon a central clear assumption that complex problems are amenable to rational solutions. What Einstein, Bohr, and Heisenberg did to physics when they introduced relativity, quantum mechanics, and the principle of uncertainty, has only, decades later, begun to be introduced into the literature of management and administrative science.[12]

We now return to Taylor.

Our first step was the scientific selection of the workman. In dealing with workmen under this type of management, it is an inflexible rule to talk to and deal with only one man at a time, since each workman has his own special abilities and limitations, and since we are not dealing with men in masses, but are trying to develop each individual man to his highest state of efficiency and prosperity.

Commentary: Despite the humanitarian aspect of "developing each man to his highest state of efficiency and prosperity," the bias toward leadership (and indeed tight and absolute direction) of the individual worker (who, as we have seen, is in reality no more than an intelligent gorilla) by those who "know better" is clear. Masses of men must not be dealt with, and all unions, by implication, must be opposed, suppressed, or co-opted. The individual working man should trust the intentions of the man who knows more than he does since that man frequently tells the workers that what he is trying to do is in their interests. Thus management, in both capitalist and socialist societies—one in the form of corporate leaders and the other in the form of party leaders—has the best interests of the workers at heart. Or so went the argument from Frederick Taylor and Lenin.

Let us return once again to the narrative.

Our first step was to find the proper workman to begin with. We therefore carefully watched and studied these 75 men for three or four *days, at the end of which time we had picked out four men who appeared to be physically able to handle pig iron at the rate of 47 tons per day. A careful study was made of each of these men. We looked up their history as far back as practicable and thorough inquiries were made as to the character, habits, and the ambition of each of them. Finally, we selected one among the four as the most likely man to start with. He was a little Pennsylvania Dutchman who had been observed to trot back home for a mile or so after his work in the evening about as fresh as he was when he came trotting down to work in the morning. We found that upon wages of $1.15 a day he had succeeded in buying a small plot of ground, and that he was engaged in putting up the walls of a little house for himself in the morning before starting to work and at night after leaving. He also had the reputation of being exceedingly "close," that is, of placing a very high value on a dollar. As one man whom we talked to about him said, "A penny looks about the size of a cart-wheel to him." This man we will call Schmidt.*

The task before us, then, narrowed itself down to getting Schmidt to handle 47 tons of pig iron per day and making him glad to do it...

Commentary: Two underlying themes are stated and restated by Taylor. They are (1) the organization of work through the determination of the "one best way" and (2) the adoption of certain procedures such that the work can be so controlled as to provide no escape from the direction of a manager who has already determined the "one best way." Management is thus for the purpose of control. This is the central dilemma facing administrative science both as it has emerged in the United States and as it has been emulated in the Soviet Union. Ever since Taylor wrote about Schmidt and the loading of pig iron, the literature of administrative science has been overwhelmed by the search for ever more efficient and effective *management control systems*. Little examination of underlying assumptions (such as that there really is only "one best way") appears to have been accomplished. Instead, there has been a straightforward movement toward control systems such as PPBS, MBO, ZBB, and the like. As Landau and Stout have remarked, "That these have not as a group produced striking successes, that many of them show a sustained record of failure, has not served to diminish either the expected utility or the normative appeal of the concept. Enthusiasm remains high, efforts to secure foolproof management control systems continue unabated, promising to perpetuate what must now appear as an unending cycle of vaunted introduction and veiled discard."[13] Frederick Winslow Taylor sent administrative science on a century-long search for the will-o'-the-wisp of the perfect control system. Only in the last few years has this effort begun to be questioned.

This last passage also adds more evidence to the normative values that Taylor and his system rest upon. Taylor argued that his discoveries were free of value judgments, yet the worker is described as a gorilla, or, as in the quote at the beginning of the chapter, an ox. Clearly, a high degree of Social Darwinism is exhibited here. Social Darwinism was a body of thought that gained great popularity in the late nineteenth century. In an obvious misunderstanding of the theory of evolution (or a convenient recasting of it into the social setting), Social Darwinists claimed that those who are "fit" in any society are those who materially advance. Failure to so advance is due to the fact that the individual is flawed. Inherited money, family station, educational advantages, parental occupation, and so on have nothing to do with success. The belief that people have only themselves to blame if they have difficulties, however false, has been one of the sustaining forces in American social and political thought.[14]

We will now return to Taylor's narrative, noting that in the following conversation, the dialect is exactly as printed in *The Principles of Scientific Management.*

> *This was done as follows. Schmidt was called out from among the gang of pig-iron handlers and talked to somewhat in this way:*
> *"Schmidt, are you a high priced man?"*
> *"Vell, I don't know what you mean."*
> *"Oh yes, you do. What I want to know is whether you are a high-priced man or not."*
> *"Vell, Idon't know what you mean."*
> *"Oh, come now, you answer my questions. What I want to know is whether you are a high-priced man or one of these cheap fellows here. What I want to find out is whether you want to earn $1.85 a day or whether you are satisfied with $1.15, just the same as all those cheap fellows are getting."*
> *"Did I vant $1.85 a day? Vas dot a high-priced man? Vell, yes, I vas a high-priced man."*
> *"Oh, you're aggravating me. Of course you want $1.85 a day— everyone wants it! You know perfectly well that has very little to do with your being a high-priced man. For goodness' sake answer my questions, and don't waste any more of my time. Now come over here. You see that pile of pig iron?"*
> *"Yes."*
> *"You see that car?"*
> *"Yes."*
> *"Well, if you are a high-priced man, you will load that pile of pig iron on that car tomorrow for $1.85. Now do wake up and answer my question. Tell me whether you are a high-priced man or not."*
> *"Vell—did I got $1.85 for loading dot pig iron on dot car to-morrow?"*
> *"Yes, of course you do, and you get $1.85 for loading a pile like that every day right through the year. This is what a high-priced man does, and you know just as well as I do."*

"Vell, dot's all right. I could load dot pig iron on the car to-morrow for $1.85, and I get it every day, don't I?"

"Certainly you do—certainly you do."

"Vell, den, I was a high-priced man."

"Now, hold on, hold on. You know just as well as I do that a high-priced man has to do exactly as he's told from morning till night. You have seen this man here before, haven't you?"

"No, I never saw him."

"Well, if you are a high-priced man, you will do exactly as this man tells you to-morrow, from morning till night. When he tells you to pick up a pig and walk, you pick it up and you walk and when he tells you to sit down and rest, you sit down. You do that right straight through the day. And what's more, no back talk. Now a high-priced man does just what he's told to, and no back talk. Do you understand that? When this man tells you to walk, you walk, and when he tells you to sit down, you sit down, and you don't talk back at him. Now you come on to work here to-morrow and I'll know before the night whether you are really a high-priced man or not."

This seems to be rather rough talk. And indeed it would be if applied to an educated mechanic, or even an intelligent laborer. With a man of the mentally sluggish type of Schmidt it is appropriate and not unkind since it is effective in fixing his attention on the high wages which he wants and away from what, if it were called to his attention, he would consider impossibly hard work.

Commentary: Here again we see Taylor's view that the worker has to be guided, and guided rather firmly at that, by those who are, in Taylor's mind, obviously superior. And, of course, Schmidt will not be able to figure out that he is working approximately four times as hard for a pay increase of about 60 percent. Because he is of "the mentally sluggish type," he will not ask what has happened to the fruits of his fantastic increase in productivity. Perhaps even more prophetic is Taylor's argument that each worker should be trained carefully. As we shall see, what happened along Henry Ford's assembly line was very different. The idea that management could, or would if it could, spend such a large amount of time in training workers was ludicrous.

Schmidt started to work, and all day long, and at regular intervals was told by a man who stood over him with a watch, "Now pick up a pig and walk. Now sit down and rest. Now walk—now rest," etc. He worked when he was told to work, and rested when he was told to rest, and at half-past five in the afternoon had his 47½ tons loaded on the car. And he practically never failed to work at this pace and do the task that was set him during the three years that the writer was at Bethlehem. And throughout this time he averaged a little more than $1.85 per day, whereas before he had never received over $1.15 per day, which was the ruling rate of wages at that time in Bethlehem.

That is, he received 60 percent higher wages than were paid to other men who were not working on task work. One man after another was picked out and trained to handle pig iron at the rate of 47½ tons per day until all of the pig iron was handled at this rate, and the men were receiving 60 percent more wages than other workmen around them.[15]

Commentary: Taylor achieved his objective. Productivity increased by 400 percent while labor costs rose only 60 percent. When Henry Ford took Taylor one step forward and built the assembly line, labor costs actually went down because the higher productivity that was demanded as well as the introduction of labor-saving machinery reduced the number of men employed. Of course, the price of Henry Ford's product also dropped dramatically. Labor savings helped produce vast sums of capital—in capitalist societies, these were paid out as profits to investors; in centrally planned economies, they were used by the government for its own purposes. For any nation, the process of industrial growth requires the creation of capital, and Taylor succeeded spectacularly in that. It was the result—the increase of capital—that led Taylorism to be accepted by Lenin.

Soviet Response to Taylorism

In an article in *Pravda* on 28 April 1918, Lenin wrote:

> The task the Soviet Government must set the people in all its scope is—learn to work. The Taylor system, the last word of capitalism in this respect, like all capitalist progress, is a combination of the refined brutality of bourgeois exploitation and a number of the greatest scientific achievements in the field of analysing mechanical motions during work, the elimination of superfluous and awkward motions, the elaboration of the correct methods of work, the introduction of the best system of accounting and control, etc. . . . We must organise in Russia the study and teaching of the Taylor system and systematically try it out and adapt it to our own ends.[16]

Lenin's exhortation to organize and emulate Taylor was heeded, and thus the process of Soviet emulation of American administrative science began almost immediately after the Soviet revolution in Russia.

Lenin's statement also reminds us that Taylorism did not simply deal with changing the rate at which the worker was to work (although this was the core of his writing). In order to increase the rate at which work was accomplished, fundamental changes in industrial organization had to take place. We have chosen to introduce Taylor from the perspective we have because of Taylor's normative values that are so visible in the extended quote on training Schmidt to handle pig iron at four times his previous rate for only 60 percent higher wages without bringing on a strike. As the dominant writer in the founding of administrative science, Taylor laid down "principles," which we have commented upon. These principles may be summarized as follows:

- The findings that result from the application of scientific principles to the workplace are universal and neutral and therefore should be accepted by all once they have been demonstrated to be true.
- The worker cannot possibly understand the nature of the task to be performed by him and must therefore be guided from above by men better educated and more fit to be managers.
- Management consists of developing systems of control, both of the worker and of the processes (accounting, etc.) of industrial management.
- Workers are motivated exclusively (or nearly exclusively) by economic considerations and will work at vastly increased rates if offered adequate economic incentives; workers are not interested in other aspects of work, nor should they be, because that is the province of management.
- The task of management is to increase productivity.

Taylor's principles cannot be demonstrated. In fact it is clear that they are false. Modern research has shown that the findings of scientific management were not neutral and far from universal; that workers can indeed understand their jobs and are motivated by many other values than material or economic ones; and that management is often interested in many other things than increasing productivity (e.g., in high management salaries and benefits at the expense of profits, or in avoiding too large a share of the U.S. market so as not to be broken up under anti-trust provisions). But Frederick Taylor, perhaps more than any other writer, influenced administrative science and continues to do so today. In the invention of the assembly line, Henry Ford put Taylorism into full practice and changed the twentieth century.

Henry Ford and the Assembly Line

As we have noted, Taylor died in 1915, the year the assembly line created by Henry Ford came to full fruition. The practical consequences of his ideas were never visible to Taylor. But they were visible to Henry Ford and other managers of both socialist and capitalist societies, and they were felt by workers in both types of societies as well. Ford's mass production lines, which emerged first in the automobile industry and then in other industries, led to the worst conditions imaginable on the assembly line. Even Ford's introduction of the $5-a-day wage in 1914, widely heralded at the time as a breakthrough in wages, faded as inflation destroyed its value. By the 1920s, the wages being paid along Ford's lines were lower than the industry average. But "Ford's concept of mass production, his belief that lower prices and ever-widening markets would make steadily rising wages possible came some twenty years before Keynes' emphasis on consumption as the key to economic growth."[17]

Ford made three crucial judgments that were to form the basis of the automobile and mass-production revolution that changed the face of society. Each of these decisions went against the dominant thinking of the time. In 1905–1906, when the automobile was still viewed as a gadget or toy for the well-to-do, Ford dreamed of an automobile that was so low in cost that most people could afford it, and, after dreaming of it, he decided to build it. In 1908, he discovered one of the key steps toward the goal of a car that was low enough in price to be afforded by the middle class when he froze the design of one of his models—the Model T. By freezing the design—that is, permitting no changes in the design to be made as time went by and refusing to develop countless variants on the basic model that would increase the unit costs during production—Ford introduced his version of the annual model change, the price cut. Instead of a slightly different car each year, Ford would lower his prices as the unit cost of production kept going down. In 1908, as the assembly line began, Ford built 10,000 cars; in 1915 (the year that Taylor died), Ford produced over 470,000 cars; and in 1920, Ford built over 933,000 cars. The last decision—to expand and to flood the market with low-cost (and ever-lowercost) automobiles—created a market where one had previously not existed. The change in concept of the automobile from that of a toy of the elite to the vehicle in which millions of people moved has had massive social, economic, and political consequences, now being felt intensely in the world of the 1980s.[18]

In the early days of the Ford Motor Company, Henry Ford was also surrounded by extremely talented men.[19] That he would later drive his talented men out and replace them with sycophants was part of the tragedy of Ford and his company as it lost its pre-eminent place in the market to General Motors. Under the driving leadership of Alfred Sloan, General Motors countered Ford's unchanging Model T in the 1920s with a host of different cars at different price ranges, annual model changes, introduced the used car trade-in and began installment credit.[20] General Motors moved into the dominant position in the automobile market in the 1920s.

Some Problems of Taylorism and Innovation

Although Ford ultimately could not adapt to the changing market, General Motors did. Fifty years later, however, as the market began to change once again in the 1970s, neither Ford nor General Motors was able to cope with the flood of imports. Ironically, those Japanese and German imports emphasized quality and durability over annual changes and planned obsoles cence. The Japanese and German firms were able to do this because they had read Frederick Taylor and observed Henry Ford's assembly line and brought those ideas to their assembly lines of the 1970s. The inability of American producers to adapt raises profound questions about the ability of organizations which have operated in a stable environment to respond to changes in that environment.[21] We shall discuss this problem in more detail throughout the book but have raised it here to introduce a problem that, in different form, has been very difficult for both capitalist and centrally planned economies to deal with.

Henry Ford succeeded, as he knew he would, through the mass production of cars, which resulted in ever-lower prices. Yet the Model T, with its frozen design, eventually went out of favor with the consuming public, as General Motors introduced a series of innovations—annual style changes, a variety of models built from the same frame, a trade-in allowance, and installment credit. Decades later, in the 1970s and 1980s, the market changed, and the producers of autos were seemingly flat-footed even though there was substantial warning that the market was about to change. In fact, it can be pervasively argued that were it not for the intervention of the U.S. government in the automobile business in the mid-1970s (when the government, for pollution reasons, insisted that the industry produce more efficient cars), the American auto industry might have completely collapsed in the early 1980s. If this is true, what is the key to innovation in capitalist society?

In centrally planned economies there is no competition as such. When the Soviet Union adopted Ford's techniques, the producers of automobiles were not faced with competition from within, so, at least in the short run, one of the principal stimuli to design changes and production improvement is removed. Without the incentive to change produced by competition, what ultimately is the source of innovation in a centrally planned economy? It is obvious to those who have traveled in Eastern Europe and the Soviet Union that consumer goods are almost always of substantially lower quality than those in the West. As Charles Lindblom has remarked, "The simplest answer [to this question] is that communist enterprises are without the incentives to innovate that propel enterprises in market-oriented systems."[22] But, as Lindblom also remarks, ". . .that answer is incomplete [and] pressure for innovation comes down from above, from party and specialized institutions for encouraging innovation. . ."[23]

Ford's Production Strategies

The methods that Ford developed came after Ford had conceived of the car and had envisioned the market. As a production process it was so

associated with Ford that in the Soviet Union it was called *"Fordizatsia."*[24]
And it was also regarded, like Taylorism, as an industrial philosophy.
At the core of this philosophy of production was the assembly line:

> in which the car moved from the raw state to the finished product
> through a sequence of men and machinery. By 1913 the sequence of
> men and machines was already supplied by gravity slides; within months,
> moving conveyors would be introduced and the process line itself mech-
> anized. The production system in other plants in the industry was still
> tied to the grouping of machinery by type; drill presses or milling ma-
> chines, for instance, were herded together, and the flow of work in
> progress was made to conform to the location of departmental opera-
> tions. A single part might move back and forth between departments
> before it was finally completed, contributing to higher costs in time and
> in-process inventory.[25]

The assembly line permitted other advantages, too. Volume allowed the
rapid amortization of machine tools, and the length of the production run
permitted the introduction of better steels, which, in turn, improved the life
of the tools and the quality of the product. The company's engineers had
time to break down the process of production, as Taylor did the process of
labor, into its smallest parts and eliminate unnecessary steps and time.
Newer and better machine tools replaced old machines and individual workers. A network of assembly plants spread across the entire country; this
network dramatically reduced the cost of freight, since previously, entire
cars had to be shipped across the country. Now trainloads of parts, which
took much less room per part than if assembled into cars, were shipped to
the assembly plants, where they would be put together into the final product.
Yet the buyer would still be charged f.o.b. Detroit, so the savings went to
the company. Purchases of raw materials were made in such quantity that
suppliers would quote lower prices in order to get the contract. And Ford
helped its suppliers by sending in Ford engineers to improve *their* methods,
helped them obtain high-volume machine tools, and often took over *their*
purchasing in order to take advantage of volume price discounts from Ford
Motor Company's supplier's suppliers. Because Ford paid in cash, he demanded and received further price discounts.[26] And so it went, in what now
seems a dizzying and rapid shift in the industrial heartbeat of the country
as the pace of production escalated rapidly.

Ford also changed the management infrastructure surrounding and guid-
ing the production and assembly processes; he introduced management control systems such as accounting and inventory control; and he used terror
to keep labor peace. The following example illustrates life along the assembly
line as Ford management had spies (called "spotters") placed among the
workers on the line. At the end of the production line a worker drives the
fully assembled car away from the line and parks it, then walks back to the

line and gets another, drives it to the parking space, returns again and so on. This worker

> frequently commenced work five or ten minutes early (for which he was not paid) so that the line would be clear and all in readiness when the department swung into action.
>
> One day just about thirty seconds before lunch period, he delivered a car. . . and knowing he did not have time to deliver another before the bell rang, he stepped over to a lunch wagon and bought a bottle of coffee. As he was paying for it the bell rang.
>
> That evening when he went to punch his clock-card it had been removed from the rack. The time-clerk referred him to the superintendent, who at once ordered the clerk to make out a quit slip for this employee because he had bought a bottle of coffee before the lunch bell rang. Once more a "spotter" had done his deadly work as an aid to natural attrition.
>
> No one was big enough or little enough to feel sure he was exempt from these spotters. So the haunting fear that their every movement was being watched was present in the minds of all.[27]

Yet Henry Ford claimed in 1923, "The Ford factories and enterprises have no organization, no specific duties attaching to any position, no line of succession or authority, very few titles, and no conferences."[28] When Ford wrote this, he had purged his companies of most of the men who helped build them and was running his organization as a personal empire. The fact that Ford purged his bureaucracy of all those who, in his view, could challenge him from within was the central reason for the company's near collapse, which came only a few years after Ford made that statement.[29]

Clearly, in any complex organizational system such as Ford's, a high degree of specialization is required in administrative tasks. For Taylor, the problem was to increase productivity by changing the nature of work and the workplace. For Ford, the objective was to change the process of work and thereby to change industrial control systems. For those who followed Ford and Taylor, the task was to increase productivity by rationalizing the administrative structure.

Classical Administrative Theory

The essentials of Fordism and Taylorism were developed prior to World War I. Between the two world wars, Taylorism was extended into the administrative structure, by Luther Gulick and Lyndall Urwick, among others.[30] It was Gulick who introduced the famous acronym POSDCORB, which will be discussed later in this chapter. POSDCORB was to represent the core of public administration for many years, even though it would be challenged on many fronts. Since Gulick's work summarizes this school as well as those who can be grouped into what we call classical administrative theory, we shall quote from Gulick's important article "Notes on the Theory of Organization."[31]

Gulick first espoused a set of principles, which, in his view, constituted a theory of organization. By organization, he meant a "structure of co-ordination imposed upon the work division units of an enterprise." Thus, as work is specialized it must be co-ordinated, and co-ordination requires planning.

> Organization as a way of co-ordination requires the establishment of a system of authority whereby the central purpose or objective of an enterprise is translated into reality through the combined efforts of many specialists, each working in his own field at a particular time and place. . . The problem of organization thus becomes the problem of building up between the executive at the center and the subdivisions of work on the periphery an effective network of communication and control.

There are four steps in this process:
- Define the job.
- Hire a director to achieve the job.
- Determine the nature and number of individualized and specialized work units into which the job will be divided (thus Gulick believed that as the tasks of labor could be divided into smaller and smaller units, so could administrative tasks be broken into smaller pieces and reorganized more efficiently.
- Establish and perfect the structure of authority existing between the director and the ultimate work subdivisions.

It is the last step that is crucial since the organization should enable the director to organize all the subdivisions to achieve the major objective. Once the process of problem solving is understood, Gulick argued, a series of principles emerged. Among them were "the span of control" and "the unity of command." The span-of-control principle, briefly stated, is that:

> Just as the hand of man can span only a limited number of notes on the piano, so the mind and will of man can span but a limited number of immediate managerial contacts [and] as a result, the executive of any enterprise can personally direct only a few persons. He must depend upon these to direct others, and upon them in turn to direct still others, until the last man in the organization is reached.

In the principle of the span of control, the basis for the mega-hierarchies of modern complex organization was established. If a director can direct only a limited number of people (and, like Taylorism, this is so because the director must pay close attention to those being directed rather than delegating authority) and the organization employs tens of thousands of people, then by definition the organization will be many layers deep. The larger the organization, the more the layers. Taken to its logical extreme, it is possible to construct a situation where the addition of a few individuals at the bottom of a very large hierarchy would require many supervisory personnel to properly direct them. The few additional workers (who were actually producing something) would result in many administrators (whose salaries added to the cost of the service or product and whose paper work slowed the process of accomplishing the productive work). This situation is not uncommon in modern public organizations. In many public organizations there are far more administrative personnel than wokers. The span-of-control principle is at the heart of the present crisis in public administration and management. When applied to large-scale public bureaucracies, the span of control has resulted in organizations so unwieldly that leaders and participants do not understand how their organizations work. The policy initiatives of leaders are ground into pulp. Not much will be accomplished, but thousands of people will be employed in the process.

The principle of "unity of command," also known as "one master," is stated by Gulick as follows: "A workman subject to orders from several superiors will become confused, inefficient, and irresponsible; a workman subject to orders from but one superior may be methodical, efficient and responsible. Unity of command thus refers to those who are commanded, not to those who issue commands." To ameliorate conflict within the organization that develops when one subunit receives orders from more than one superior in the organization, Gulick's solution was to create an intermediate layer in the hierarchy to coordinate the numerous orders. Furthermore, additional staff would be added to support decision makers. Thus, the organization would grow vertically and horizontally.

"POSDCORB"

Working within what by now has become a very complex administrative structure, the decision maker must perform a series of functions designed to ensure that the many principles of management are fulfilled. Those functions are summarized by POSDCORB. POSDCORB stands for:

- "*Planning*, that is working out in broad outline the things that need to be done and the methods for doing them to accomplish the purpose set for the enterprise." Note the assumption that the enterprise has clearly definable objectives that are presumably agreed upon by the organization's members and clients.
- "*Organizing*, that is the establishment of the formal structure of authority through which the work subdivisions are arranged, defined and coordinated for the defined objective." Note the assumption that it is

through the formal structure of authority that decisions are made—the informal organization apparently does not exist.

- "*Staffing*, that is the whole personnel function of bringing in and training the staff and maintaining favorable conditions of work." Note that, like Taylor, Gulick apparently assumes that "favorable conditions of work" can be objectively defined.
- "*Directing*, that is the continuous task of making decisions and embodying them in specific and general orders and instructions and serving as the leader of the enterprise." Note the assumption that general and specific orders will suffice and that, presumably, they can be made clear enough for all to understand.
- "*Co-ordinating*, that is the all important duty of interrelating the various parts of the work." Note that how co-ordination is to be accomplished is not spelled out in any detail.
- "*Reporting*, that is keeping those to whom the executive is responsible informed as to what is going on, which thus includes keeping himself informed and his subordinates informed through records, research and inspection." Note the assumption that managerial efficiency will be increased by increasing the information flow—many organizations and senior leaders are overwhelmed by the flow of paper.
- "*Budgeting*, with all that goes with budgeting in the form of fiscal planning, accounting and control."

As Herbert Simon noted thirty years ago, the principles that Gulick developed are not principles but proverbs.[32] Much of our criticisms of POSDCORB is drawn from Simon's seminal article, which marked the transition from early approaches to the study of organizations and administrative science to the modern approaches (which we shall discuss in later chapters), those concerned with finding out why organizations and people in them behave as they do, not as one wished them to behave. POSDCORB does not help a manager make a concrete decision, nor does it describe what a manager actually does. For example, it is intuitively obvious that a manager should organize, but how? By region? By product? By service? And so on. It is equally obvious that management also involves planning, staffing, directing, co-ordinating, reporting, and budgeting. But how should each of these be done and who should do them? And the organization that Gulick envisions is one in which there is agreement among members and clients over goals (which seldom actually exists), in which the formal structure of the organization is crucial (when in fact the informal structures may be even more important than the formal apparatus)[33] and in which there is one acceptable way of defining acceptable conditions of work. As Nicos Mouzelis has noted, "Very often when one reads in textbooks on business or public administration about the functions of a department or of the executive, one is not sure if reference is made to what the executive does or what he should do."[34] That the principles of classical administrative theorists such as Gulick are tautologies has not reduced their popularity. Modern textbooks still utilize them.[35] This is the case because administrative science still, after years of research, cannot provide a systematic understanding of organizational behavior, and, without that understanding, a true science of management cannot be devised. Thus, generations of public administrators have been routinely taught that these principles are the means by which one organizes a complex system, have employed them in their careers, and are not about to abandon them. In one of the world's largest organizations, the United States Department of Defense, the span-of-control principle is probably the dominant organizational concept. Thus, the Department of Defense is many layers deep and, as a result, is plagued by inefficiency, foul-ups, confusions, delays, and the like.

Human Relations

At about the same time that classical administrative theory was emerging, a fourth major approach to administrative science also began to be developed. This approach—human relations—was based on the intuitively appealing ideas that a happy worker is a good worker and that a good worker produces more. Many of the early researchers in human relations were reacting to the horrifying application of Taylorism in the automobile assembly lines and elsewhere in industry. Where workers were terrified and brutalized by Henry Ford's "spotters"—or so the argument ran from those advocating human relations—productivity would improve in a more humane workplace. No matter how appealing this idea, researchers have been unable to demonstrate any significant relationship between worker satisfaction or morale and productivity. Indeed, there are situations in which authoritarian management may result in higher productivity than participatory management.[36]

Human relations as an approach to administrative science emerged from studies that were originally designed as Taylor-type experiments designed to improve productivity. Taylor and Ford had demonstrated that the organization of work was crucial to productivity. Near Chicago, at the Hawthorne plant of American Telephone and Telegraph, engineers were measuring the effects of lighting intensity on the productivity of workers. A select group of workers were assembled in a special area where illumination could be varied and compared with worker output. In addition to the experimental group, a control group was also placed in a room and used—or so the researchers thought—to ensure accuracy. In the experimental area, the illumination was increased a bit. Productivity increased a bit. Illumination was increased a bit more and productivity went up a bit more. The illumination was gradually increased until it reached extreme intensity and with each increase in intensity came an increase in productivity. At this point, the experimenters decided to lower the illumination under the expectation that productivity would also decrease. Contrary to their expectations, productivity continued to increase even as the lighting was gradually decreased to the equivalent of bright moonlight. Even more confounding was the fact that the control group's productivity also increased when compared to production in the main plant. After the experiment was repeated twice, with similar results, the findings were examined. Given that the initial r̲e̲s̲u̲l̲t̲ surprised them, a number of additional experiments were conducted over the next few years.[37]

In what seems an obvious finding to the late-twentieth century reader, the experimenters found that work groups have informal structures. Those informal structures sometimes operated to resrict highly productive members to the norms that the group had established, by putting pressure on those who deviated from those norms. Additional research has confirmed what was found at Hawthorne—group pressure on individuals and the desire of individuals to belong to groups are among the most important factors motivating people.[38] Thus, the research was extremely significant. Howeer, it was also misleading, for many of the apparent results of the Hawthorne experiments were in fact wrong.

One finding later proved to be incorrect was crucial. It was the conclusion of the researchers that if management was obviously interested in the workers, their morale would increase and improved morale would lead to improved productivity. Thus Taylorism—with its view that workers were interested only in monetary rewards—was cast aside, and in came an army of social psychologists, consultants, and other social scientists. They argued that the social and psychological needs of the workers were as important as or more important than their financial needs. Once the dehumanization of Taylor was abolished—or so the argument went—and workers were treated with dignity rather than as cogs in a machine, productivity would increase. This appealing idea was the classic case of the researchers seeing in their data what they wanted to see. In fact, the Hawthorne experiments proved nothing because they were so flawed in the way they were carried out that too many intervening variables made any results unverifiable. Alex Carey, in 1968, and ten years later, Richard Franke and James Kaub, using statistical techniques not available when the experiments were carried out in the 1920s, completely demolished the Hawthorne experiment's findings.[39] In a similar manner, Maslow's conclusion that workers need fulfilling jobs in order to maintain their self-esteem, however popular, has never been demonstrated (it may be that the need exists, but it has not been yet proven).[40] That these "findings" were destroyed, like the precepts of classical administrative theory, has not reduced the popularity of human relations among many students of organizational behavior. Even though many positive findings on the role of the small group in the workplace have been, and continue to be, developed, administrative science and organization theory were sent off on another wild-goose chase, humanizing the workplace. Much of this literature is psychobabble at best and, at worst, huckstering, but it nevertheless flourishes.

Conclusion

We have reviewed the emergence of administrative science from Taylorism to human relations. Four major schools that developed early in the twentieth century—scientific management, Fordism, classical administrative theory, and human relations—played important roles in shaping the direction of industrial and public organizations. That their findings were built on sandbars has not deterred their widespread application today. No one would deny the tremendous impact these approaches have played in the increase in productivity and the dramatic change in the standard of living. But the ultimate questions are, At what cost, and, Were there other means to the same end? Early approaches promised what they could not deliver, and their failure bedevils administrators and leaders to this day. The hope of an efficiently and effectively running administrative apparatus achieved through ever-more-sophisticated management-control system has proved illusory.

In the next chapter, we shall trace administrative science as it emerged in the Soviet Union. One of our major themes will be that the Soviet Union borrowed from American thinking.

3

Administrative Science and the Rise of Soviet Power

> *The country that is more developed industrially only shows . . . the less developed [country] an image of its own future.*
>
> —Karl Marx

> *We, the Bolsheviki, have convinced Russia. We have won Russia from the rich for the poor, from the exploiters for the working people. Now we must manage Russia.*
>
> —V.I. Lenin

Introduction

Russian leaders had tried to reshape their society long before 1917. They proposed nothing less than the total transformation of a sprawling, multinational, largely peasant land into an industrial giant. From a global perspective, the Czarist regime had little choice but to follow and overake, the advanced states of the capitalist world. To be sure, the West had demonstrated time and again the superiority of its industry, technology, and military might. Thus, Kremlin leaders in the mid-nineteenth century reluctantly concluded that if Russia did not modernize, and do so quickly, then the balance-of-power system would crush her. Westernization would be the necessary price for survival.

The dramatic political and administrative reforms advanced by Tsar Alexander II in the 1860s represent a definitive point of departure in Russian history.[2] Recognizing that Russian national interests could no longer be served by the traditional agrarian system, Tsar Alexander sought to establish a socioeconomic framework within which advanced Western technology and organizational forms could take root and flourish. But the leadership was unwilling to blindly copy the Western model. Industrial techniques and military technology were thus detached from accompanying institutions as well as politcal values and then adapted to "fit" existing structures. The regime dogmatically insisted on propping up the defining traits of autocracy, even as socioeconomic changes were making them increasingly irrelevent and vunerable. Hindsight has shown that the greatest social and political unrest occurs precisely in times of greatest economic advance. Russia proved to be no exception. In fact, the regime strengthened, and even created, its own internal enemies by ruthlessly forcing the pace of industrialization without adequate regard for political change.

Strategies of Sergei Witte

Nevertheless, Russia became a pioneer in centrally directed economic development under Sergei Witte, Finance Minister in 1892–1903.[3] Government sponsorship, if not outright control, was a basic feature of his system. Labor legislation was designed specifically to minimize disruptions. Strikes and even attempts to organize unions were illegal. An ambitious program of railroad construction, including the 5000-mile Trans-Siberian line, raised the productivity of Russian industry. In turn, this led to burgeoning growth in heavy industry and machine building. The Ukraine became the most dynamic economic region of the empire. Soon it boasted a powerful industrial infrastructure—chemicals, textiles, mining, metallurgy, etc. And by the turn of the century, Russia's growing commercial centers came to resemble the grimy mill towns in the West. This situation represented progress to both capitalist and Marxist revolutionaries, but for quite different reasons.

A central feature of Witte's system rested upon the massive export of grain to finance the purchase of Western machines and technology. And these exports continued even in the face of food shortages and famine in the Russian countryside. The tax burden on the rural populace assumed staggering proportions. Although coercion and oppressive living standards remained the price of industrialization carried out at a breakneck pace, the alternatives were clear, if sobering to the Kremlin leaders: catch up or be crushed.[4] The forced march into the twentieth century was intended to stamp out the docile conservatism of old Russia as well as the casual indifference of its huge state bureaucracy. To be sure, those changes would alter forever the cultural values of a backward people, traditionally accustomed to an almost medieval orientation to life.

Henceforth, the self-discipline and scientific rationality of Western culture—traits widely acknowledged as "progressive" and "modern"— were to become inextricably linked to Russia's social structure. Since illiteracy stood in the way of industrial progress, a massive commitment to education began; and, to its credit, despite fears that widespread literacy might undermine popular loyalty to the autocracy, the regime made impressive gains in educating its people.[5] Advances were expected at all levels of society. For example, Russian scientists and engineers were strongly encouraged to learn from their Western counterparts, especially in the area of industrial organization and production technology.[6]

Introduction of Taylorism

By the outbreak of World War I, the works of Frederick W. Taylor had gained substantial recognition as well as an enthusiastic following in the scientific community. The Moscow Polytechnical Institute set up a special department to examine Taylorism and to speed its practical application. Studies in the scientific organization of labor (*"NOT"*) soon found a captive audience among Russian specialists and several, including M. Arapov, P. Bogodarov, A.K. Gastev, B. Zheleznov, made impressive contributions to the world literature. By 1914, at least eight major industrial enterprises were purposively organized according to scientific principles.[7]

Russia was woefully unprepared for the total mobilization required by World War I. Her armies were brave, but poorly equipped and miserably led. The semi-industrial economy was strained beyond its limits. Nevertheless, the war induced the first large-scale applications of *NOT* in factories producing military equipment—rifles shells, grenades, cartridges, and the like. This scientific movement peaked in 1915–1916 with the introduction of quality-control inspectors in certain plants and the establishment of a special school for their instruction. Soviet commentators have unabashedly concluded, in retrospect, that Russian achievements in organizing labor and industry during World War I were no less impressive than those of the West.[8]

By 1917, Russian cities were collapsing into anarchy and the Romanov dynasty, master of the land for centuries, was swept away in a flood tide of discontent and revolution. Among those contending for power were the Bolsheviks—a disciplined, paramilitary political party dedicated to a Marxist *Weltanschauung* and Leninist organizational recipes. Their subsequent triumph, unanticipated by most foreign and Russian observers, promised dramatic changes in politics and society. But few analysts could then envision the impact that capitalist organizational forms and Russian history would have on future economic development. Although Marx had brilliantly described the dynamics of capitalism, his remarks on the new proletarian order were brief, vague, ambiguous, and sometimes even contradictory. Thus, Bolshevik leaders were forced by unanticipated circumstances to improvise and learn by trial-and-error methods. Marxist–Leninist doctrine nonetheless created expectations that had real behavioral and policy consequences, especially regarding the organization and management of production. A detailed portrayal of Bolshevik administrative theory clearly belongs in another study, but this theory's substantial contribution to Soviet management science cannot be appreciated without a brief review.

The Marxist–Leninist Theoretical Heritage

Marxism is a sociopolitical theory seeking to explain the course of human history.[9] It does so by *describing* a given society (capitalism) and then *predicting* paths for its inevitable development (socialism). The major organizing concepts of Marxism—the dialectic, historical materialism, class struggle, economic base—point to the conclusion that social changes are not caused by ideas, but rather by material processes. Most important here are changes in humans' relationship to the means of production and exchange. Thus, the economic structure of society largely determines the legal, political, and ideological constructs, which, in turn, constitute a definite form of social consciousness. As a general rule, Marx paid little attention to the bureaucratic nature of modern states. The few times he did, however, resulted in a contradictory amalgam of sophisticated analysis and naive utopianism. His descriptions of administrative behavior, although partial, reveal many characteristics which were later examined in depth by Weber and others. Marx found the typical bureaucrat ignorant, haughty, incompetent, and adverse to risk taking. Likewise, bureaucrats jealously guarded their prerogatives, mystified their own positions and authority, and attempted to expand their administrative domain whenever possible.

Marx's findings have not been successfully challenged, and the behavioral traits he defined for bureaucrats apparently exist irrespective of social system. Bureaucratic traits have persistently frustrated efforts (and good intentions) by Soviet political leaders to increase the responsiveness and effectiveness of their own massive state bureaucracy. Such difficulties were unforeseen by Marx, since he regarded bureaucracy as a *consequence*, rather than a *cause*, of society's power structure. Thus, his trenchant analysis of capitalism's administrative machine is displaced by blind faith and naivity when talking about the role and character of bureaucracy under proletarian rule. The administrative apparatus, according to Marx, although not a social class in itself, functions as an instrument whereby the bourgeoisie exercises its control over others. Its major task is to uphold the status quo and privileges of the ruling class. This will prove self-defeating in the long run, however. An oppressive bureaucracy can only sharpen the tension and conflict between classes. As a result, the proletariat will suffer greater degradation and, hence, become more alienated from society and more *conscious* of its own distinctive interests. Revolution will occur precisely when workers recognize that they have "nothing to lose but their chains." Bureaucracy is assumed to be irrelevant for a classless society and it will soon "wither away" and be absorbed by the social order itself. The demise of capitalist domination also means the end of role specification and the division of labor. Administrative tasks can be performed by the "average" citizen once they have been demystified of their artificial complexity. Alienation will disappear and governance over people will be replaced by administration of things. Indeed, under socialism, societal and/or production management are considered functions of technology. And the technical requirements of management do not entail radical changes, even as its social basis undergoes revolutionary transformation.

Lenin's Theories on Bureaucracy

Lenin was *a priori* committed to Marxist theoretical categories and naturally refused to consider alternative possibilities in the historical evolution of society. While preoccupied with organizational problems, he made no effort to examine bureaucratic phenomena apart from the societal framework in which they were found. In his *State and Revolution*,[10] Lenin advocated smashing the repressive organs of the bourgeois state, but he nonetheless found managerial and economic agencies capable of fulfilling legitimate functions under socialism.[11] Industrial organizations were sufficiently productive under the old regime, so few changes would be required. Even if bourgeois specialists were needed to staff key administrative positions, the Bolshevik leadership—by manipulating rewards and through selective threats—expected to elicit their cooperation.

Events after 1917 soon demonstrated that Lenin's vision of socialist bureaucracy rested on a static, oversimplified notion of management and the organizational tasks of future socialist construction. Contrary to expectations, the size of the new bureaucratic apparatus expanded at a rapid rate. Lenin characterized its performance as pitiful, if not disgusting. Although severe problems were plainly evident in production enterprises, Lenin reserved his sharpest comments for state agencies. This growing administrative malaise could only be overcome, in the long run, by further economic development in Russia. But since there was no visible objective basis for final victory over bureaucracy in the early 1920s, Lenin proposed that the party's Central Control Commission and the Working Peasants Inspection (commonly known as *RABKRIN*) be reorganized into a super-control agency with the dual function of scientific research and systematic checking.[12] Its staff of competent professional—well versed in the latest Western techniques— would enable the reorganized agency to inject scientific management into the state administration as well as party apparatus.

Lenin was an orthodox Marxist in that he stressed the revolutionary nature of the working class and its preeminent role in sociopolitical change. But he was temperamentally ill disposed to accepting his mentor's deterministic views. Instead, Lenin stressed the centrality of purposive, organizational behavior in shaping human destiny. His voluntarism was embodied in the Bolshevik party or "organizational weapon"—a paramilitary political instrument, which could transform members into deployable agents.[13] The party's main task was to infuse "objective" class consciousness into a sluggish proletariat, which could do no better by its own efforts than to achieve trade-union awareness. Lenin believed that correct organizational principles would lead to correct decision making. His notion of democratic centralism was an ingenious, albeit largely rhetorical, device to combine the hierarchical virtues of centralism with the democratic virtues of participation. Indeed, one does Lenin no disservice by calling him a "revolutionary with a bureaucratic mind."[14]

Good socialists, including Lenin, never doubted the ability of the capitalist system to create and manage large-scale production. They were, in fact, largely unconcerned about questions of industrial organization after the revolution, since its basic structure and technology were already present under the ancien regime. While the economic mechanism as a whole would be adapted to serve proletarian interests, there would otherwise be few changes. Of course, one would expect greater centralization and more comprehensive planning to exist under socialism. But these were quantitative, not qualitative, changes and consequently did not call for radical technological or organization adaptation. Thanks to the immeasurable *social* advantages of proletarian rule—e.g., public property and state ownership—the conditions for effective macromanagement of the entire economy would be present for the first time. No longer would anarchy in the market place and/or cut-throat competition among private firms distort society's optimum distribution of resources. Dramatic changes under socialism were expected, however, in the class content of those occupying managerial posts. Thus, reliable proletarians would replace bourgeois specialists and holdovers from the Tsarist regime. And in those cases where trained personnel with proper class standing were unavailable, the professional status of bourgeois engineers and technicians would ensure their apolitical status and, hence, de facto loyalty to the revolution.[16]

Bolshevik theorists as a rule did not underestimate the complexities of managment in the industrial era.[17] It was recognized as an organic part of large-scale production—a vital function existing apart from the specifics of a given social order. From here, it was a small step indeed to acknowledge, if not actively preach, the benefits of capitalist administrative techniques for socialist management science. By stripping away their oppressive class base, the concepts, experience, and technology of bourgeois management could be profitably recast into the new proletarian order. And there was no stronger advocate of selective borrowing from capitalist experience than

Lenin himself: "The working class should not fight against scientific and technological progress or the achievements shown in the Taylor system, but only against the capitalist application of this system."[18] Thus, while "squeezing sweat" could not take place under socialism, many capitalist ideas would be adopted by management theorists and practitioners in the USSR.

There was a danger, nevertheless, that capitalist "techniques" could displace the socialist "system," if analysts were not careful to be selective and identify that which was incompatible with Marxist–Leninist class principles. Not only was it impossible for administrative specialists to neatly separate "techniques" from the capitalist "system," but it remained inherently difficult to specify when and under what conditions "bourgeois contamination" was actually taking place. Bolshevik doctrine simply offered little more than vague expectations that Western concepts would not detract from building socialism in one country. But even during the New Economic Policy (1921–1928), when vestiges of capitalism were tolerated along with the "dictatorship of the proletariat," ostensible limits were placed on the selective borrowing of Western techniques in the scientific literature. These constraints substantially restricted the content and conduct of inquiry in the early years of Soviet power. Later on, those theorists who dealt with things and not people—to the neglect of politics and of recognition of class struggle—found themselves tragically out of step with the emerging Stalinist system.[19]

Socialism and Taylorism in the 1920s: Political Constraints on Inquiry

It was difficult, if not impossible, to identify the major elements of long-term Bolshevik economic policy following the October revolution. This should not be surprising; the civil war and foreign intervention forced the beleaguered leadership to contend with one emergency after another. Thus, the regime's initial approach to organizing production—isolated and sporadic nationalization—later gave way to the wholesale nationalization of entire industries. During War Communism (1918–1921),[20] when counterrevolutionary forces were at high tide, some fifty governmental agencies *(glavki)* directly managed Russian industry.[21] And since their finances were absorbed into the general state budget, individual enterprises lost their former autonomy. Henceforth they functioned as mere operating units of the Soviet government. Indeed, economic organizations were directed to satisfy the priority requirements of the political leadership and, consequently, resources were allocated largely in physical terms at specified targets. Ignoring economic analysis in the conventional sense, command decisions replaced the self-adjusting market mechanism, while Bolshevik élan and/or trial-and-error practice did the same for "scientific management."

Having endured virtually every disaster that could befall a country—invasion, famine, civil war, economic dislocation—the Bolshevik leadership, at Lenin's insistence, begrudgingly recognized the practical necessity of dismantling the overcentralized command economy. And by reversing the practice of forcibly extracting grain from the peasantry, Lenin expected the New Economic Policy (NEP) to secure a breathing space for the hard-pressed regime. Of course, NEP was never intended to be anything more than a tactical, and temporary, retreat—fraught with political and economic perils, to be sure. By reinstituting individual (profit) motivation in small-scale production, the new line would create a group of small entrepreneurs or "NEPmen" in towns as well as wealthy peasants (known as kulaks) in the countryside. While such developments would have sobering political consequences for a system dedicated to proletarian class principles, social control, and the fundamental manipulability of economic life, policy makers found no feasible alternatives after the ominous Kronstadt rebellion in March 1921.[22] Henceforth, until 1928, the Bolshevik leadership withdrew from its extreme over-commitment to social control and granted relative autonomy to various sectors of Soviet life. Preoccupied with its own internal affairs, the Communist party was unable and/or unwilling to direct the major currents of socioeconomic development. And widely varying norms of acceptable attitudes and behavior soon emerged in the USSR. As a result, there was a tremendous burst of creative energy in the 1920s. Numerous innovative, and often archaic, ideas evolved in education, the arts, religion, morality, and the like. Administrative science, economics, and the scientific organization of labor *(NOT)* enjoyed a proverbial "golden era" which would not reappear again for nearly half a century. Whereas former capitalists occupied important bureaucratic positions, management specialists and consultants—including many sporting bourgeois credentials—examined and sometimes enthusiastically advanced Western concepts to "rationalize" the foundering Soviet economy. Despite the strong support, and even encouragement, given to these "Westernizers" in certain political circles, they always faced various doctrinal as well as political constraints on their studies. Taylorism could not be permitted to displace socialist principles, but certain bourgeois ideas would nonetheless flourish in the USSR.

Intertwining of *NOT* and Taylorism

Lenin's insistent pleas to adopt "all that is progressive" from the capitalist managerial repertoire set the stage for subsequent developments under the New Economic Policy. *NOT* (and Taylorism) burgeoned, along with substantial ambiguities over its proper role in the new socialist order. Thus, Bolshevik ideologues and political leaders alike would often uncover "erroneous views on the content, methods, and possibilities of NOT under . . . dictatorship for the proletariat."[23] Even among mangement specialists sharp disagreements arose over the conceptual basis and scope of *NOT* under socialism. And these differences—many of which went far beyond mere scholarly disputes—had ostensible roots in antagonistic political forces. At bottom, the conflict pitted those allegedly representing hostile class interests against either doctrinal purists or skeptics who (mistakenly) asserted that Taylor's ideas could not be successfully transplanted into the Soviet Union. The former were likely to conclude that Taylorism could be utilized by good socialists without "critical" examination and/or "selective" adoption. And the latter either found Taylor anathema or argued that the Russian economy was simply ill equipped to absorb "advanced" capitalist ideas.

Whatever one's ideological persuasion, the omnipresent shadow of Frederick W. Taylor permeated the socialist debate on the scientific organization of labor *(NOT)*. The observer could find enthusiastic supporters, doctrinaire foes, and even outright skeptics of his scientific method—time-and-motion studies.[24] Self-serving conclusions on *NOT*'s preoccupation with the worker, his health and working conditions, as well as questions of fatigue *(utomlenie)* could not hide the basic similarities of approach and subject matter to that existing under capitalism. For obvious doctrinal reasons there would be little talk of "intelligent gorillas" and, to their credit, many Soviet theorists felt more comfortable dealing with technical rationalization than labor intensification.[25] But for those spirited defenders of Taylor, including some who called him a genius,[26] there were no *social* obstacles to spreading his work throughout the Soviet Union. Indeed, it was the legitimate property of socialism.[27] Nevertheless, a consensus position on *NOT* failed to emerge in the early 1920s, despite strong promotion in official circles. What did evolve, however, was a veritable jungle of sharply contrasting views. To be sure, this was a time of rich and diverse scientific activity in administrative science.

The first major bibliography on *NOT* appeared in 1921, and the Central Institute of Labor was established later in the same year.[28] Its journal, *Organization of Labor*, was highly respected in scientific circles and was edited by the institute's renowned director, A.K. Gastev.[29] By 1924, there were 108 organizations working on problems of scientific management. Special state agencies were created and given the task of monitoring research work. Besides *RABKRIN*, the Council on *NOT (SOVNOT)* assumed a central place in coordinating the research agenda of numerous institutes.[30] It maintained close ties with counterpart agencies in France, the United States, and other countries. Prompted by a discussion of scientific management in *Pravda*, the League *Vremia* ("Time") emerged in 1923. It represented efforts to broaden *NOT* into a mass social movement consisting of party workers,

scientists, engineers, and ordinary citizens devoted to finding ways to economize on time and resources at the workplace. Spreading rapidly, *Vremia*
soon had branches in 75 cities and totaled over 2000 members. Renamed
the League of *NOT*, it was unceremoniously liquidated in 1925 after clashing
with the trade unions, thus providing a harbinger of things to come under
Stalin, when entire institutes and their staffs would disappear.

Approved Status of Looking to the West

Bolshevik theorists did not shirk from canvassing the West for relevant
ideas on how to order the growing administrative malaise they had helped
to create. But this emulative posture vis-à-vis capitalist experience, while
strong medicine indeed for doctrinal purists, caused relatively little soul
searching among professional specialists dedicated to building a more efficient Soviet state machine. In fact, attempts to gather and disseminate information about Western techniques were officially sanctioned, vigorously
promoted, and enthusiastically received by the community of specialists
during NEP. Thus, the Bureau of Foreign Science and Technology *(BINT)*
was formed in March 1921, and began publishing a reference collection
shortly thereafter.[31] A high-powered Soviet delegation was sent to Prague
(July 1924) to learn about Western approaches to scientific management.
Rhetorical bombast aside, the trip represented an important "educational
experience," especially a chance to exchange views with American specialists.[32] Of course, this was neither the first nor the last delegation to visit
Western Europe. Trips abroad became standard practice for scientists from
prestigious institutes in Moscow, Leningrad, Kazan, Kharkov, and elsewhere.[33] The Central Institute of Labor was particularly active in exchanging
information with counterpart Western organizations; unfortunately, the record of this correspondence was largely destroyed by Stalin.[34] It comes as
no surprise, then, to find Soviet research and theorizing heavily influenced
by Western schools of public administration and industrial management.
And certain political leaders would point to Germany and the United States
as role models, while bourgeois management specialists— by temperament
and prior training—looked westward for inspiration as well as for relevant
ideas.[35]

However, overzealous emulators sometimes accepted more "ideological
garbage" than useful techniques from the capitalist repertoire. Since many
sported bourgeois credentials themselves or were holdovers from the ancien
regime, their ultimate political loyalty to the revolution was suspect. Not
surprisingly, vigilant Bolsheviks could always find pure Taylorism in the
USSR; the blatant, indiscrimminate use of bourgeois concepts; and even
recognition that *NOT* was a *universal* system of labor organization. Such

notions were no doubt sufficiently compromising on strict doctrinal grounds to give political leaders cause for alarm, but they could be tolerated, if begrudgingly, as long as NEP remained official policy.

The tenuous balance between deviance and orthodoxy was strikingly evident at the Second Conference on *NOT*, 10–16, March 1924.[36] There, Gastev's approach, *rubka zubilom* ("carving with a chisel") was vigorously taken to task. No only did *rubka zubilom* examine excessively narrow subject matter—separate work operations and/or the individual worker—but it simply ignored the broader social environment. Opponents could justifiably charge that Gastev had elevated naked empiricism to the forefront of scientific inquiry; consequently, they found his work equivalent to Taylorism. Other major controversies emerged at the conference. For example, certain irresolute theorists mistakenly called *NOT* a general system of labor organization. And by doing so, they ignored the distinctive traits of socialist construction—dictatorship of the proletariat and the politics of class struggle. Naturally, they were accused of displacing the ideological basis of the socialist system—Marxism–Leninism—with capitalist technique. While these charges could be tolerated under NEP, they later—when the political climate became more repressive—proved fatal to thousands. But even in the mid-1920s there were indications that the Bolshevik leadership was growing restive with excessively bourgeois outlooks and mechanistic models:

> It is a harmful, non-Marxist illusion to consider NOT a system of principles for organizing labor . . . . It is considerably more modest . . . And it is essential to theorize less [and] borrow from capitalist cultures only that which raises the general productivity of labor without violating the principles of dictatorship of the proletariat.[38]

It is no exaggeration to conclude that scientific research conducted in the early years of Soviet power actually outstripped that accomplished in many Western countries.[39] And Gastev's micro-level approach was not the sole research focus. One can identify a steady expansion of the specialist's research domain—from individual-in-workplace, to production section, to enterprise, to national economy as a whole.[40] Nevertheless, theorists in the 1920s typically adopted a machine model or "production treatment" of organizations.[41] This view, which was vigorously advocated by the Institute of Administrative Techniques, dealt exclusively with the technical aspects of management and largely ignored human behavior and/or the psychological attributes of individuals. It also assumed that there were fundamental uniformities between production and nonproduction organizations involving natural resources, technical instruments, and the work force. These common elements meant that both industrial enterprises and state agencies could be rationalized along similar lines, using identical principles. And based on the systematic observation of existing organizations, theorists advanced various "principles" of successful management—specialization, standardization, mechanization and the like. Others identified the "functions" of management and then linked them to the whole organization. Based on the notion of mechanization, some specialists would even predict the "withering away" of management as a separate command function.[42] Although this was an ideologically palatable conclusion, those dealing with "principles," "functions," etc, were treading on insecure turf. They would be accused of ignoring class analysis as well as the distinctive features of socialist production.[43]

FAYOL AND SOVIET EMULATION

Many Soviet theorists emulated the renowned French administrative specialist Henri Fayol, who, at the turn of the century, focused on alleged "universal principles" of internal organization in a manner similar to Taylor. E. Drezin was a typical Russian Fayolist.[44] He examined organizational structure, rules for internal routine, and various accounting procedures. The core of his approach, however, rested on the match between the psychological attributes of each worker (e.g., intellect, technical knowledge, general health) with a particular task within the enterprise. The ideal establishment, according to Drezin, would connect each worker to that position for which he was ideally suited, both physically and psychologically.[45] While acknowledging that Western scientists already knew how to do this, he naturally concluded that the exploitative essence of capitalism precluded humane application of such knowledge. In this case, capitalist technique could be fruitfully adapted to the egalitarian social norms of proletarian rule.

These approaches, although drawing liberally from Western experience, did not purport to explain organizational phenomena in general. Nor did they aspire to create a universal framework whereby problems of organization and management could be examined. That task remained for Marxist–Leninist doctrine. Consequently, most Soviet work dealt with nuts-and-bolts issues and/or hardly ventured past the practice of management. But although advocates of these lower-level, inductive approaches were most influential in the 1920s, there were prominent exceptions, notably the radical philosopher A.A. Bogdanov, who had parted company with Lenin on philosophical and political grounds before the revolution. He was unprepared to accept dialectical materialism as a universal framework and, instead, advanced his own scheme between 1912 and 1928—general organizational science or *Tektology*.

Bogdanov's theorizing constituted an explicit challenge to the political leadership and clashed head on with socialist doctrine. By rejecting the ever-narrowing focus of scientific knowledge into separate disciplines, Bogdanov promoted *Tektology* as an integrative, interpretive "science of sciences." It dealt with important similarities of structure and process found in physical, biological, and even *social* systems.[46] These were not simply analogies, but rather fundamental principles operating according to discernible laws. Not only should systems be analyzed as integrated wholes, but the goal of human activity itself is to increase the organizational state of a given system, i.e., to make it more "organized." Such a conclusion went far beyond mere philosophy:

> . . . the aim [of *Tektology*] is not to represent the world as a single whole, but to transform it into an organizational whole . . . . [H]uman activity . . . from the most simple to the most complex form leads to organizational processes. *Mankind has no activity apart from organizational ones.* [Emphasis added.][47]

Nowhere in Bogdanov's work could one find class analysis or acceptable criteria for separating socialist from capitalist society. Such neglect did not rest well with orthodox Bolsheviks. But even more challenging, *Tektology* reputedly had a *universal* character and was applicable to all natural and social phenomena. Denounced as a heretic and buffoon, Bogdanov was charged with philosophical idealism and was unable to play any significant role in social and political life. Had he lived beyond 1928, he surely would have fallen victim to Stalin's purges, as many of his contemporaries did for much less serious "crimes."[48]

Virtually every approach or school of thought in the 1920s, when examined closely, could be classified "deviant." For example, Gastev's microlevel view and preoccupation with separate work operations simply ignored the broader socioeconomic environment in the USSR. And it proved difficult, if not impossible, to clearly separate this view from pure Taylorism, despite claims that it dealt with the worker's health and welfare. Soviet Fayolists were criticized for overemphasizing the subjective factor (human will) and thus were wide open to charges of idealism. The "production treatment" reputedly contained a fatal defect. It took Taylor's mechanistic approach to shop-level organization and applied it to analysis of the USSR's production and state apparatus as a whole.[49] Macrolevel theorizing, especially that done by mathematical economists, had too many advocates of "balanced" growth and equilibrium to suit those dedicated to "catch up and overtake" the advanced countries of the West.[50] That these heretical views survived, even prospered, under dictatorship of the proletariat, illustrates the relatively free inquiry in the 1920s. However, should NEP "wither away"—and it was always envisioned as a temporary measure—then these views would drastically part company with socialist orthodoxy.

DEBATES OVER NEP

Party leadership struggles increasingly involved questions of industrialization, planning, and economic priorities (e.g., heavy vs light industry) in

1921–1930. The latter half of the decade found NEP the focal point of strident debates among rival factions. Although NEP had brilliantly achieved its overall goals, particularly the relaxation of intolerable pressures on society, serious problems were emerging for this political system, doctrinally opposed to the free interplay of "bourgeois" market forces.[51] Since the chief beneficiaries of NEP were private traders and especially land-owning peasants, their gains and those of other private (class) interests were beginning to clash with the long-term needs of socialist construction. And not only did growing kulak strength engender a severe malaise in Bolshevik circles, but morale plummeted among the party rank and file because of official policy that seemed to defend "profit-seeking" enterprise directors against the trade unions.[52] Most challenging—and disheartening—to the Bolshevik leadership, however, was the somber realization that the pace and even direction of economic development was largely outside its control. This was bitter medicine indeed for a regime dedicated to production and accumulation. If NEP were to continue, then the party had no choice but to depend on hostile class interests to implement policy decisions. This situation could not be tolerated indefinitely.

The struggle over control of the party machinery must not obscure the fundamental policy alternatives that confronted a divided leadership. NEP would either continue (the 'right")—and with it the peasantry's stranglehold on industry—or it would be replaced by a strategy directed towards rapid industrial growth and control of the peasantry (the "left"). After prolonged debate and maneuvering in high leadership circles, Stalin finally chose the "left," but not until first discrediting, then purging (and ultimately liquidating) those favoring development of heavy industry as well as those pushing NEP.[53] Indeed, Stalin was determined to gain complete mastery of the political system before attempting to remake society. He transformed Bolshevik consensus into conformity and served notice on any deviations from the general line.[54] He was prepared to go further, and faster, in his industrialization drive than even the most zealous advocates of the "left."[55] Attempting to "revolutionize" society from above, Stalin did much more than establish the organizational framework of the modern Soviet economy. He forged the basic sinews of the totalitarian state.

From 1928 onwards, the relatively sophisticated analysis of economic science and development strategy was superseded by demands for "vigilance," "discipline," and, most of all, Bolshevik élan. According to economist Strumilin: "Our task is not to study economics but to change it. We are bound by no laws. There are no fortresses which Bolsheviks cannot storm. The question of tempo is subject to decision by human beings."[56] This revolutionary attitude toward economics drove the radical effort to accelerate the growth of heavy industry. Production became an end in itself. Informal and even quasilegal practices were tolerated as long as they would lead to successful plan fulfillment. Meanwhile, the casualty list of those liquidated grew ominously—kulaks, NEPmen, various class enemies, party cadres, bourgeois management specialists and their research centers "mechanically" borrowing administrative techniques from abroad. Taylorism and other Western concepts were not to interfere with *socialist* administrative experience, e.g., storming, democratic centralism, shock-labor, socialist emulation, one management, and the like. Consequently, research institutes were shut down (Taganrog in 1927, the Institute of Administrative Techniques in 1931), their staffs were dispersed, publications were suspended, and leading scientists fell under the pall of suspicion. Many were linked, ᵣᵣᵣ ᵢᵢᵢcally, to the "right deviation" and disappeared during the Great Terror. Somehow, Gastev's Central Institute survived until 1940, but was then liquidated "as an organization hindering the development of the Stakhanovite movement in light industry."[57] Most of the 558 Soviet journals dealing with organization and management met their demise in the 1930s.[58] Those few survivors passed from the control of management scientists dedicated to rationalizing the administrative apparatus into establishments promoting rapid industrialization. Thus, *Organization and Management* was transferred to the Commissariat of Heavy Industry. This symbolic change pointed to the future: rationalization could no longer be applied to administration (and politics), but would henceforth be sharply restricted to the technical aspects of industrial production.[59] To be sure, a qualitatively new era of Soviet management science was about to dawn, that of "high Stalinism": Stalin's domination of the political system reached high tide in 1934 and continued more-or-less unabated until his death in 1953.

"Cadres Resolve Everything"[60]

Bolshevik élan almost completely displaced scientific management and organizational rationality as a leadership value in the 1930s. For Stalin and his entourage, there could be no technical expertise apart from the "correct" political line. Thus, administrative science suffered near-total demise, except for a badly truncated branch of technical-engineering knowledge. And the economic literature became increasingly sterile, descriptive, or preoccupied with technical detail. By pursuing short-range policy benefits, scholars gingerly avoided theoretical analysis and, instead, concentrated on microlevel questions of intrafirm planning, control, accounting, bookkeeping, and the like.[61] Their neglect of theory was, in Soviet jargon, "not accidental." Stalin had consciously divorced theory from practice and pronounced the latter sole criterion of theoretical truth. (Today, Soviet administrative specialists openly acknowledge that this artificial separation had a disastrous impact on theoretical developments in the fields.) From this doctrinal standpoint, "[to] foist upon political economy problems of economic science is to kill it as a science."[62] What survived of theoretical inquiry remained safely tucked away in administrative law (for examination of the state apparatus) and did no more than provide ex-post-facto theoretical justification for Stalin's policies, as political economy did for economic "analysis." Henceforth, until the mid-1950s, administrative specialists would engage in "agitprop" and were completely replaced by economic practitioners (mainly engineers) who made decisions on a trial-and-error basis. And their organizational goals were dominated by a single imperative—the irrational forcing of heavy industry.

Developments in the 1930s

Administrative specialists in the 1930s abandoned an interbranch perspective and concentrated on specific industrial sectors—steel, chemicals, machine building, mining, etc.[63] The leading research center of the era— the Central Scientific Research Institute (TsI0)— was established in 1931. Given the task of elaborating socialist theory, it in fact dealt exclusively with practical matters of organizing heavy industry. In 1934–1938, several articles on production control appeared in Organization of Management.[64] TsI0 was also responsible for what one Soviet researcher, has called the first major textbook on production management published in the USSR (1937).[65] Intra firm planning made important strides, namely the genesis of *tekhpromfinplan*.
[66]   Technological centers and branch institutes sprang up. Their objective was to assist enterprise managers in dealing with new industrial techniques. The first All-Union conference on planning in the electrical-machinery industry was held in Leningrad (1931). Over 600 economists and engineers attended. It was not until seven years later that Moscow and Leningrad factory directors met to discuss common problems, especially those involving new technology. Several conference reports tried to *generalize* experience and, as such, were atypical of the 1930s.

To the extent that administrative personnel retained their status, they did so as industrial cadres and/or engineering specialists. Higher schools demanded technical expertise and all but abandoned theoretical questions in their course curricula. There was simply no time to ponder that which did not promise immediate practical benefits. Managers were taught their functional responsibilities—planning, organizing, accounting, finance, etc. Engineering–economics institutes were set up in Moscow, Leningrad, and Kharkov. Separate departments were established in other institutes to deal specifically with industrial mangement. Of course, the industrial academy (*promakademiia*) had already been founded in 1927; it concentrated on raising the qualification of those industrial cadres already in leadership positions. Trained under socialist conditions, the "red directors" remained personally loyal to Stalin. Other centers were closely tied to priority industrial sectors and their training programs lasted from six months to one year.[67] The Institute of Management Problems (IPU) was founded in 1939. Drawing heavily from an interdisciplinary research program, researchers at *IPU* concentrated on technical control processes found in mechanical and/ or social systems.

THE DAMPER OF STALINISM

There was little relief from adroit citations and sterile economic discourse in the 1930s, the indisputable nadir of Soviet administrative science. The few exceptions warrant scrutiny, especially since they represent "windows" in the totalitarian edifice that later developed into important, relatively autonomous schools of thought in the USSR. No single individual did more to support modern economic thinking and management science in the 1930s than N.A. Voznesensky. Installed as director of Gosplan, the state planning agency, in late 1937, Voznesensky called for more creative approaches to economic theory.[68] He might have concluded that the absence of objective criteria to guide decision makers could no longer be tolerated; in any event, he quietly began to resurrect interest in pricing policy, indicator construction, and the interrelationship among major sectors in the economy. Earlier, in his role as economic "boss" of Leningrad, Voznesensky protected a small group of mathematical economists, including V.S. Nemchinov, V.V. Novozhilov, L.V. Kantorovich, and several others. Although mathematical economics had flourished in the 1920s, it became highly suspect under Stalin. And Kantorovich's remarkable breakthrough in linear programming in 1939 (which implied constraints on Bolshevik will and the absolute freedom to set objectives) remained isolated, circulating only among a small circle of enthusiasts.[69] The day would come, however, when such thinking would be accepted in the Soviet Union.

There were also several modest efforts in the 1930s to elaborate a theory of *socialist* production management. The "science on organizing production"[70] brought to light several important points that would eventually constitute the basis for a rebirth of management science some twenty years hence. Basic questions included: What are the distinctive features of management under socialism? What are the subject matter and scope of an autonomous field of inquiry? How can they be linked to adjacent disciplines? Is management a science or an art? Indeed, these were *not* typical questions asked in the 1930s. That they were raised at all at that time is surprising, given the severe penalties of those years for nonconformity and/or abstract theorizing; however, Liubovich raised the same questions during the rebirth of administrative science during the period 1957–1966.

Nevertheless, I.O. Liubovich strongly criticized the narrow, technical specialization of Soviet managers as well as their tendency to equate engineering with organizational skills.[71] He found that technical knowledge, in fact, bore little relation to leadership or managerial ability. And on that basis, the regime's cadre policy was misguided because it neglected the "organizational factor" and—by the third five-year plan—this deficiency was having a disastrous impact on economic development. A remedy was to "completely overcome the neglect of organizing production in the educational training of our engineers . . . so that [they] can successfully carry out their tasks as organizer of socialist production"[72]

Unwilling to focus on techniques or to take Engels's prediction of "administering things" literally, Liubovich and B.I. Katsenbogen concluded that management dealt with the cooperation of people in the labor process. Not only did their treatment stress social factors, but it raised the possibility of separating socialist management from that existing under capitalism. Their insights did not end here, however. A holistic approach was clearly required:

> [Management science] examines the factors of production as combined elements of a single "production body": the implements of labor . . . and work force [are] a system of the complex cooperation of people [examined] from the perspective of the harmonization of separate organs.[73]

Although management was an interdisciplinary field borrowing liberally from biology, psychophysiology, and administrative and labor law, it was most closely related to economics. Unlike political economy, however, it dealt with the *concrete* expression of general laws, particularly those manifest in separate socialist enterprises.[74] In this sense it was an applied discipline taught to administrative personnel. And the relevance of Western "techniques"—a central issue in the previous decade—was gingerly avoided by specialists concerned with their own personal safety and, hence, content to restate "eternal truths." They could no longer apply the rhetorical device of separating "system" from "techniques": the whole package, so to speak, was out of step with the political and psychological needs of high Stalinism. Only the rich, if poorly mastered, experience of constructing socialism in the USSR could provide the theoretical basis of socialist management science. Those lacking sufficient vigilence were presented with an ominous warning: "Whoever contends that socialist production organization does not have its own theoretical base is profoundly in error[and] is unaware of the real content and meaning of [that] science, or underestimates its tremendous theoretical wealth.[75] Thus, Soviet theorists had to formulate a different approach to administration than those heavily trodden paths of bourgeois specialists. But time would prove this an unwieldy, even demoralizing, task.

Correctly fearing for their personal safety, most simply avoided any issue that might compromise their good socialist credentials. It was prudent to deal exclusively with narrow, technical issues, or simply repeat ad nauseam Stalin's ideological pronouncements. Administrative specialists learned a hard lesson in the 1930s: their survival depended upon silence and luck.[76] To be sure, cadres would resolve everything.

Conclusion

Hitler's *Drang nach Osten* (22 June 1941) stamped out the miniscule remnants of Soviet administrative science and almost destroyed the USSR itself.[77] The unprecedented Soviet mobilization that followed the German attack marked in its every aspect—the tempo, scope, and ruthless determination by which it was pursued—an ultimate shift in the strategic balance between the two contestants. No one doubted the immense *potential* power of Soviet Russia, but few envisioned a cohesive sociopolitical system (especially after the Great Terror), defended by a well-equipped and capably led army. And the organizational achievements of the Stalinist leadership, notably Ustinov,[78] in transferring a significant portion of the country's industrial capacity eastward under the most difficult wartime conditions, were remarkable indeed. Despite enemy occupation of the most intensively developed sections of Russia and the Ukraine, Soviet industry actually outproduced that of Nazi Germany in several categories of military equipment. If nothing else, the awesome bloodletting of the Great Patriotic War had vindicated Stalin's 1931 prediction: there would be ten years to either catch up with advanced capitalist states or else be crushed by them. Consequently, the victory day celebration (9 May 1945) symbolized much more than justifiable pride in military success: An entire social system and political ideal had withstood the test of battle. And with this triumph came the tested forms of industrial organization and managerial practice developed by Soviet political leaders and economic planners—five-year plans, centralized control, shock labor, storming, etc. Nevertheless, the real measure of their staying power lay in the future. Meanwhile, in the United States, no such political suppression of management concepts and practices had taken place. Instead, the American victory in World War II was felt by most American leaders to be a vindication of the closed-system perspective of scientific management, the mastery of the assembly line, and the "principles" of management that had been developed between the 1880s and the 1940s. Thus, when Herbert Simon published "The Proverbs of Administration" shortly after World War II ended, the piece was both widely hailed and ignored in management practice. Nevertheless, American administrative science was about to go through a second conceptual revolution that would revitalize it. To this revolution we now turn.

4

The Revitalization of Administrative Science

> *It is a fatal defect of the current principles of administration that, like proverbs, they occur in pairs. For almost every principle one can find an equally plausible and acceptable contradictory principle. Although the two principles of the pair will lead to exactly opposite organizational recommendations, there is nothing in the theory to indicate which is the proper one to apply.*
>
> *—Herbert A. Simon*

> *Considerable misperception is a standard part of the functioning of each government. Any proposal that is widely accepted is perceived by different men to do quite different things and to meet quite different needs. Misperception is in a sense the grease that allows cooperation among people whose differences otherwise would hardly allow them to coexist.*
>
> *—Graham T. Allison*

Introduction

As we noted in Chapters 2 and 3, Herbert Simon's "Proverbs of Administration" marks the transition between early American administrative science—which was based, in the main, on invalid assumptions, and whose practitioners attempted to find the method to create the "perfect organization" (something as feasible as a perpetual motion machine)—and modern American administrative science. Modern U.S. administrative science is grounded in more rigorous, though in many cases still flawed, attempts to describe, explain, and predict the behavior of large-scale, complex systems. Administrative science changed from that of a *closed-systems* perspective to a *social, open-systems perspective*. This transformation led to modern ad-

50

ministrative science and to current approaches toward the comprehension of complex organizational systems, approaches that permit far more powerful explanations of how systems actually behave. Perhaps the most dominant attribute of modern approaches is their emphasis on *uncertainty*, both in the narrow statistical sense of applying modern analytical techniques to the process of problem solving, and, more recently, to the larger problem of a complex system operating in a larger complex world, much of which cannot be controlled, understood, or confidently predicted.

From Rational to Open-System View of Organizations

As administrative science emerged in the late nineteenth century, its early practitioners were consumed with the notion of a perfectly operating system that could be described through the "wiring diagram" of the organization. The concepts that were developed do not describe how an organization does operate, they describe how it should operate. Modern approaches have revealed the vast chasm between these types of descriptions. Formal research into the wiring diagram of an organization as well as its rule books and procedural manuals help our understanding of what was intended by management; but analyses of what actually happened, how people in the organization behaved, and how the organization itself behaved are very different matters. Furthermore, the question of alternative organizational structures and processes that produce more effective outcomes (we will leave open at this point the definition of "more effective," to return to it later in this chapter) disappeared in early administrative science because of the assumption that there is only one best way. With only "one best way," we are unable to examine the attributes of an organization and the environment in which it operates because there is no point to be gained by such an examination.

The early approaches of administrative theory assumed that a single structural form was adequate for all tasks that faced the organization. Whether the organization was engaged in the production of a simple product (e.g., paper bags) for a market or had a production goal well understood (e.g., X units this year and Y units next year) by managers and workers or was engaged in a area requiring high technology (e.g., fabricating advanced aircraft) and rapid innovation to stay even with or ahead of the state of the art (e.g., microchips and other electronics) in a highly fluid or uncertain market, the structure to perform these tasks was assumed to be essentially the same. The task of innovation, for example, would be carried out within the same structure as that for day-to-day tasks and simple operations.

At this point, we should make clear that we are not dichotomizing organizations into mutually exclusive categories. Rather, the closed-systems view dominant in the early writers must be viewed as one extreme in a continuum. As James Thompson has observed, the closed and open characteristics of organizations vary even within organizations, depending on separate levels of responsibility and control.[1] Talcott Parsons divides these levels into technical, managerial, and institutional levels.[2] The technical level is at the lowest level in the hierarchy of authority and is concerned with ensuring that the technological processes of the organization operate efficiently. This work, routine in nature for the most part, is characterized by attempts to create closed systems so that uncertainty is reduced and production efficiency increased. At this level, Taylorism as applied in the United States and the Soviet Union—in such forms as PERT, operations research, mathematical economics, network analysis, and the like—remains a useful technique for solving microproblems associated with the maintenance of technical efficiency.

At the managerial level, the central concern is the administration of the technical level so that the relationship of the organization to its environment is a favorable one. That is, all organizations, whether public or private, must obtain resources (such as people, materials, and money) from the environment that is external to the organization.[3] They then transform these resources into a product or service, which is then exchanged with the external environment so as to obtain new resources. In a market economy an organization must have a favorable rate of exchange as measured in profits and losses. In public-sector organizations, the exchange ratio is far harder to measure and indeed an organization providing public services may continue to obtain resources from the external environment because organizational momentum, political considerations, and other criteria obivate the necessity for a profit-and-loss statement. This latter problem is one to which we shall later in this chapter.[4]

At the institutional level, the "top" of the organization in a formal chart is concerned with the legitimacy of the organization in terms of its environment. Thus corporate executives will be concerned with product changes in order to anticipate changing markets, changing environments in terms of governmental regulations, and the like. (The inability of American automobile manufacturers to react to a rapidly changing environment can be isolated here; thus, despite complaints from the American automobile industry that federal regulations caused the near collapse of the industry, it is relatively easy to determine that the real reason for that near-collapse lay with the institutional level within the industry. In fact, it can be argued that if it were not for the intervention of the U.S. government into the industry with regulations requiring improved gasoline mileage after the 1973 OPEC embargo, the industry would have collapsed completely as it approached the 1980s. These regulations forced the recalcitrant auto industry to begin the lengthy design and engineering process that led to the ability of American car makers to sell low-mileage autos at about the time of the second great economic shocks, brought on by additional increases in the price of oil in the late 1970s and early 1980s.) It is at the institutional level that the power of the open-systems explanations is most clearly seen.

A system so described is prone to internal conflict as well as conflict with its environment.[5] The top level is supposed to be change inducing (although in the automobile industry it has not been), so that the organization can continue to successfully obtain resources from the environment. Yet the technical level, demanding stability through reduced uncertainty, will resist change.

Differences between Systems View and Taylorism

As Alvin Gouldner and Charles Perrow have noted, a systems view has three critical differences from the rational model of applied Taylorism and its descendants.[6] The first, which we have noted, is that organizations operate in an environment that is uncertain. This uncertainty prevents full control of the "organizational weapon." Second, because each part of the organization is part of an organic whole, changes in one part will affect other parts. The third major part of the open-systems view is that the organizational structure may behave in ways that are not planned when the structure was organized. Thus what is important is not what was planned but rather what behavior (by both individuals in the system and the system itself) actually emerges. The structure of the organization cannot be separated from the functioning of the organization.[7] And because the organization is a structuring of events rather than of tangible parts, "It has no structure apart from its functioning."[8] Thus, one can never hope to learn how an organization actually functions by examining organizational charts ("wiring diagrams"), procedural manuals, and other physical aspects. Rather, organizations acquire inputs, process those inputs so as to increase their value, and then exchange them as outputs. To do this, the system must maintain itself, it must be able to adapt, and it must manage its own external and internal functions through coordination and control.

The organization is a social system composed of various subsystems, which are, in turn, linked to the larger organization by mutually interdependent bonds. The organization is then linked both to other organizations and to the general environment.[9] Systems approaches open the perspectives by which organizations can be viewed, since through the flow and content of communications within the organization the "glue" that holds the organization together and permits it to function in its environment can be examined.[10] The open system shifts focus from the internal structure and properties of individual subsystems to "their interaction and its relevance to the larger systems."[11]

To describe organizations as simply constituting the sums of their parts is to fall prey to the fallacy of composition: each level does share certain characteristics of the whole, while it maintains some selected properties unique to that level.[12] Various subsystems are linked together but are also semiautonomous.

By focusing on the flow of information both within the organization and between the organization and its environment, the concept of feedback moves to center stage. The organzation monitors its output (its exchange of resources with its external environment) through the feedback concept—in a rational administrative situation the organization will move to change its behavior if the effect of the output is a negative exchange with the environment. What Karl Deutsch, using the metaphor of the driver of an automobile moving down an expressway, has called the ability to steer through the utilization of the feedback mechanism is critical to open-systems approaches.[13]

Yet while the open-systems approach was a great step forward in the understanding of how organizations actually behave, many of the questions raised suggest that a different focus of vision might yield additional insights. We earlier suggested that it was the U.S. government's intervention in the automobile industry that "saved" the industry from its own self-induced bankruptcy—that is, political action forced the industry to modify its feedback systems in such a way that the industry, kicking and screaming all the way, was dragged to the altar of the energy-efficient vehicle. Thus, despite its ability to "steer" and thus to be "adaptively rational,"[14] the industry was so only because of outside intervention. Deutsch has analyzed the possibility of organizational collapse and has identified six major areas of inquiry to explain such collapse. However, a vulnerable organization may not actually collapse because it has the power required to control the environment. In one of the more interesting definitions of power, Deutsch argues that power means "not to have to give in, and to force the environment or the other person to do so. Power . . . is the ability to talk instead of listen. In a sense, it is the ability to afford not to learn."[15] The question then becomes, just when does an organization have enough power so that it does not have to learn because it can manipulate the environment rather than making difficult and painful internal changes so that output can be adapted to the realities of the environment. This question suggests that political models, which focus on conflict within the organization, and a distinction between market-oriented (private) organizations and non–market-oriented (public) organizations may be useful. We will examine these questions in greater detail later in this chapter. First, however, a final review of open systems is necessary.

REVIEW OF SYESTEMS THEORY

When analysts discuss self-destroying systems, nonviable systems, viable systems, and self-developing systems, what is not clear is whether they are discussing the ability (or lack thereof) of the systems to control the environment or the internal attributes of the organization that permit it to be viable or self-developing or cause it to be nonviable and self-destructing.

The open-systems view focuses on links between units of the organizational systems and between the system and its environment. This perspective tends to "black box" the internal characteristics of those subsystems of the organization by focusing on the exchange between them. Thus, the nature of the exchanges can be analyzed, but the questions how or why a given policy originated in a subunit cannot be attacked with confidence. The political-conflict and decision-making approaches fill this void because they examine the internal activity and characteristics of the subunits. In the political-conflict model, policy output is tied to internal conflict within and between subunits of the organizational hierarchy. In those conflicts, participants pay only marginal attention to the external environment. What is required is an examination of the social aspects of the human beings who play the bureaucratic game. Thus, a social-systems perspective can broaden open-systems insights through an examination of the intentions of people and their intended and unintended behavior. A "comprehensive view of organizations must take into account the fact that sometimes conflicting, sometimes congruent, and sometimes unrelated intentions of human actors are important ingredients of organizations."[16] To this perspective we now turn.

Political-Conflict Perspectives

Conflict within organizations has traditionally been viewed as something undesirable, something for managers to avoid. In our earlier analysis of human-relations approaches (see Chapter 2), the normative bias against conflict is evident. And the search for the rational organization has been dominated by the search for ways to reduce or eliminate conflict. Taylor held that once the "one best way" was identified, there would be no conflict because no rational being could argue with "scientific truth." Thus, the rational argument has been that organizations must be designed in such a way that conflict is limited. Even the open-systems view suggests that although conflict will be present in all organizations, it is not a permanent attribute but something to be overcome through adaptation.

Although we do not intend to enter the normative thicket of whether conflict is always something to be avoided, we do believe that conflict can play a positive and vital role in the functioning of an organization; and there is some evidence for this point of view. That evidence suggests that tension can produce positive emotional effects in individuals and that some individuals seek out situations of stress because of curiosity.[17] Indeed, many strikingly successful political leaders in both the United States and the USSR (such as Franklin Roosevelt and Stalin) have deliberately introduced conflict, into their immediate environments so as to ensure that the warring parties in the circle of immediate advisers, and the larger bureaucracy as well, will come to them for resolution of these conflicts. Thus, while the American culture tends to view conflict as a negative attribute and emphasizes harmony, uniformity, and a lack of tolerance for alternate or divergent views, the real world of politics is filled with the rough-and-tumble affairs of government, which are almost always in a state of conflict, whether about the location of a sewer line or about foreign policy. Politics is, after all, the resolution of conflict. To belabor this point a bit, it is possible to imagine a society where harmony and uniformity are so highly valued that the society could be viewed as a collection of blissfully happy and contented idiots joyfully headed for disaster.[18]

The political model brings to center stage the everyday fact of life of conflict between people and organizational subunits, between subunits of certain organizations and subunits of other organizations, between organizations themselves, and between organizations and their environments. In fact, some analysts have suggested that conflict within organizations can become so bitter and intense that the individuals engaged in the infighting want the organization or its efforts to fail, so that the other side can be blamed. Part of the difficulty in organizing and carrying out the U.S. bombing campaign against North Vietnam was rivalry between the Air Force and the Navy over which service had the right to fly planes over water.[19] Daughen and Binzen argue that the main reason for one of the biggest and most important bankruptcies in recent American business history—that of the Penn Central railroad—was the struggle between persons previously associated with either the old New York Central railroad or the old Pennsylvania railroad prior to the merger of the two. The New York Central group, for example, refused to consolidate data-processing operations if the consolidation meant using the Pennsylvania railroad center and programs.[20]

The focus on political conflict as an aspect of organizational behavior opened a "new perspective of organizational analysis . . . [and] constitutes one of the most significant theoretical developments in recent organization theory . . . [It is] badly needed in order to reinvigorate organization theory . . ."[21] As Graham Allison has remarked and our experience confirms: "The gap between academic literature and the experience of participants is nowhere wider than at this point."[22] Academic literature has tended to concentrate on rational aspects of organizational behavior and has generally failed to describe how organizations and people in them actually behave. The political model is closest to the experience of those who have actually been involved. It focuses on the immense number of variables and the subtle nature of problems involved in decision making and problem resolution. Time pressures are intense and information is seldom adequate. Conflict occurs because "men share power. Men differ about what must be done. The differences matter."[23] Conflict over the differences can be resolved only in a bargaining process, whether the organization is a production-centered concern or a governmental one. Samuel Huntington has described the process as legislative in nature but executive in locale.[24] In that political process:

> Sometimes one group committed to a course of action triumphs over other groups fighting for other alternatives. Equally often, however, different groups pulling in different directions produce as a result, or better a resultant—a mixture of conflicting preferences and unequal power of various individuals—distinct from what any person or group intended . . . . Hundreds of issues compete for players [sic] attention every day. Each player is forced to fix upon his issues for that day, deal with them in their own terms, and rush on to the next. Thus the character of emerging issues and the pace at which the game is played converge to yield . . . "decisions" and "actions" as collages.[25]

Conflict is frequently hidden from the observer outside the organization and even from some of the participants. Warring participants use the "official" language and the ideology of the organization to mask their intent. Conflict objectives are thus cast in the language of the "rational" model's language—that is, maximizing official organizational goals. But actual objectives may in fact be very different.

The formal organization chart with its neat lines of communication and authority masks the real centers of power within any organization because of an informal structure composed of cliques that cut across organizational lines both vertically and laterally, the membership constantly changing depending on the issue that tends to dominate decision making.[26] For participants, today's enemy on Issue A is tommorow's ally on Issue B. This awareness among the players influences the manner of conflict. Cliques are crucial to the explanation of what the organization does and why it does it because they form the dominant coalition within the organization. This dominant coalition defends the "organizational essence" from attack both from within and without the organization. Organizational essence, a term first used by Morton Halperin in his study of foreign-policy bureaucratic politics, refers to "the view held by the dominant group within the organizational structure of what the missions and capabilities [of the organization] should be."[27] In the U.S. Department of Defense, for example, the dominant coalition tries to protect its view of organizational essence by controlling the promotion patterns of junior officers so that those who share the view of the dominant coalition are promoted into its ranks.[28] According to Melville Dalton, the same phenomenon occurs in corporate organizations.[29]

EXAMPLES OF THE POLITICAL MODEL

The power of this perspective can perhaps be best understood by reviewing the weapons acquisition process of the U.S. Department of Defense. The fact that the United States acquires weapons systems that may or may not be appropriate to the threat faced and may or may not be effective on the battlefield is a rational question but one that *is essentially irrelevant from the political perspective*. The weapons-system procurement process is directed by a dominant coalition of government officials, industry managers, and congressional barons, all protecting vested interests. In fact, in all nations, various ministries of defense have acquired, in peacetime, weapons which, when put to the test in battle, failed miserably (and cost many lives) but were procured because those were the systems favored by the dominant coalition.[30] In the automobile industry, the dominant coalition favored production of large, fuel-inefficient, but highly profitable cars, dismissing until the late 1970s any demand for small cars as "the teacher trade"—a small market for low-to middle-income individuals that was hardly worth the effort.

When American presidents are sworn into office, they believe that they have a mandate as they confront entrenched coalitions. The entrenched coalitions also believe they have a mandate from their clients, congressional committees, industry groups, and bureaucrats. Presidential attempts to penetrate and deal with these coalitions is, to say the least, an interesting spectator sport. In part, the "success" of a president simply reflects his ability to break through dominant coalitions.

The cliques in the bureaucracy can cut across organizations laterally and vertically, as Dalton found, but, as Michael Crozier discovered in his study of the French bureaucracy, they can also be organized around and within subunits of larger organizations. Unlike Dalton's description of groups that emerge to fight over an issue and then disappear only to reform with somewhat different participants to fight on another issue, Crozier found highly cohesive and long-lasting groups operating in a highly stratified bureaucracy. Conflict occurred between these groups over interpretation of formal organizational rules and regulations.[31] Because coalitions can be temporary *and* permanent, organized informally across and up-and-down the organization (or in a web between organizations) *and* formally composed of subunits warring with each other, and have a major impact on policy and program implementation, analysts face a nightmare in trying to reconstruct events. Individuals and groups pursue interests that are, by definition, parochial in nature, because those interests tend to be perceived by those individuals and groups as the most critical problems facing the organization as a whole. These narrow interests are defended by those coalitions even at the cost of larger goals. In the 1960s, for example, the U.S. Army intensely resisted the adoption of a rifle that was cheaper, easier to operate, more jam-resistant, lighter in weight, and more effective (the AR-15) than the army's standard rifle (the M-14) because it was not developed by Army small arms bureaucrats, the "traditional" source of army small arms (the AR-15 was developed by a small arms maker instead). There is evidence that the refusal to adopt this better rifle played a role in the deaths of American soldiers in Vietnam, the extensive disillusionment with the war by the GIs fighting it, and the subsequent disorder and organizational decay that caused intense internal problems in the army. The army ordinance group simply would not adopt the AR-15 until it had been modified into the M-16 by that ordinance group itself and the modifications forced on the rifle dramatically reduced its performance.[32]

The strength of the political approach to understanding organizational behavior is that it permits explanations of actions that the rational and open-systems approaches do not. Yet a glaring weakness is related to its assets: the focus on conflict tends to mask the fact that conflict is strongly influenced by the formal organizational structure. Although factions may form across vertical and horizontal formal lines, the shape of the hierarchy grants authority to decide to those at the top of the organization and power to implement to those in the intermediate and lower ranges. This distinction is, of course, a source of conflict when the right to decide is separated from the expertise to decide[33] or lower-level bureaucrats refuse to implement or try to subvert policy guidance from higher levels when they translate policy into programs.[34] Nevertheless, there is a general relationship between formal position and power. Organizational theorists who have studied the decision-making process in organizations note that one of the constants of that process is the attempt to mute conflict within the organization. This "quasi-resolution of conflict," in Richard Cyert and James March's terminology,[35] results from the fact that organizations are collections of subgroups with differing perceptions about what needs to be done and what is important. Inconsistency in the policy output or program implementation of complex bureaucracies results from the decision process in which demands of the subgroups are met sequentially. For example, the production elements within the organization require stability for planning purposes, while the sales elements may be rewarded for exceeding quotas, although the sales push, in turn, disrupts the smooth functioning of production through sudden demands for acceleration to meet unexpectedly large sales. At the same time, the research and development group may develop a new product that sells beyond any expectation, further disrupting production by requiring new tools and production runs. The natural conflicts that emerges among sales, research and developemnt, and production are dealt with through changing sales quotas to stabilize production, restructuring sales reward systems, establishing a new plant for the new product, and so on. But the process of decision making does not fit in the political model of organizational behavior. Decision making in itself is another approach, to which we now turn.

Decision Making in Complex Bureaucracies

Modern analysis attempts to describe how decisions are actually made in practice and does not attempt to prescribe how managers should make a rational decision. In the real world, it is not possible to make a completely rational decision because that decision requires information that can never be obtained—exact knowledge of the future and all possible consequences of all possible alternatives. Consider the impact of this statement on the drive of early organization theorists for the perfectly functioning organization. If completely rational decisions cannot be made, the very assumptions (e.g., goal-directed behavior) that guided classical administrative theorists and applied Taylorism are invalid. People may act for reasons that appear non-rational to the observer but that are perfectly rational to the individual acting. Thus, much of organizational behavior is "Hardyesque in nature; it depends upon the fortuitous, complex and obscure confluence of many distantly related streams; it depends upon solutions that happen to be there when the problems arise . . . and is therefore not goal-related."[36]

Herbert Simon, perhaps the towering figure in developing explanations of actual decisions made by people in organizations, argues that rational decisions are constrained by the capabilities of individuals to process, store, and retrieve information, and further, that these capabilities are subject to distortions and errors.[37] As a result of those errors and distortions, as well as short time limits to make decisions, individuals tend to select the first alternative that *appears* to offer a solution. Simon and his colleague James March label this decision process "satisficing" as opposed to making the optimal choice. The process of satisficing is how decisions are really made.[38] Because satisficing decisions will have some consequences that were not intended by the decision maker, organizational decision making is best described as a sequential process of satisficing decisions, each having unanticipated consequences, which must be dealt with by additional satisficing decisions. Charles Lindblom has labelled this process "The Science of Muddling Through,"[39] in which the organization bumps along, never able to function completely rationally because of constraints on information processing that individuals suffer. When one adds the notion of quasiresolution of conflict developed by Cyert and March to this description, a picture of how decisions are made emerges. For example, the American automobile makers were unable to forsee to forthcoming rapid change in the market place because they could not possibly know the future, so their decisions were satisficing in nature in that they could not possibly know the future, so their decisions were satisficing in nature in that they continued to produce large, fuel-inefficient automobiles because it appeared to be the "best" decision at the time. American foreign-policy decision makers did not foresee the quagmire that became American involvement in Vietnam, so their decisions were satisficing with the hope of muddling through.

These explanations, widely offered by those who were in charge when these disastrous decisions were made, have plausibility but they ignore one additional powerful constraint on decision makers—that of the small group. Decisions in large, complex bureaucracies are seldom made by individuals in isolation. Rather, there are groups of people advising the actual deciders and these people tend to form small groups, which in themselves have powerful impacts on each individual.

ASCH'S SMALL-GROUP THEORY

Beginning with the writings of Muzafer Sherif and Solomon Asch, students of small group behavior argue that the small group (roughly, between 5 and 12 persons) serves as an anchor for each individual in it and helps establish a framework for the making of decisions.[40] In a series of experiments, which Robert Zajonc has labelled "one of the most disturbing discoveries of social psychology,"[41] Asch found that the pressures exerted on individuals by peers in the small group could lead those individuals to deliberately imitate "a judgment that they knew was contrary to the facts, contrary to what they perceived, or both."[42] Asch's experiments were so organized that a subject was asked to make a judgment alone, then to make another judgment in a group after all of the other members of the group (confederates of the experimenters) had given a deliberately incorrect response. When the individual was making his decisions alone, correct responses averaged 93 percent; when the individual was subjected to the peer pressure of unanimously wrong judgments, the correct responses rate dropped sharply to 67 percent. Other students of the small group have found that as the difficulty of the decision increases, so does individual conformity to the group, even though the group response is in error.[43] As groups place pressures on individuals to conform to group norms, individuals tend to conform or the group will reject those individuals holding views contrary to the group norms. People want to belong to groups and to be accepted by their peers, so they adjust their views to conform.[44]

The study of the small group is not yet at the point where it can be determined under what circumstances small groups will have a positive or negative impact on the operations of the organization. If the norms of the group are in consonance with the norms and larger objectives of the organization, small groups may reinforce organizational operations.[45] On the other hand, the desire to conform can contribute to a negative overall result.[46]

From the perspective of small group theory, the American auto industry's failure and the involvement of the United States in Vietnam take on still another perspective. The auto industry failed to adapt because the small group at the top of the organization refused to admit that the external environment, the market, had changed and that small cars were now required or would be in the very near future. Dissidents such as John Z. DeLorean (one-time president of the Pontiac and then the Chevrolet divisions of General Motors), who argued for small, down-sized cars, were forced out of the organization because they did not conform.[47] In a similar vein, the United States blundered into Vietnam because the small group of advisors surrounding Lyndon Johnson forced out dissidents such as George Ball, the under secretary of state.[48]

CENTRALIZATION vs. DECENTRALIZATION

Other students of the decision process focus on the structure of the organization and thus are related to the classical administrative theorists of an earlier time. However, their descriptions of how the structure influences the decision-making process and how that influence contributes to the gap between the ideal decision and the observed decision sets the two groups apart.

Harold Wilensky, for example, examines the dilemma of organizational centralization and decentralization.[49] This problem is a simple one but has profound implications. In highly centralized decision systems, such as those of the Soviet Union, problems of coordination are reduced because of a central location or a central management group. However, operations at the local level will suffer because guidelines issued from the central group may be inappropriate to the local situation. In the United States, for example, a common complaint of local officials is that many regulations of the federal bureaucracy are simply inappropriate for local conditions. In an apocryphal example (which we believe to be aprocryphal because we cannot confirm it), the Occupational Safety and Health Administration (OSHA) was reported to have issued a regulation requiring stretchers at all entrances to mines so that injured miners could be quickly removed. This regulation is appropriate for large mines but inappropriate for the single-miner mine in isolated areas, since the single miner could not possibly carry himself out of the mine on the stretcher. Yet a permit for the mine could not be granted until the stretcher requirement was certified. So individual miners had to purchase a stretcher and place it outside the mine in order to obtain the permit. This story illustrates the frustrations inherent in central direction's insensitivity to local needs.

Decentralization leads to new problems. Although it allows the "man on the spot" to deal with local problems, the criteria used at the local level may "not be closely related to higher-level criteria."[50] For example, if federal government educational assistance funds are not specified and are instead given to local communities without requirements, nothing formally prevents the local decision makers from responding to pressures of local elites and spending those funds for improvements to the wealthy (largely white) school rather than to the poor (largely black or Hispanic) school. If federal officials attach detailed regulations, then the movement back to the centralization end of the spectrum is clear, and soon centralization's problems reappear.

The dilemma of centralization and decentralization is simply not solvable in any known manner, particularly when the problem requires centralized control and decentralized problem solving. This latter difficulty is particularly acute in the Soviet Union, where ideology constrains decentralization. A cumbersome and inefficient central bureaucracy—one that restrains and frustrates innovation from below—dominates Soviet society. In the United States, where ideology calls for a highly pluralistic decision system, the solving of problems has also led to a cumbersome and complex intergovernmental structure that consumes a large portion of the monies allocated to it for substantive programs. The result is that decision makers in both societies must constantly experiment with degrees of centralization and decentralization. Large organizations are therefore constantly undergoing marginal organizational changes as decision makers develop satisficing methods of dealing with current problems through adjustments in the organizational structure. The problem is that the goal set in concrete in early organization theory has proved difficult to abandon; that is, the smoothly functioning organization attending to its goals in an efficient and effective manner. Constant reorganization on "efficiency" grounds leads, of course, to increased political activity, as jurisdictional disputes flare up and procedures are disrupted.

PROBLEMS OF THE HIERARCHICAL STRUCTURE

Typically, problems of coordination and control and the accomplishment of work are accomplished through rewards available to leaders—status, power, and wealth. Control over information in a bureaucracy is a source of power. The hierarchical structure itself becomes a maze of concealment and misrepresentation as individuals try to maximize their status, power, and wealth. Superiors ignore subordinates in order to maintain the appearance of authority while those subordinates tend to try to "please the boss" by not reporting problems. The problems of the flow of information and of distortions in that flow are also of interest to analysts of decision making. As bureaucracy expands, large numbers of middle-level positions are created (largely due to the early administrative concept of span of control). Thus information has to pass through ever more filters and the isolation of top officials from organizational realities is increased. Wilensky notes that there "are many time servers at the lower ranks who have neither information nor the motive for acquiring it. In the middle, among the non-mobile, there are many who restrict information to prevent change, many mutual aid and comfort groups who restrict information because of the resentment of more ambitious colleagues, and many coalitions of ambitious men who share information among themselves but pass on only that portion that furthers one or more of their careers."[51]

The formal hierarchy also allows leadership to control what issues will rise to the top for review because the leaders control the formal communication system, which is hierarchical in nature. Control of these formal information systems makes it more difficult for issues not popular with elites to penetrate the higher levels of the bureaucracy.[52] The picture of organizations that emerges from this view is one filled with middle-level officials who do not want to tell senior officials and senior officials who do not want to be told "bad news." This, of course, is a vast distance from the concept of the rational organization capable of massing highly specialized skills in a coordinated manner in seeking organizational goals. If literally true, it is a picture of organizational confusion, failed programs, and long-run disaster. That this does not occur on the whole (although it does in specific situations) provides fertile ground for the examination of which organizations are able to "muddle through" and which organizations fail.

Comparison of Government Organizations and Corporate Organizations

The analysis of the decision-making process in complex bureaucracies has occurred largely through the study of corporate (private) organizations. Largely by inference, conclusions developed in the study of private organizations have been applied to government bureaucracies on the ground that many of the formal characteristics of government organizations are identical to those of private ones. Up to this point, we have drawn evidence from both public and private organizational studies and applied those observations to illustrate our points. Evidence is emerging, however, which suggests that in some very important areas it may not be possible to transfer findings from one group of organizations (private) to another group (public) without serious reliability and validity problems. For one, public and private organizations have vastly different objectives. For another, they are financed differently. For a third, they have different abilities to measure their output and their success in meeting their objectives.

Private organizations exist to meet "narrow" goals such as production, sales, and service. Public organizations have much broader social objectives, such as providing for defense or promoting the general welfare. To do that, public organizations develop complex programs, which are assumed to meet the more general goals. Activities such as constructing waterways, subsidizing mass-transit systems, acquiring and deploying intercontinential ballistic missiles, and establishing public-health centers, are examples of those programs. To finance these operations, governments extract wealth from the remainder of the society. Private organizations, on the other hand, are financed through the sale of output, from income charged for service, through the sale of securities and the issuance of bonds. Information flowing from subunits in private organizations is generally far easier to quantify and therefore numeric in form. Because it is numeric, it is more easily understood by personnel than is information flowing in government organizations, which tends to be more concerned with quality and therefore less numeric. For example, after the 1980 general election in the United States, the new president called for a build-up of American military forces and a scaling down of social programs. Yet the defense increases and the corresponding reduction of social efforts is difficult to justify in quantitative terms—it is rather one based on judgment, which is in turn based on a theory of the role of the central government in a plural society and another theory about the relationship between military power and international politics and foreign policy. In private organizations, no manager would authorize a similar drastic change of direction for the organization without extensive market analyses and profitability estimates because a shift of such magnitude could be very dangerous to the ongoing viability of the organization. In reviewing the financial information arising from such studies, the private decision maker would ask three critical questions in making the decision as to alter the change in course:

- Score-card questions: Is the organization doing very well or not so well?
- Attention-getting questions: With what problems should the organization be concerned?
- Problem-solving questions: Which is the best alternative among available options?[53]

Because profits and losses act as a standard for evaluation of alternatives, the manager in the corporate organization answers the critical questions with hard data based on extensive previous experience. The government manager asks the same questions but the answers are more difficult to obtain. For example, will the build-up of defense forces in the United States strain the economy to such an extent that high rates of inflation result because of labor shortages and critical backlogs? Even after the proposals for the increases were made, the answers are uncertain. A specialist for a research firm was quoted as stating that "nobody can really tell for sure yet . . . There's been very little hard analysis."[54] No corporate manager would propose a similar build up without much better analyses to back up the decision.

With profits and losses acting as a standard for private organizational decision makers, managers can and do delegate authority downward in the organization when they structure the management situation. Because authority is delegated, the amount of information that must flow vertically between subunits is considerably lower than in organizations where delegation is not possible.[55] Using the comptroller, corporate headquarters can guard (not always completely successfully) against biased information flowing upward from subordinate units. As Cyert and March have noted, in this manner "the system does not become hopelessly confused."[56]

Government managers cannot accomplish the same control because, unlike corporate organizations, there is now narrow objective similar to profits and losses and there is widespread disagreement between governments and citizens over just what programs should operate and how they should be funded. It is not possible for public decision makers to compare day-to-day behavior with ultimate objectives because no large group can agree on what are those ultimate objectives. So, it has been stated that it is not possible to:

> apply such tests as "maximum well being from available resources." Without more precise definitions, this is merely saying we want the best. And when we spell out tests of preferredness more precisely, we find that we are using proximate criteria—that is, practicable tests which are not necessarily or obviously consistent with ultimate goals. The fact that we use such criteria makes it easy to adopt erroneous ones.[57]

PUBLIC ORGANIZATIONS: THE PROBLEM OF OUTPUT MEASUREMENT

The lack of adequate output measurement is a major distinguishing characteristic of public organizations. It is for this reason that input measurements are frequently substituted—that is, guestimating that if enough resources are devoted to (or thrown at) a problem, the problem can be ameliorated. In the 1980 election campaign in the United States, the argument advanced by the Republican party was that the throwing of money at social programs produced little tangible benefit (except to the administrators of those programs) and that they therefore should be eliminated. The Republicans proposed to throw money at defense instead, apparently assuming that there was a connection between input and success in foreign-policy programs that was not present in domestic programs.

Because there is a lack of appropriate output measures, government managers cannot delegate authority so that lower levels perform as desired and the centralization–decentralization question is generally settled in favor of higher centralization in public organizations and greater decentralization in private ones. It is obvious to us that "good government"—a battle cry to political aspirants—cannot be modeled on the private-sector model. This fact helps explain why successful corporate leaders have difficulty running public organizations. Having "met a payroll" may sound appealing in political campaigns, but that experience may not be helpful in managing public-sector organizations. With the combination of the lack of adequate performance indicators and the lack of anything but the most general agreement about what public-sector organizations should be doing, it is clear *that there is no one best way to organize.*[58] The search for the perfect model of an organization is a fool's errand. No matter how an organization is structured, government managers are forced to measure performance with measures that are gravely flawed (such as input) or with intuition and rules of thumb (defense needs to be increased while social programs should be cut back). To control behavior, leaders of public-sector organizations develop extremely detailed set of organization rules and operating procedures. They measure performance of lower level officials by their adherence to the rules and procedures. Because those lower officials know this, lower level officials treat the rules and regulations as an end in themselves, not as means to a supposed larger end. Robert Merton identified this as "goal displacement," in which the means to an end becomes the end itself.[59] Goal displacement is a powerful force in public organizations.

Yet program performance must be somewhat measured. And as we have seen, the measures adopted (such as input) can be and are gravely flawed. Arthur Ross, once a government data expert, noted "how public officials deceive themselves with statistics of impeccable quality."[60] Because of this deception, a "performance gap"—that is, the difference between what an organization is in fact accomplishing in terms of its programs and what individuals in it think it is accomplishing—will almost inevitably develop and lead public-sector managers to major errors in their decision making.[61] The performance gap will tend to grow very large because of inadequate performance indicators.[62]

Conclusion

This last section should have made clear that we believe there are very important differences between public and private organizations. Yet organization theory as a body of knowledge has only recently begun to explore them. It is also clear that the views of more recent students of organizational behavior have led us a long way from the early approaches with their emphasis on rationality. Organizational behavior is perhaps best viewed as the process of solving short-range problems with short-range solutions that are only poorly linked to longer-range objectives. Short-range solutions generate new immediate problems with which the coalitions that dominate organizations must deal. And they must deal with them in a structure that is heavily influenced by internal political processes and an inability to measure program effects in an adequate manner. Yet this view has one great problem. It assumes that there is a connection between behavior and objectives, and in this sense, although the political model, the open-systems approach, distinguishing between public and private organizations, and the decision analysis approach are all related. We will address the problem of an assumed link between behavior and objective in Chapter 7.

In the time that American organization theory was undergoing this behavioral revolution, the Soviet Union was slow to follow. In fact, for over a decade after the close of World War II, Soviet administrative theory was at first set back into orthodox indeological lines and then was in a period of near paralysis that lasted until the Twentieth Party Congress in 1956. From 1956 through the 1960s orthodox political economists resisted the introduction of more modern concepts but gradually lost that struggle. The struggle in the Soviet Union is the subject of our next chapter, after which, in chapter 6, we document the acceptance of these ideas.

5

From Stalin to Kosygin: The Reemergence of Administrative Science

To be always "different" does not in itself mean doing things right. In the early days of the revolution some enthusiasts demanded, in a flush of infantile leftism, the abolition of the railroads because [they] had been built under capitalism. Quite recently I talked with a character who argued passionately that our automobiles take better account of the political aspirations of the people than do American automobiles. I couldn't decide if he were a demagogue or a fool.

—Leonid Likhodeyev

[T]he insulation of Soviet theoretical thinking in economics has at last come to an end. Undoubtedly, mathematically formulated ideas, "imported" from the West, have by now made a major contribution to the change in this thinking; it is a change in an amazingly short period. . . . The two way channels of communication are at last open.

—Alfred Zauberman

Introduction

Although wars often lead to dramatic technological and managerial innovations, their sociopolitical implications can just as often portend a return to traditional practices. Such was Soviet experience in the immediate postwar era. After Stalin had given his last address to the Russian people as supreme military chief (24 June 1945), he began to persistently chip away at those concessions which had been reluctantly granted under wartime duress. The officially tolerated flowering of religious sentiment was stamped out; famous military leaders were unceremoniously put back into their place; political control over the armed forces was reintensified vigorously; every indicator of ethnic autonomy was brutally suppressed. Doctrinal phraseology returned full force—back to "class vigilance," "discipline," "enemies of the people," "capitalist encirclement," and the like. By 1948, the forced march back into Stalinist orthodoxy was virtually complete. Andrei Zhdanov—boss of Leningrad and the epitome of an anti-intellectual party cadre—assumed the task of imposing new and heretofore unattained standards of conformity and dullness on writers and artists. The brutal reassertion of "socialist realism" in the arts led to dreary, repetitive tales of devoted workers, peasants, and soldiers led by an infallible Stalin who possessed unique insights on Marxism–Leninism. By 1949, the grim prospect of renewed purges swept over the political landscape, reminding everyone of their perpetual vulnerability. Many would soon disappear, including Gosplan chief Voznesensky and other prominent economic leaders. There is even some indication, albeit of a sketchy nature,[1] that a widespread purge of industrial managers was being contemplated at the time. By 1953, after the arrest of several influential Jewish doctors for allegedly plotting to kill top government and party leaders, the liquidation of the entire Politburo seemed a frightening possibility.[2] Indeed, the totalitarian imperative never appeared more powerful, and compelling, than in the period before the great kahn's death.

CONSEQUENCES OF THE RETURN TO STALINIST ORTHODOXY

As in other areas of Soviet life, a return to standard economic theory and practice also occurred. The observer of communist affairs could find no *liberalizing* changes in the hierarchical command system. Central planning, physical allocations, and the plethora of bureaucratic control agencies had advanced too far and were simply too deeply imbedded in Soviet reality. Consequently, even in the face of staggering war losses (e.g., almost 25 percent of capital assets in Soviet industry had been destroyed), postwar reconstruction would proceed in traditional fashion, stressing investment in heavy industry, hierarchical command, and rigid control in agriculture. But unlike an earlier era when Lenin had made substantial concessions to the peasantry and NEPmen, now there would be no reassessment of conventional wisdom, even for tactical purposes. Soviet politicians were convinced that improvements could be derived only by tightening the screws on the old Stalinist system. And predictably, planners and managers—knowing how to deliver more rather than better products—stumbled badly when it came to reducing costs and/or manpower, developing new goods and services, and improving production efficiency. Although Stalin refused economic assistance from the capitalist states and was content to trade off Western cooperation for a stable buffer zone of "peoples' democracies," he ruthlessly stripped Eastern Europe of its capital stock. This ultimately solidified a cold-war mentality on both sides and destroyed any prospect for economic cooperation between East and West for years to come. Nevertheless, to Stalin's credit, the Soviet economy attained its 1941 output level halfway through the second postwar planning period.

However, the traditional economic recipes started to break down. The command system depended, increasingly, on widespread rule breaking and informal, quasilegal activity to reach its short-term production goals. Adaptation proved exceedingly difficult, especially since economists, planners, engineers, and ideologues had been trained under Stalin and often were personally dedicated to the command system's survival. However, the complexity of a rapidly maturing economy was outpacing the capacity of bureaucratic control to successfully manage change. Literally thousands of enterprises depended on a maze of technical and administrative agencies for supervision and even detailed planning of their internal operations. Consequently, even the most routine, prosaic transactions were planned and then closely monitored from the administrative center. But still worse, planners had no theoretical model on which to rationally base their calculations and/or policy decisions. Those who searched for practical guidance in the scientific literature found little but glib phrases and adroitly manipulated doctrinal citations. Indeed, high Stalinism had become a nightmare for analytical economics and administrative science. The dictator's message of the 1930s was brutally reasserted throughout the 1940s: economic science bore absolutely no relation to economic policy and/or the practice of management. Under such conditions, there could be no reciprocal influence between scholars and political leaders. Stalin simply furnished major policy departures himself, and then an army of loyal planners, managers, and engineers carried them out dutifully. Efforts by certain "progressive" specialists to link theory with the practice of management under socialism were attacked as "anti-Marxist," "idealistic," and "voluntaristic" distortions of objective economic laws.[3] Of course, management scientists had played virtually no constructive role in improving planning and administration in the national economy since the early 1930s. And by the immediate postwar period, most capable specialists had been discredited, driven underground, or simply liquidated. Those who still managed to contest orthodox views were either ignored or suppressed, and their informal groupings made little, if any, impression on the larger scientific community.[4] But unknown to many casual observers at the time, the seeds of a miraculous rebirth were already present.

Meanwhile, the situation deteriorated further when several leading economists became embroiled in high Kremlin politics. One of the most notorious cases involved E.S. Varga, head of the Institute of World Economics.[5] He was attacked by conservatives for the heretical argument that the advanced states of the capitalist world need not suffer imminent economic collapse. He dared to suggest that state intervention in the previously anarchical marketplace might prop up and stabilize the United States and Britain, at least for a time. *Pravda* soon launched a full-scale attack on such views and, presumably, on any political forces that stood behind them.[6] Before long, Varga was officially censured, his journal—*World Economy and International Politics*—suppressed, and the Institute of World Economics merged with the conservative Institute of Economics. The latter's power structure remained totally dominated by orthodox political economists willing and able to do Stalin's bidding. Varga and his allies were assailed by *Questions of Economy* for their ideological sins. Hereafter, extraordinary vigilance was exercised to guard doctrinal purity and, to underscore such a commitment, the Institute of Economics was given no specified task to research policy-relevant questions.[7] In Soviet political culture, this injunction was surely "not accidental."

Despite his tyrannical dominance over Soviet society, Stalin still managed to uncover political rivals as well as skeptics who questioned, if only implicitly, his economic sagacity. The dictator's views were comprehensively reiterated in *Economic Problems of Socialism in the USSR* (1952).[8] There, he restated that economic science had no relationship whatsoever to administrative policy. He also dogmatically reiterated the fundamental "principles" of Soviet industrialization, which, although put into practice in the 1930s, were now concretized as eternal truths—absolute priority for heavy industry, highly differentiated wages and prices, and rigid controls on collectivized agriculture. The socialist economic plan functioned as an economic law and, as a result, the spontaneous market mechanism had irrevocably given way to planned, orderly proportional growth. Tha planners were (allegedly) in complete control over the pace and direction of economic development. And since those "principles" had successfully industrialized Russia, Stalin was committed to their perpetuity. From the political standpoint, however, *Economic Problems* became a diatribe against N.A. Voznesensky and his "liberal" ideas, as well as his followers.[9] One could easily interpret Voznesensky's writings, especially *The War Economy of the USSR during World War II* (1947),[10] as a plea for "rationality" in planning, "balance" in growth, and more realism in planned output targets. But it was less the cogency of these ideas than the politico-psychological implications of Voznesensky's deviance that ultimately led to his downfall.[11] To be sure, Stalin would tolerate no rivals, even imaginary ones—Voznesensky was dismissed from Gosplan in March 1949, then shot in July 1950. Soon, other economists were accused of pernicious "anti-Marxist" views in support of their fallen chief. They came under severe pressure and many were forced to officially recant their ideas in a series of scholarly meetings.[12] By Stalin's death (5 March 1953), he had eliminated potential adversaries, plotted the infamous Leningrad affair,[13] hatched plots in his own Politburo, and dogmatically insisted that archaic ideas like economic rationality were anathema to the socialist way of life.

The Battle against Inertia: 1953–1961

Stalin's death created the necessary conditions for a dramatic rebirth of administrative science in the Soviet Union. The immediate beneficiaries were Politburo members slated to be purged, if not liquidated, Jews and other "rootless cosmopolitans" implicated in the so-called doctor's plot,[14] and errant economists determined to reassess the conventional wisdom. Nevertheless, few changes could be found in administrative science or economics for several years, despite a rush of articles on improving the quality of consumer goods and even public recognition that largely unwanted items were being produced by Soviet industry. Doctrinal views remained firmly entrenched in economic science and orthodox political economists continued to hold key academic, editorial, and institutional positions. Thus, enlightened debate was still fraught with political dangers. Those committed to reform or even to the idea that economics should be relevant to policy analysis were "atomized," entirely cut off from each other, and unable to exert collective influence on the field, much less on decision makers. Little was expected—or heard—from Soviet political economists, save their endless platitudes to ideological truth.

But Stalin's death had an immediate and demonstrable impact on high politics. His erstwhile lieutenants soon became entangled in a bitter struggle for power: who had the right and capacity to rule the country? The dictator's sudden passing meant that once again policy questions could have a significant bearing on the basic issue of Soviet politics—*"Kto-kogo"* "Who [does in] whom?").[15] Soon, genuine differences of position surfaced among leading politicians. Not only would they conspire against one another, but it became clear that the "leader" could be challenged, and perhaps defeated, on certain issues. While inherently unstable, "collective leadership" revealed that each member shared a common interest in discouraging another emergent dictator, who might gain absolute control, and subsequently threaten the security of everyone else. And to underscore that fear, Lavrenti Beria—the dreaded leader of the secret police—was arrested and shot in July 1953, allegedly by Khrushchev himself.[16] Immediately thereafter, the institutional powers of the security apparatus were downgraded substantially. This had profound consequences for Soviet society. The *expectation* among party cadres, scientists, and ordinary citizens that "deviant" behavior would be met with arbitrary, and usually severe, treatment began to diminish after 1953. The political climate that emerged henceforth, although harsh by Western standards, injected an element of *predictability* into Soviet life that had been missing since the late 1920s. Those criticizing certain aspects of the socialists system or even advocating various reform measures could now seek allies in high places who might be anxious to protect compatible views. In short, a more traditional type of politics had returned to the USSR, and with it came a growing complexity of communications processes, group interactions, and eventually a reciprocal influence flow between political leaders, scientists, and opinion groupings. Once again a reform movement emerged in the politburo, suggesting that the economic mechanism be streamlined along lines indicated decades before. (Many ideas of economic rationalization that surfaced in the post-Stalinist years had been thoroughly reviewed in the 1920s.) And authoritative "rationalizers" surfaced in the Politburo; they were top party leaders whose role had been intimately linked with state economic functions, including Bulganin, Pervukhin, and Kosygin.[17] Although it would take Western Sovietologists nearly a decade to recognize the meaning of these political changes, the totalitarian model's congruence with Soviet reality had, in fact, passed with Stalin.[18]

The leadership struggle in the Politburo involved two major contestants— N.S. Khrushchev and Georgi Malenkov. The latter, thought to be Stalin's personal choice for party general secretary, had his political base in Leningrad and professional experience in the state economic apparatus. By contrast, Khrushchev had broad experience in agriculture and would soon champion an expansion of the party's role in economic affairs. A central political issue quickly emerged in their sparring, that of correct proportions for national economic development. Of course, under Stalin, the priority of heavy vis-à-vis light industry remained indisputable. No longer. Malenkov, pursuing an idea that has periodically resurfaced in Soviet politics (so far without gaining official ascendency), insistently argued that heavy industry had been sufficiently built up so that a rapid increase in light industry and consumer-goods production was not only possible but desirable. Khrushchev entrenched himself firmly behind orthodox (Stalinist) economic preferences. And he successfully mobilized traditional interests in the Soviet establishment (e.g., the armed forces, industrial ministries, enterprise management) against Malenkov's policy innovation. Accusing his rival of a "rightist" deviation like Bukharin and various fellow travelers, Khrushchev eventually forced Malenkov to step down as premier in 1955. While the party leader's own political problems were far from over, his victory demonstrated that Stalin's policy could be defended (much more easily than could the man himself), and that traditional priorities could be "used" as a political instrument against would-be change agents.

CRITICISM DURING THE "SUCCESSION CRISIS"

The public controversy over investment priorities indicated that, in the background, substantial differences existed between and among national leaders. Such differences as well as their public airing would soon exert a profound impact on all facets of Soviet life, including economics and administrative science. During the "succession crisis" (1953–1957), it was possible (and fashionable) to openly criticize the deplorable condition of the

Soviet economy and the state of the art of economic science. In that dialogue, a substantial gap between aspiration and real organizational performance was revealed.[19] Specialists readily admitted that they had no analytical language that could adequately *describe* the economic malady, much less *prescribe* a diagnostic cure. From an objective standpoint, this situation called for nothing less than a revolution in those sciences dealing with every facet of organization, management, and planning in the national economy. But economists themselves were in no position to launch such a revolution. Indeed, neither individuals nor groups dared press the political leadership too far. The Stalinist legacy was still fresh and vivid in their minds. And a fundamental part of that legacy was the reality of rigid hierarchical control exerted by Politburo members (especially the party's general secretary) upon political cadres, managers, and academic specialists. Thus, few economists were willing to propose new tasks for their discipline (such as the notion that it should have a direct bearing on policy questions) without clear signals that the changes would be, in fact, accepted by some faction at the top. Once those signals were forthcoming, however, substantial progress would be registered in administrative science.

Tangible evidence finally emerged in 1955 that the party had new, and strikingly different, tasks for economic science. By then, the more relaxed political climate had led to a relative profusion of journal articles forewarning specialists of a possible new era. Soon, party leaders would begin to *explicitly* place demanding policy-relevant challenges before economic theorists. In May 1955, an all-union industrial conference was held. It proved to be a crucial milestone on the road to economic reform, representing as it did a turning point in the reemergence of administrative science. Great attention was given to geographical and functional decentralization as well as to broadening the rights (and responsibilities) of enterprise directors.[20] To be sure, these notions represented, in part, Khrushchev's attack on the state apparatus (Malenkov's political stronghold), but they also constituted genuine attempts to improve the economic system. Then, the July 1955 Central Committee Plenum led to serious party attacks on the deplorable status of Soviet economic science. In September, the presidium of the Academy of Sciences convened a special session in which economists well as the Institute of Economics were sharply assailed for their mediocre research and theorizing.[21] And the Institute itself was directly ordered to undertake studies that could assist planners and economic policy makers.[22] Shortly thereafter, a separate economics research center was set up in Gosplan.

But if the party's message to economists needed more forceful promotion, or perhaps a more authoritative forum, then both were provided by the historic Twentieth Party Congress in 1956. There, delegates heard much more than the staggering revelations about Stalin's "crimes" against loyal party members. There were endless protests about the overcentralized industrial ministries. Other comments were directed toward expanding enterprise prerogatives in the economic system. And the party's plea to upgrade economic science was vigorously reasserted. For example, A.N. Kosygin, an emerging "rationalizer", bemoaned the lack of sophisticated planning methodology; Khrushchev himself publically scorned Stalin's *Economic Problems of Socialism*; and Anastas Mikoyan pointedly uncovered the lack of qualified economic specialists by comparing their miniscule numbers in the USSR to the mass of American scholars examining Soviet developments.[23] Following this barrage and now armed with the expectation that party leaders demanded analytical studies, specialists began to delve into their "brave new world" of policy analysis. The situation has changed dramatically since then. Unlike an earlier era, economists are now censured precisely because of their neglect and/or inability to deal with real problems of the national economy.

Progress since the Twentieth Party Congress

From the Twentieth Party Congress onward, the resurgence in economics and administrative science in the USSR has been impressive. Having finally accepted the absolute futility of relying simply on Stalinist economic dogma, the political leadership authoritatively communicated its new preferences for policy-relevant studies to the community of specialists. The spirited debates which were to follow involved so many issues and so many participants that analysis through fragmentary, haphazard citations is inadequate. Specialists were directed to examine questions like the basis of price formation, the law of value's role under socialism,[24] new performance indicators (e.g., "profitability") for industrial organizations, the automization of production, mathematical methods in economic research, the use of material incentives, way to promote technological progress, and innumerable others. After securing his victory over the "anti-party" group in the Politburo, Khrushchev would proceed apace in his efforts to dismantle the hierarchical Stalinist command system.[25] His *sovnarkozy*, or regional economic councils, were designed to shift the locus of decision-making powers from the central ministries in Moscow to regional centers around the country.[26] Although this macrolevel organizational reform would prove unwieldy and eventually collapse, it did much to encourage an "agonizing reappraisal" of orthodox thinking and led to serious investigation of the optimal balance between centralization and decentralization. And before long, the observer would discover Soviet specialists closely examining Western perspectives on organizational science.

Soviet economic science fell into great turmoil after 1956 as several distinct (and competing) trends quickly made their appearance. Each would battle against hostile elements, especially orthodox political economists and conservative politicans. Of course, bureaucratic inertia as well as lethargy in the scientific community would place constraints on the legitimization of any particular approach and also hinder rapid institutional developments. Nonetheless, specialists desiring to explore new and/or archaic views could find political backing and, potentially, the scientific resources to overturn Stalinist orthodoxy in administrative science.

The first identifiable trend to emerge and take shape was economic-mathematical methods (*ekonomiko-matematicheskie metody*) or simply *EMM*. By applying mathematics to economic problems, specialists would try "to model the process of socialist production in all branches of the economy and [to develop] methods of optimal decision-making for planned economic objectives."[27] While conservative political economists railed against market socialist tendencies in the East European literature,[28] their mathematically inclined brethren in the USSR were developing even more radical notions of price formation. In fact, they were introducing ideas into the internal Soviet dialogue that, functionally, were equivalent to efficiency prices, opportunity cost, marginal costing, and interest rate.[29] Mathematical economists drew inspiration as well as concrete ideas from retrospective studies of Soviet research conducted in the 1920s and input–output analysis done in the West. The renowned work of Wassily Leontief was once again seriously examined and, even before 1957, a modest body of American literature on EMM had been translated and privately circulated among interested specialists.[30] Grouping themselves around L.V. Kantorovich, V.V. Novozhilov, and the politically astute V.S. Nemchinov, a coterie of analytical economists stressed the Russian roots of EMM as well as the prospects for constructing "optimal" economic plans. EMM promised to give politicans, administrators, and economic planners an invaluable tool—empirical indicators which could link, in rational scientific fashion, goals of the central planning apparatus with those of regional and/or local agencies.

EMM enjoyed meteoric growth and diffusion in the Soviet Union. In 1957, although the number of specialists did not exceed "several tens," by 1961, there were over 40 institutes examining the application of mathematical techniques to economic problems.[31] Five years later that number had risen to 213. Mathematical economists were promoted to important institutional positions, an unambiguous *political* message to orthodox forces that EMM had official sanction as well as strong backing at the top. In 1958, the Academy of Sciences publically announced creation of the Institute of Economics and Organization of Industrial Production in the Siberian branch of the academy, headed by a "rising star" in Soviet economics—Abel Aganbegyan. In that same year, Kantorovich was sent to Novosibirsk to take charge of the newly established Laboratory of Mathematical Economics. In 1960, a mathematical economics laboratory was set up in Moscow under

Nemchinov. It soon evolved into the prestigious Mathematical Economics Institute (*TsEMI*) and began publishing its journal—*Economics and Mathematical Methods*—two years later. And *TsEMI* remains one of the leading "think tanks" in the USSR today, despite occasional charges of abstract theorizing and changes in editorial policy.[32] These institutes, and others like them, were instructed to develop tools of economic analysis that could improve the practice of planning and management under socialist conditions. Their establishment provided specialists with a powerful organizational fortress from which to "market" their innovative research techniques. As a result, the conservative Institute of Economics found itself increasingly out of step with the mood, conceptual needs, and analytical language of the burgeoning new field. In addition, several crucial publications strongly advanced the good fortunes of EMM in 1957–1960. Thus, although it had been written nearly two decades before, Kantorovich's classic *Economic Calculation of the Best Use of Resources* finally appeared in 1959. In that same year, Nemchinov edited *The Application of Mathematics to Economic Research*. That collection had several outstanding articles on optical planning in socialist systems and was introduced by sophisticated "political" commentary from Nemchinov himself.[33]

ROLE EXPANSION FOR ADMINISTRATIVE EXPERTS

Great administrative as well as political significance can be attached to these institutional developments and publications. Stalinism was rapidly collapsing in management science, and with this change came the portent of substantially expanded power—if not a decision-making role—for administrative experts, consultants, model builders, and the like. Even assuming that leading politicians would continue to formulate economic policy and determine the proper balance between investment and consumption, management specialists could play an important role by providing advice, information, alternative courses of action, etc. By contrast to high Stalinism, this was indeed a remarkable situation! And within the community of professional management specialists, EMM was undercutting—and would ultimately devastate—the pretensions as well as monopoly position of orthodox political economy. Still, in the late 1950s, many specialists remained skeptical of the prudence, and even legitimacy, of joining together two heretofore autonomous branches of knowledge—economics and mathematics. But the backbone of conservative resistance was finally crushed at an important economics conference held in April 1960.[34] Despite considerable acrimony and bitter jurisdictional disputes between traditional political economists and vocal advocates of mathematical techniques, conference delegates decisively resolved to continue, and expand, developments in *EMM*. Since then, mathematical techniques like linear programing and input–output analysis have among the main advances in Soviet administrative science.

Another trend that emerged and found great support in leading circles at about this same time was cybernetics. Although conservatives openly worried lest Marxist–Leninist ideology be displaced by idealistic philosophy and/or bourgeois science, leading specialists gradually shifted to a defense of the field in 1954–1958.[35] It was officially recognized as a legitimate and autonomous scientific discipline when the Scientific Council on Cybernetics was set up under the leadership of academician A.I. Berg in 1958.[36] Henceforth, the science of communication and control would attain greater status and prestige in the USSR than perhaps anywhere else in the world. Indeed, the subject matter of the field—the control of dynamic processes and prevention of increasing disorder within them—was precisely the overriding concern of Soviet planners and administrators. Cybernetics held out the promise that genuine scientific control of the incredibly complex Soviet economy could, in theory, be achieved. By using concepts like information, system, feedback, and regulation, planners were able to conceptualize how the economy actually functions at every hierarchical level. They could then prescribe potentially "optimal" recipes for improving the practice of management and organizational performance. While much initial enthusiasm over cybernetics was dissipated in fruitless semantic entanglements or attempts to precisely define key terms, the scientific debate by 1960 involved more substantial issues, such as relevant technical and social domains for applied studies.

While drawing inspiration and specific ideas from Bogdanov, and general organizational science or tektology from an earlier era, specialists have also borrowed liberally from Western theorists like Norbert Wiener, Stafford Beer, and W. Ross Ashby. There can be bo no doubt that cybernetic terminology has substantially influenced, if not outright dominated "theoretical developments" in Soviet administrative science. And the mechanistic bias of early theorizing has been largely replaced by a viewpoint stressing the complex relationships existing in cybernetic systems. This is particularly evident in descriptive studies of the *process* of management, particularly those focusing on steering, self-regulation feedback, and the like. Naturally, cybernetic definitions of *upravlenie** reflect such concepts: *"Upravlenie* is the processing of information into signals which correct the activities of machine or organisms,"[37] or "[It] is the process of transferring a complex, dynamic system from one state to another by [purposively] influencing its variables."[38]

From the standpoint of practical activity, however, cyberneticists have been preoccupied with applying computers and data-processing techniques to resolve administrative problems. Many regard the computer itself as an instrument whereby the traditional central-planning apparatus can be reinvigorated and streamlined. Thus, centralizers envision a vast national computer network which connects local agencies to Moscow by transferring

*This broad term is defined on p. 7.

pertinent information between and among various computer terminals. This would, in theory, connect the thousands of production units and administrative control agencies into a single, gigantic coordinated production organism. While such an objective has not yet been reached, and is unlikely to be attained in the future, many have remained convinced that hard- and soft-ware developments are the key to optimal economic performance in the USSR.

The Long-Term Struggle with "Orthodoxy"

Having successfully overcome the long-standing inertia in administrative science, mathematical economists and cyberneticists nonetheless continued to battle against orthodox political economy—the "science" regarded as a basic part of official socialist ideology in the USSR. To be sure, the brugeoning growth of quantitative methods forced traditional specialists well versed in Stalinist rhetoric to scramble frantically to protect their institutional, doctrinal, and political turf. And political economists had good reason to fear these intruders:[39] their presumed right to formulate the doctrinal basis of the regime's economic policy and/or the theoretical core of economic science was being directly challenged. By dealing with aggregate economic behavior in socialist society, both *EMM* and cybernetics provided an analytical language that not only was competitive with political economy but permitted the conceptualization of "optimal" performance. Despite the insistence of orthodox Stalinists that only political economy, not certain "technical-engineering" fields, could address the fundamental issues of economic science, the quantifiers held an important trump card, namely, the promise of vastly improving the practice of management under socialism. Since only a few, other than ideologues or party hacks, seriously believed that political economy could resolve pressing administrative difficulties, it was not surprising that leading politicians generally ignored orthodox protests and instead promoted the rise of new approaches.[40] Even shrill cries that EMM and cybernetics were bourgeois fields, "mechanically" emulating capitalist experience, made little impression in official circles. Nevertheless, despite this near-fatal political blow and virtual intellectual confinement, political economy has still managed to retain a truncated position in the official Soviet *Weltanschauung*.

Its spokesmen are not content to wage a fruitless rearguard action against EMM and cybernetics. By rethinking several important "methodological" issues, they have demonstrated that socialist doctrine has not played a static, immutable role in the metamorphosis of Soviet administrative science. Their attempt to interpret management in acceptable Marxist–Leninist categories—to develop a managerial interpretation of political economy—represents the third major, sequential development in Soviet administrative theorizing. The debate centers around the character of managerial relations (*upravlencheskie otnosheniia*) under socialism. Seeking a way to distinguish socialist management from that existing under capitalism, political economists usually uncover "objective" economic linkages between the defining traits of socialism (e.g., social property, national planning, proletarian rule) and the nature of its administrative system.[41] But this view is persistently challenged by juridical specialists, sociologists, data analysts, and others who regard *upravlenie* as essentially a "superstructural" phenomenon, i.e., one involving leadership (*rukovodstvo*) of people in organizational-production processes.[42] Such a treatment creates severe doctrinal tangles for political economists, since the "objective" foundation of socialist management disappears and, hence, it becomes impossible to characterize Soviet economic development as flowing from objective laws or *zakonomernosti*.[43] Because of this ideological lacuna, many now regard upravlenie as a complex intermingling of base and superstructural elements[44] which, in turn, constitute "the secondary production relations of socialism."[45] With this development, political economy has experienced a steady decline in institutional power and influence. It is unlikely to play anything more than a *pro forma* role in Soviet administrative theorizing.

Contemporary State of Theory

As one can see, a durable intellectual consensus on socialist managerial relations has eluded theorists up to this day. Indeed, the tolerance for different theoretical viewpoints is important: it shows that Marxism–Leninism in administrative science has generated *questions*, but not necessarily concrete *answers*. This conclusion is valid even in the sensitive realm of separating socialist from capitalist systems. Nevertheless, a doctrinal consensus has emerged around another issue, namely, that no one seriously argues today, as was done routinely under Khrushchev, that "upravlenie . . . is not a specific category of socialist production."[46] Most significantly, however, the preoccupation with managerial relations has not dissuaded specialists from pursuing more concrete, and sophisticated, lines of inquiry.

The scientific organization of labor (*NOT*) was one such approach and it represented the fourth trend to emerge in Soviet administrative science. Like Taylorism and previous Soviet studies, *NOT* dealt with micromanagement, i.e., shop-level organization in the production enterprise. After a lengthy hiatus, the *NOT* movement resurfaced in 1957 when, according to M.G. Babin, "the State Committee on Labor and Wages made a decision about utilizing the experience and methods of the Central Institute of Labor."[47] To be sure, the retrospective analysis of research conducted in the 1920s contained many valuable lessons for specialists who were reminded once again that select Western concepts and methods could be adapted to socialist goals. Translations of select U.S. works soon were undertaken.[48] In addition, several large volumes on *NOT* appeared in the Soviet literature, including *Voprosy Truda V SSR (Questions of Labor in the USSR)* in 1958 and *Razvitie Organizatsiia Truda V SSR (Development of the Organization of Labor in the USSR)* in 1959. But as *NOT* reemerged and even flourished in the early 1960s, so did the controversies of the interwar years. At bottom, researchers were unable to agree on the scope, much less subject matter, of the field. Should *NOT* examine the introduction of scientific methods into the workplace (technical rationalization), the optimal arrangement of equipment and space (organizational rationalization), or the creative development of workers themselves (social rationalization)?

*NOT*ists argued bitterly over these points in journals like *Socialist Labor* and *Problems of Economics*. Of course, most studies displayed a technical bias and assumed that any changes promoting organizational efficiency were fully compatible with social goals and, hence, would be favorably received in the working collective. Indeed, *NOT*ists treated worker satisfaction as simply one more factor in their complex schemes to improve production efficiency.[49] But those empirical conditions that actually lead to worker satisfaction—the normal topic of Western studies—were assumed by Soviet theorists to already exist under socialism.[50] Thus, although conflict was begrudgingly recognized in the production collective, it was considered a purely idiosyncratic phenomenon, i.e., one involving the personality disorders or incompetence of managers and/or workers, rather than a fundamental element in the organizational setting.[51]

Studies of micromanagement burgeoned and even attracted zealous proponents in the scientific community.[52] However, *NOT* was unable to regain the prestige and stature accorded to it in the early years of Soviet power. Times had changed and the economy had grown enormously in scope and complexity. Consequently, few theorists saw *NOT* as capable of addressing the basic organizational problems of the modern Soviet economy. They preferred to deal with larger aggregates—the enterprise, industrial branch, or even the entire economy. These analytical levels called for attention to *upravlenie*, rather than *NOT*, and could be more easily reconciled with the major changes that certain theorists suggested for the basic economic mechanism.

The scientific organization of labor has not been adandoned, however. Broadened by concepts like "social planning in the collective"[53] and deepened by social survey data, it still continues to play a substantial role in Soviet studies of organization and management. And *NOT*ists have been willing to take Khrushchev's seminal message to heart— " . . . the time of the personality cult is past. We should remember the instructions of V.I.

Lenin and, if necessary, must be able to learn from the capitalists and adopt that which is sensible and profitable from them."[54] They have succeeded in revitalizing a genuine (and historical) curiosity about Western management science. Many have concluded, in sharp contrast to their colleagues under Stalinism, that "a series of general principles of labor organization exist,"[55] irrespective of the social order in which they are found.

FINALITY OF BREAK WITH STALINISM

These developments in EMM, cybernetics, *NOT*, and even political economy appear to represent a clear and final break with past Stalinist practices in administrative science. The party's call for policy-relevant studies evoked an enthusiastic response from economists, engineers, jurists, sociologist, data analysts, and many other specialists. But leading politicians and academic experts nonetheless remained dissatisfied. First, most studies simply ignored the leadership of people in organization processes as well as the behavioral impact of human activity in production collectives. Second, the distinctive needs of *socialist* theory were given short shrift, especially since both EMM and cybernetics were *general* frameworks that made no attempt to differentiate socialist from capitalist management. Finally, theoretical analysis remained largely isolated from direct, practical applications. Consequently, Khrushchev vigorously attacked the moribund state of the art in economic science at the Twenty-First Party Congress, in 1959. His charges, though not new, still found their mark: theoreticians were cut off from real life situations; they ignored practical problems, and too often they merely repeated trite phrases or concentrated on descriptive analysis. Specialists were again taken to task two years later at the Twenty-Second Party Congress. Key members of the scientific establishment prodded their conservative colleagues to develop useful analytical tools and then to apply them to real problems of planning and management.

Progress could be measured in *relative* terms, however. To be sure, by comparative standards, Soviet research and theorizing remained in the backwash of world developments. Few observers in the USSR even considered administrative science a field of inquiry independent from economics, engineering, or administrative law. Consequently, specialists usually dealt with narrow "aspects" of a much broader subject matter. They neglected the role of human behavior in *upravlenie* and did not think about administration as a complex phenomenon arising at the juncture (*na styke*) of numerous fields. Unlike an earlier era, however, specialists could now openly discuss their divergent viewpoints. They built support in key academic institutes and on editorial boards, and through subtle interaction that linked party leaders and various scientists, began to promote a so-called complex approach (*kompleksnyi podkhod*) to management.[56] They began to view *uprav-*

lenie from a holistic, integrated perspective and to regard leadership (*rukovodstvo*) of people as the field's most important organizing concept. Proponents of this view found their arguments greatly enhanced by experience and examples drawn from outside the Soviet system, especially the United States.

Symbolic Emulation and the American Referent: 1962–1964

The major task confronting Soviet administrative specialists and their political patrons was no longer simply breaking through bureaucratic lethargy or even the outright resistance to change of orthodox Stalinists. By 1962, the issue was *where* and *how* the discipline should be advancing, not fruitless rhetoric about the adequacy of existing theoretical models and/or applied studies. In this sense, the reform movement faced choice problems, not inertia, since opinion groupings could now publically—and without ostensible political risk—assess the state of the art in management science and recommend possible solutions. Advancements in the field were often made in response to selective (and sometimes self-serving) perceptions of performance shortfalls between what specialists ought to be studying and what, in fact, they were doing. Thus, according to A.M. Birman:

> [A] clear gap has emerged in economic science. Studies in political economy . . . deal only with general theoretical issues [while] applied economics examine problems within individual branches [of industry]. But an unreconnoitered sphere of scientific knowledge lies between branch economics and theoretical political economy that embraces problems of management and planning in the national economy considered as a single whole organism.[57]

Administrative theorists, especially those dissatisfied with quantitative and/or macroanalytical approaches, found rich soil for their critical broadsides. Thus, if *EMM* and cybernetics were inadequate *theoretical* points of departure, which led, *inter alia*, to emasculating the social essence of economic science,[58] then *NOT* was ill equipped to examine the broad structural features of the national economy. A *socialist* science of management required analysis of people, not things, and had to account for macrolevel phenomena.[59] In sharp contrast to the study of managerial techniques, quantitative methods, industrial technology, even cybernetic systems, certain theorists looked to the administration of people (*upravlenie liud'mi*) as the most topical subject matter for the science of management. Specialists could examine, from this vantage point, organizing labor collectives, leading their activities, and improving their structure, form, and style of work, a point stressed by I.U. Liubovich since the late 1930s. By elevating people back to the forefront of theoretical analysis, "the executor of concrete managerial functions" once again would become "a distinctive area for scientific research."[60] This was an important recognition, especially since the traditional preoccupation with technical-engineering training had undercut the capacity of industrial managers to understand accounting and bookkeeping procedures, relevant pieces of legislation, and organizing and motivating productive operations. These and other deficiencies were attributable not only to an inadequately staffed and equipped educational system, but to the neglect of analyzing the rich organizational experience of early Soviet administrators (e.g., S.G. Ordzhonikidze and V.V. Kuibyshev) and successful enterprise directors like I.A. Likachëv and A.I. Efremov.[61]

The first articles suggesting that management become an independent field apart from political economy, EMM, or cybernetics appeared in 1962–1963.[62] An analytical focus on leadership raised few objections per se; by contrast, the idea of creating an *autonomous* science of management evoked a storm of protest from those fearing a substantial loss of status and/or power in the field. Naturally—i.e., by temperament, prior training, and professional experience—those specialists had traditionally approached *upravlenie* from the conceptual jails of narrow, competing research perspectives. If a new "synthetic" field were suddenly created, which could unite relevant aspects of administrative law, sociology, cybernetics, mathematics, biology, industrial engineering, and the like, then what would be the role of traditional disciplines in studies of management? How and on what basis could a central focus or principle of order be established? Who (i.e., which fields) would dominate new research institutes, departments, editorial boards, research projects, rationalization contracts, and so on? Predictably, change agents advancing the idea of an autonomous field tried to reduce conservative apprehensions by insisting that "the science of management does not represent . . . a substitute for other disciplines," but rather "represents a complex of many scientific fields."[63] Such a formulation, although not directly infringing on orthodox turf, nonetheless largely ignored questions of scope, content, and disciplinary boundaries. This confusion contributed substantially to the bitter jurisdictional disputes, semantic entanglements, and viciously argumentative theses that have plagued management studies in the USSR since the early 1960s. At times, these battles have been so abrasive that many simply backed away from autonomy and, instead, tried to advance research and theorizing in all aspects of *upravlenie*.[64]

COMPARISON OF EDUCATIONAL PLANT

Certain theorists did not hesitate to compare, in pointed fashion, the deplorable condition of management education and training in the USSR to that existing in the United States—the world's leading proponent of "scientific management." Thus, L. Kachalina examined the vast network of American universities, business schools, and private organizations, as well as conferences, seminars, and public forums devoted to the study of management.[65] She noted that, by 1960, there were over 200,000 computer analysts and over 100,000 administrative experts in the United States. Similarly, I. Kasitskii found "dozens" of associations and scientific councils designed to improve the practice of management in the United States. He spoke clearly to Soviet administrative specialists: *"It would be unreasonable to reject all those materials from study* [especially] *the experience of organizing production. . . ."*[66] (emphasis added).

Some quickly picked up this theme and recommended the outright adoption of U.S. decision-making techniques like PPBS (Planning Programming Budget System) and PERT (Program Evaluation Review Technique).[67] Other specialists began to look at American experience *symbolically*, i.e., to point out directions for behavioral and/or institutional change in the USSR. By analyzing U.S. experience, change agents sought to defuse conservative resistance to the unanticipated consequences of change. American ideas and leading specialists were consciously used as models for future Soviet work. Those referents became a "political" resource in the internal Soviet dialogue designed to enhance the good standing, persuasiveness, and power of certain ideas.[68] By quoting, citing, and illustrating U.S. works, Soviet advocates hoped to buttress their own particular views and thereby suggest optimal directions for the future course of the discipline. This corresponds to *symbolic emulation* and was intended to move the field along converging lines of U.S. research and theorizing.[69]

American management concepts did not flow spontaneously in the Soviet Union. Rather, they were borrowed and adapted through purposive organizational activities designed to reproduce behavioral patterns in a referent. Strong voices in leadership circles spoke through D.M. Gvishiani—son-in-law of Alexei Kosygin, even before the political demise of Khrushchev in 1964. A professional scholar, Gvishiani had helped to set up the Laboratory of Management Problems in Moscow State University in 1962. And his *Sociology of Business*—a survey of major trends in U.S. management science— was a genuine watershed in the metamorphosis of Soviet administrative studies.[70] Rhetorical genuflections to Marxist orthodoxy notwithstanding, Gvishiani pulled no punches about the advanced state of American theory and practice. By emphasizing the *objective* nature of advancements in the American discipline, he implied that industrial techniques and organizational forms were transferable between otherwise incompatible social systems. And to enhance his case before a skeptical audience at home, Gvishiani liberally cited from renowned U.S. management specialists—Peter Drucker, Harold Koontz, Harold Leavitt, and many others. He could authoritatively speak through them. By holding out *selective* emulation as a return to Leninist orthodoxy, Gvishiani sought to undercut conservative critics and to promote what was then an important policy innovation.[71] There were several demonstrable "lessons" in *Sociology of Business* corresponding in general, to the reform platform of those pressing for an autonomous discipline. Thus, Gvishiani pointed out that in the United States management is not only an *independent* scientific discipline, but a sphere of *professional* activity as well. It is not a domain for amateurs, however enlightened or enthusiastic their purpose. And management was clearly an interdisciplinary field drawing from numerous social sciences. By contrast to the Soviet preoccupation with things, American specialists regard social activity, especially the creative leadership of people in the production process, as the basic ingredient in the *art* of management. Quoting from American sources, Gvishiani made his pitch to change agents in the USSR:

> [P]sychologists, sociologists, mathematicians, and even economists seldom read books authored by management specialists or engineers. And vice-versa. Only in the past ten years . . . did a significant portion of scientists-sociologists start thinking about industry and representatives of industry begin to think about social science.[72]

Through U.S. specialists, he also argued that management can never be reduced to mathematical techniques, to computers, or even to cybernetic systems. The field will always retain important subjective elements and, hence, resembles art more than science. Since management deals with creative human activity, the study and generalization of leading organizational experience should constitute the analytical core of the discipline. Great theoretical and practical benefits would then result from analyzing the experience of successful Soviet (and Western) managers. Such empirical lessons could assist Soviet analysts in developing academic curricula for training and research purposes, or in improving the effectiveness of management consulting.

DEVELOPMENT OF INTERNATIONAL NETWORKING

The international isolation of Soviet management science soon began to crumble. In 1963, a Soviet delegation of economists and engineering professors visited the Harvard Business School.[73] Their report on the trip, doctrinal rhetoric notwithstanding, was not only generally positive, but included a glowing account of Harvard's case method. In 1964 Edward Lamb, a leading American industrialist, visited the USSR as "informal U.S. ambassador of modern management science and education."[74] He was enthusiastically received by Soviet officials, including Gvishiani himself. And in the early 1960s, several young Soviet specialists went to the United States on various exchange programs to study in leading universities and business schools. For instance, R. Iuksviarav spent 1963–1964 at the University of

California (Berkeley) and MIT. He now heads the department of industrial management and planning in the Tallinn Polytechnical Institute. His massive *Problems of Structure and Management in Business Organizations of the United States* provides a highly detailed account of U.S. corporate principles and managerial practices to interested Soviet readers.[75] I.M. Syroezhin spent 1963–1964 at Stanford and Cornell. He is currently chairman of the department of economic cybernetics at the Voznesenskii Finance–Economics Institute in Leningrad. His speciality is business gaming and he has drawn heavily (and creatively) from U.S. work. Vitaly Ozira spent 1966–1967 at the Harvard Business School. He has subsequently become a staunch advocate of case methods and the idea of autonomous consulting firms modeled on U.S. practice. And in the early 1960s, an influential emigree returned to his native Ukraine where he preached the benefits of American business techniques. V.I. Tereshchenko had spent 30 years in America, worked as an economist and management consultant, and was deeply impressed by what he considered the American genius in management. By insisting that American progress in industry was largely attributable to organization and management, he suggested that numerous lessons could be creatively applied under socialist conditions. His *Organization and Management: Experience of the USA* was favorably reviewed in the Literary Gazette and was often cited in the professional literature.[76]

Conclusion

Thus, by the mid-1960s, Soviet administrative specialists were scanning the American literature for relevant ideas and examples. Although most were content to promote the *idea*, rather than the specific content, of an independent field, the groundwork was being carefully set out for more durable changes in the future. Nevertheless, many conservative theorists reacted sharply, and negatively to attempts by "certain comrades" to present management as a *universal* system. Resurrecting Bogdanov's idealistic imagery and theoretical distortions, some openly worried lest good socialists *absolutize* organizational forms and depict them as the major factor in societal development.[77] Even more sobering, certain specialists came to erroneous conclusions on the content and methods of socialist management and, by implication, even rejected the basic principle of the Soviet economic system— democratic centralism.[78] And others—even as late as the mid-1970s—publically, in print, took issue with the idea of professionalizing management, regarding it as inconsistent with the entire way of life in socialist society.

These disputes notwithstanding, a vigorous debate on management had been joined by both professional specialists and laymen and competing views were publically aired in *Socialist Labor, Planned Economy, Questions of*

Economics, and other journals. While the so-called Lieberman reforms motivated critical rethinking of questions like profitability, success indicators, enterprise rights and responsibilities,[79] administrative lawyers proposed that *upravlenie* deal with rationalizing the state apparatus, rather than exclusively with production organizations. This viewpoint found enthusiastic support in Ezhi Starotsciak's *Elements of Management Science*.[80] This impressive text was heavily cited in the burgeoning literature in the USSR, and even the casual observer could not miss the Polish expert's virtual dismissal of modern Soviet contributions to the field. Indeed, prior to the collapse of Khrushchev's regime, few monographs or comprehensive treatments had appeared in the USSR. But a transitional phase was drawing to a close. Gvishiani could soon conclude that "research will doubtlessly speed up if specialists . . . cross over from declarations about the need for a science of management to concrete studies on the multi-faceted problems of organizing management. *One can say that the period of agitation . . . is over*"[81] (emphasis added). The next chapter illustrates Gvishiani's conclusion and documents the extensive transfer of modern Western concepts into the Soviet context.

6

The Brezhnev Period and "Collective Leadership"

> *At the fronts of Communist economic construction . . . the science of victory is essentially the science of management! To study the science of management and, if necessary, to learn it anew, therefore, becomes the foremost duty of our cadres.*
>
> —Leonid Brezhnev

> *Our worker often does more [work] better and faster than the American . . . . But when the economy is taken on the whole . . . then the productivity of our labor is significantly lower than the American. This does not depend on the worker, but on those who are in charge of organizing labor and managing production.*
>
> —Alexei Kosygin

Introduction

The emerging Brezhnev–Kosygin leadership did much to advance scientific studies of organization in the USSR. Certain commentators even attributed the possibility and necessity of creating a science of management (*nauka upravleniia*) under socialism to objective changes occurring after the October 1964 plenary session of the party's central committee (i.e., *after* Khrushchev's political demise).[1] Brezhnev and Kosygin minced no words—harebrained scheming, incessant organizational changes, heavy-handed administrative methods (*administrirovanie*), and the subjectivism of their predecessor were fundamentally out of step with the requirements of managing the modern Soviet economy. Henceforth, a sober "scientific" line was struck by the post-Khrushchev regime, and with it came an emphasis on economic levers, material incentives, and rationalization from above led by administrative experts.[2] And the new leaders, especially Premier Kosygin, actively sought policy advice from prominent specialists on issues like how to take supply and demand into account; how to successfully utilize the profit motive; and how to engender more decision-making authority in the Soviet enterprise.[3] Moreover, certain specialists, notably D.M. Gvishiani, gained immeasurably in the regime change. Gvishiani would lead the charge toward new methods and would scour the West for relevant techniques and administrative concepts.[4]

This cautious "scientific" leadership style had a direct bearing on economic policy. The haphazard reorganizations and reckless tinkering of the Khrushchev era had run their course. The new regime favored traditional resource allocation priorities as well as the orthodox branch principle for planning and managing the national economy.[5] This did not herald a carte-blanche return to Stalinist principles, however. Led by Kosygin, reformers wanted to restructure the industrial system so that enterprise management would have greater responsibility and decision-making powers. These objectives could be accomplished, they believed, by reducing the number of planned success indicators and stressing "profitability." While the macro-economic consequences of enterprise-level reform were judiciously side-stepped in public statements, Gosplan, the ministries, and orthodox political economists openly worried lest the party lose overall guidance and control over economic planning.[6] Although analysis of the rise and eventual decline of the reform clearly belongs elsewhere, bureaucratic foot-dragging and conservative resistance made substantial contributions to its failure.[7]

But if the reform did not lead to fundamental structural change in the economy, much less upgrade organizational performance, then it did foster closer collaboration between policy-makers and management specialists. Mathematical economics received a strong boost from the leadership and a lively, even contentious, debate sprang up over numerous policy issues. Some conservative theorists, including Lev Gatovskii, jumped on the bandwagon and strongly promoted economic–mathematical methods at the Institute of Economics.[8] Of course, the Central Mathematical Economics Institute (TsEMI)—created in 1963—remained in the epicenter of creative thinking and continued to attract the most capable quantitative specialists. From 1965 onward, theorists possessing "modern" skills—mathematics, systems analysis, familiarity with Western techniques—received substantial support and encouragement in the official media. And one does not exaggerate in suggesting that the "agitation" of management specialists had at last found sanction in official policy, especially in statements made at the September 1965 central committee plenum.[9] At the Twenty-Third Party Congress, management specialists and economists were issued a direct challenge: "to concentrate attention on further elaboration on the theory of planned leadership in the national economy on the basis of the deep study and utilization of economic laws."[10]

The debate over economic policy had not shown such vigor and diversity since the 1920s. Analysts also argued over the subject matter, scope, and disciplinary boundaries of an independent science of management. An avalanche of articles, pamphlets, and books hit the market. Kruk notes that in 1965–1968 more than 30 branch and regional conferences were held on management and the scientific organization of labor.[11] Perhaps the most significant of such conferences was "Problems of the Scientific Organization of Managing Socialist Industry" (7–10 June 1966).[12] This was an unprecedented forum in the evolution of management science in the USSR: 1056 people representing 514 organizations were present, and 148 papers were delivered.[13] The diversity, even disarray, in the field are reflected in these papers. Several prominent themes emerged, including the growing gap between (socialist) theory and the practice of management (Western "techniques" were relevant here), the preoccupation with technical issues, the "administration of things" bias, and dissensus on the meaning of key terms. While the marginal attention given to theoretical questions was noted in Soviet reviews,[14] the "aspect" approach adopted at the conference was harshly criticized.[15] Certain analysts openly wondered how far *upravlenie* could be broken down into so-called aspects without blurring fundamental relationships and/or processes?[16] The aspect approach contained another serious flaw, namely, that "research into . . . the managerial aspects of political economy becomes a treatise on a controversial issue of political economy itself."[17]

Several papers delivered at the conference dealt exclusively with American theory and practice. In the main, they examined relatively narrow technical issues, e.g., quality control, the training of administrative personnel (the case method was strongly promoted), and intrafirm planning. Some dealt with broader issues, however. Thus, N.V. Adfel'dt surveyed the early history and development of Taylorism and its diffusion throughout the world. R.K. Iuksviarav categorized the contrasting American approaches to management science and noted topical research areas—the principles of organization, various traits of successful leadership, organizational design, centralization vs decentralization, data-processing systems, and decision making. In standard fashion, Iuksviarav insisted that rational decision making could only occur under socialism, but nevertheless, "a certain part of the ideas and practical results of the experience of the USA can beneficially be borrowed . . . [and applied to] conditions of industry in the USSR."[18]

The planned, purposive "organizational search" for useful Western administrative techniques stands in sharp contrast to the self-imposed exile of Soviet economic science in the Stalin years. And under Brezhnev–Kosygin the attention to Western administrative experience assumed unprecedented dimensions. Business terminology—MBO, case methods, feedback, econometrics, PERT, management simulations, sensitivity training, organizational design—became intertwined with the traditional jargon of political economy. An identifiable "grouping" of Americanizers emerged, which has tried to adapt various techniques to the socialist system. This has proved no mean task, and success must be measured in relative terms.[19] Not only does a great language barrier separate Americanizers from traditional specialists, but an intense, protracted political struggle between them has ensued over who would dominate the turf in economic science, if not economic policy itself. While Americanizers advance ideas promising to improve managerial practice, traditional theorists maintain powerful bastions on editorial boards and in leading research and teaching institutes, and have close ties with conservative politicians. They have been able to slow down, and even frustrate in some cases, progress toward more analytical rigor in management science.

Of course, one should not underestimate the growing diversity in economic science as well as the complex interplay between and among various trends. To be sure, serious analysis goes far beyond fragmentary study of citations found in the Soviet literature. At bottom, however, "modernists" played their trump card (i.e., concepts which could improve organizational performance), while "traditionalists" resorted to the litmus test of Marxist orthodoxy. Indeed, virtually all new concepts had to pass a legitimacy test and be accepted into a broader community of specialists.

The diversity in Soviet management science notwithstanding, a basic cleavage between (socialist) theory and those (Western) concepts promising to rationalize the practice of management is readily apparent. The "communications differential" between these extremes has substantially reduced the diffusion of new ideas in the Soviet management science community. Our task in this chapter is to examine some of the channels by which Western ideas have penetrated the USSR. In Chapter 7, we will examine the major Western concepts adopted by Soviet theorists; in Chapter 8, we will review the "synthesis" of Western practice with the needs of socialist theory.

The Transfer of Administrative Science from West to East: Journals, Exchanges, and Agreements

Soviet efforts to gather and process information about foreign management developments have expanded greatly since the early 1960s. This has enabled specialists to familiarize themselves with the concepts, methods, and techniques of Western management science. The first major effort to review and summarize both Western and Soviet materials in one journal was *Reference Collection: The Organization of Industrial Management* (1967–1970). This journal was published by the All-Union Institute for Scientific and Technical Information *(VINITI)* and was narrowly focused on operational questions of industrial management. The editorial board was headed by A.M. Lisichkin and included several corresponding members of the Academy of Sciences. With an absolute minimum of critical commentary, the articles in *Reference Collection: The Organization of Industrial Management* reviewed and summarized selections from the management literature. The distribution among Soviet, East European, and Western sources is instructive. In the first year of publication (1967), the proportion of Soviet articles was quite modest; only in economic–mathematical methods did the reviewers concentrate on internal Soviet sources (52 percent). For the other categories (organization of industrial management, organization of management in industrial associations, and management of industrial enterprises), the proportion of Soviet articles was, respectively, 27 percent (n = 255), 14 percent (n = 109), and 28 percent (n = 143). On the other hand, the proportions of Western articles (i.e., Western Europe, USA) in the same period were 39 percent, 63 percent, and 35 percent. Reviews of East European developments were, in some cases, quantitatively more prominent than Soviet sources.

Noting the importance of high-quality information in promoting the rapid introduction of the latest achievements of science and technology in production management, *VINITI* and the USSR Academy of Sciences broadened the format of this reference journal in 1971. This monthly publication was renamed *"Reference Collection: The Organization of Management,"* and reviewed articles from 130 economic journals in 30 countries. By 1977, however, the scanning of foreign journals was further expanded, and over 110 American economic and managerial periodicals were included. The categorization of articles reveals an effort to broaden the scope of inquiry: reviews were now directed to theoretical issues as well as the social and psychological dimensions of management. Articles were organized under the following rubrics: (1) general questions, theory, and methodology; (2) the basic functions of management; (3) organizational forms and management structures; (4) economic methods of management; (5) legal methods; (6) sociological–psychological aspects of management and the leadership function; (7) management information systems; and (8) the training, selection, and placement of managerial cadres. Such a format was accompanied by major changes in the editorial board as Gvishiani assumed the general editorship and other positions were filled with prominent specialists of the empirical persuasion. B.Z. Mil'ner, a well-known Americanizer, was also included. These changes are indicative of the rising prominence of Soviet empiricists and their efforts to reorient the discipline away from its traditional technical-engineering bias. Moreover, while there have been occasional reviews (less critical commentary) of Western organization theory, these remain quantitatively insignificant.[20] Nevertheless, if a review appears in *Organization of Management*, then the full article can also be found in the USSR.[21]

In addition to these reference books, Soviet journals have given considerable attention to Western managerial developments. While empiricists have thus far failed in their efforts to obtain a separate management journal, *Organization of Management* has appeared yearly since 1971. This journal has a special section on foreign administrative experience and a bibliography on Western literature. The editorial board accepts articles from both political economists (these are usually "theoretical" treatments) and management empiricists. Furthermore, the journal of the Siberian branch of the Soviet Academy of Sciences, the bimonthly *Economics and the Organization of Industrial Production* (since 1970), often contains articles that examine Western theory and practice. An important theme has been the education and training of administrative executives. In January 1970, the Institute of the USA and Canada began to publish *USA: Economics, Politics, Ideology*. An important part of the institute's research program is devoted to management questions: quality control, organizational design, systems analysis, quantitative methods, data processing, the legacy of Taylorism, and so on. Both D.M. Gvishiani and B.Z. Mil'ner have made significant contributions. Finally, *World Economy and International Relations* (since 1957) examines American administrative experience, albeit often with propagandistic intent.

Although a comprehensive listing of the massive Soviet translation of American management literature is beyond the scope of this study, several major efforts warrant closer attention. For instance, D.M. Givishiani has served as editor-in-chief in the ten-volume series *Novoe v Upravlenii Proizvodstvom za Rubezhom [New Features in Production Management Abroad]*. This was, in the main, a serious effort to translate Western studies of intrafirm planning, the modeling of production processes, data processing, the training and placement of managerial personnel, and various questions of production organization. The volume *Kriticheskii Analiz Teorii i Praktiki Menedzhmenta [Critical Analysis of the Theory and Practice of Management]* (1976) is clearly propagandistic, but most volumes contain a substantive introductory article written by a leading Soviet management specialist. For example, in *Sovremenye Tendentsii v Upravlenii v Kapitalisticheskikh Stranakh [Modern Tendencies in Management in Capitalist Countries]*, G.Kh. Popov suggests several research departures for Soviet specialists. He also finds considerable support for his own views from American theorists like Herbert Simon, Peter Drucker, and Stanford Optner. In addition, Gvishiani was editor-in-chief of the reference book *Itogi Nauki: Seriia Organizatsiia Upravleniia [Review of Science: Organization of Management Series]*. This work surveyed American data-processing and optimal-decision techniques, emphasizing one point:

> [T]he borrowing [*zaimstvovanie*] of concrete methodology, techniques, and also a series of ideas, which are developed by management science abroad, can considerably enrich the economic–mathematical methods

and economic cybernetics in the socialist countries, and quicken the process of the development of these sciences [emphasis added].[22]

The Soviet institutes put out books as well as periodicals. The Mil'ner group at the USA Institute has published fourteen books on American and Soviet management practices. One important study of American experience is *SShA: Organizatsionnye Formy i Metody Upravleniia Promyshlennymi Korporatsiiami [USA: Organizational Forms and Methods of Management in Industrial Corporations]* (1972). Researchers from the Institute of World Economy and International Relations have also written widely on the American system of management.[23] In their efforts to gather information about American management, Soviet researchers can not find a modest assortment of topical periodicals from American sources in many libraries. Moreover, an intra-institute system to gather and categorize relevant publications exists as specialists at the Management Center of Moscow State University pepare and distribute bibliographies of current Soviet and foreign works.[24]

The state of the art in the USA has been periodically surveyed by various Soviet specialists,[25] most prominently by D.M. Gvishiani. The popularity of Gvishiani's books on this topic testify to the growing familiarity of Soviet specialists with the main features of American analytic approaches. His second major work, *Organization and Management* (1970; 1972 in English translation), is a comprehensive review of the major schools of thought in the American repertoire: managerism, human relations, social systems, the empirical approach, the "classical" principles of management, and operations research. According to Gvishiani, there are three ways to improve managerial performance in the USSR—(1) develop a theory of management; (2) generalize from Soviet experience; and (3) "critically" study advanced Western experience. His "critical" commentary on American approaches has demonstrated the potential utility of American concepts, methods, and research departures. As a general view, "systems analysis is the correct scientific methodology for managing complex systems, it is a comprehensive, integrated approach."[26] Gvishiani further argues that this formulation is entirely compatible with Marxism-Leninism:

> *The attempt of some bourgeois researchers to counterpose the general theory of systems to materialist dialectics and, in particular, to its categorical apparatus is . . . completely illogical.* It only shows that they do not understand dialectics and, what is more, that they interpret the principles of the systems approach metaphysically. . . . Naturally, systems analysis relates to materialist dialectics as a special theory relates to a general one. The methodological function of systems analysis is generally reserved for individual problems and applied tasks, notably, complex systems. *However, this distinction between systems analysis and the dialectical method, which reveals the universal laws of the development process, provides no reason for counterposing it to dialectics* [emphasis added].[27]

ADVOCACY FOR EXPLORING WESTERN THEORY

Although Gvishiani reassures bureaucratic interests like Gosplan that the growing importance of management presupposes an enhanced role for planning, he indicates that virtually every American approach has significant "lessons to be learned" and should be "critically" studied by Soviet specialists. Organizational design is one area of particular interest: "[These] views are of interest to the theory and practice of management in socialist conditions, since they reflect . . . the need for a strict coordination of subunits, the priority of general tasks over particular ones, and also provision for control and measurement of work . . ."[28] Since the human-relations approach is the normal whipping boy for Soviet reviewers, Gvishiani's endorsement is understandably circumspect:

> Some of its [human-relations] propositions continue to have fundamental importance in the present-day American theory of management and have some positive aspects, which should be *critically studied and incorporated into socialist practice when they have been freed from their ideological and class-biased implications* [emphasis added].[29]

Moreover, Gvishiani suggests that despite their utilitarian empiricism, certain American specialists have followed generally useful lines in analyzing management problems. Such a formulation acknowledges, at a minimum, those uniformities that exist irrespective of social systems in managing large-scale industrial production. Thus, relevant questions for *both* socialist and capitalist management are: (1) the classification and analysis of managerial functions; (2) the organization of the executive's work; (3) the establishment of an optimal relationship between human and technical elements; and (4) the selection and training of managerial personnel. The author finds certain American specialists worthy of careful attention. Peter Drucker is referred to as a specialist with an unusually profound understanding of the complexity of managerial–organizational processes. Chester Barnard is similarly treated:

> The point he [Barnard] makes about the constant need to consider strategic factors in taking managerial decisions is worthy of attention; so is his formulation of the so-called "zones of indifference" concept, etc. His description of the intricacy of studying social systems is of particular importance. Here he rightly stresses that the social sphere has no powerful magnifier like the balance sheet, no universal device which would make it possible to picture social aspects of an organization in a formal and simplified way.[30]

Unlike some American theorists, Gvishiani does not feel that American studies are marking time. Although the field of American management science may still be in its formulative stages, future directions are quite evident. These will entail a systems or comprehensive approach to management problems and will concentrate on information-gathering techniques and computer technology. Greater information capabilities will affect organizational structure and enable companies to recentralize. The role of middle management will sharply decline and information specialists and programmers will move up in the hierarchy. This scenario, which has also been outlined by Harold Leavitt and Thomas Whistler, has unusual appeal in the Soviet Union.[31] The selective utilization of American methods and techniques, it is hoped by Soviet specialists, will assist in its realization.

To the extent that the American referent has played a prominent role in Soviet management developments, the Soviets have borrowed experience and analytic concepts. Since the early 1960s, a small but growing number of Soviet specialists have attended a number of American universities. Certain specialists have made only short-term visits of two weeks or less, but others have stayed for an academic year. These research trips have familiarized the visiting Soviets with the essentials of American business education and appear to have contributed to their good standing and prestige within the management-science community in the USSR. Some have become advocates of specific ideas and techniques (such as V. Ozira and case methods), whereas others have utilized the American experience to popularize certain general ideas. For example, after living in the United States for over three decades, V.I. Tereshchenko returned to the Soviet Union in the early 1960s and promoted certain advantages of the American approach to management. His "American credentials" gave him the prestige to address questions of organization and management. Thus, research visits to the United States and familiarity with American approaches can both increase the information base of and enhance the standing in the scientific community of Soviet administrative specialists. Some American experience may be an important "ticket punch" in the career development of these individuals.[32]

EXCHANGE OF SCHOLARS

The most important of these programs, in terms of numbers, has been the exchange of young scholars and graduate students administered by the International Research and Exchanges Board (IREX). For each of the last several years, about 50 individuals from each country have spent from six to ten months in the other country. Most of the Soviet participants have been narrowly trained specialists in the natural sciences or applied engineering, whereas the proportion of Americans trained in the social sciences has been increasing. The Soviet participants have not, in the main, been those interested in topics of administrative science and management but some managerially relevant topics are of interest. One of the rising stars in the Soviet Union—R.L. Raiatskas—spent the 1967–1968 academic year at Harvard where his advisor was Wassily Leontief.

In addition to the exchange of junior scholars, a second program between the Ministry of Higher and Specialized Secondary Education and IREX is the exchange of senior scholars. This program is considerably smaller than the junior faculty exchange. As in the junior exchange program, the senior scholar exchange has only a few management specialists. The largest number of management-related exchanges occurs between the Soviet Academy of Sciences and the American Council of Learned Societies. Through this program, some of the most prominent members of the Soviet management science community have visited the United States. Nikolai Fedorenko, Mikhail Bermant, Vladimir Joffe, B.Z. Mil'ner, Vladimir S. Dadaian, Lenoid Evenko, and others came to the United States during the 1970s. Not only are these individuals attached to prestigious institutes in the USSR, they visited important management centers in the United States, including Harvard, MIT, the National Science Foundation, the University of Michigan, and the Office of Management and Budget.

The extent to which these research visits to the United States influence the learning capacity of Soviet administrative specialists is difficult to assess. For the senior Soviet participants, the extended research visit may be a capstone to their careers and their exposure to the American system may not significantly change their general conceptual orientation. For younger researchers, however, there is prima facie evidence indicating that not only have certain specialists adopted American analytic modes, but their standing in the Soviet management science community has thereby been enhanced. For example, V.S. Dadaian, an important mathematical economist spent two months at Northwestern University in 1974. He is now articulating innovative research departures in mathematical modeling. Along with R.L. Raiatskas, who was at Harvard during 1967–1968, Dadaian has presented a powerful challenge to the optimization model of the Central Economics–Mathematical Institute, the dominant paradigm of Soviet management. Given the recent increase in tension between the two governments since the intervention in Afghanistan and the election of Ronald Reagan, the long-range viability of these programs is open to question. In the middle of 1982, allegedly as an economy move, the Reagan administration was in the process of drastically reducing the IREX and Fulbright programs. Whether congress will reinstitute a larger program is still in doubt at this writing.

COOPERATIVE ARRANGEMENTS

In addition to faculty exchanges, the United States and the Soviet Union signed an agreement for scientific and technical cooperation on 24 May 1972. Part of the cooperative agreement deals with management science under the "application of computers to management" part of the understanding. The topics covered are a good indicator of important issues and concepts for Soviet administrative specialists and include econometric modeling, computer analysis applied to the economics and management of large systems, computer applications for management of large cities, theoretical foundations of software for application in economics and management, and computer-aided refinement of decision making and education of high-level executives.[33] These programs provided the first major opportunity for American management specialists to systematically exchange views with their Soviet counterparts and has led to the first reviews of management course curricula and training centers in the Soviet Union by American specialists.[34] Thus, the state of the art has been assessed. Although preliminary visits by Americans have revealed a considerable lag in Soviet developments (McKenney has likened Soviet management training to American practice in the 1930s),[35] there is an intense interest with active training techniques, particularly the case method as practiced at the Harvard Business School. In the late 1970s, the outlook for an expansion of these efforts appeared bright. But the election of the Reagan administration has changed the relationship. Academic and data exchanges with the Soviet Union have been greatly curtailed.

Finally, Soviet administrative specialists have participated in various international institutes dealing with questions of organization and management. These forums are an important component of Soviet efforts to modernize their administrative sciences and may have indirectly promoted the establishment of an institute of systems analysis in the USSR. In any event, such international endeavors have provided opportunities for Soviet theorists to exchange experience with foreign counterparts, to assess heretofore scarce information, to participate in joint research projects and publications, and to take part, informally at least, in advanced training and education programs. To the extent that Soviet specialists were less familiar with the methodology of systems research than Western scientists, at least during the 1960s, these forums have been learning experiences.[36]

One such international endeavor is the European Centre for Research and Documentation in Social Sciences currently headed by Adam Schaff (Poland) and Riccardo Petrella (Italy).[37] Strictly speaking, the center is not an institute, but rather a clearing-house for collaborative research projects between Eastern and Western specialists. It was established 6 April 1963 in Vienna by the International Social Science Center (a branch of UNESCO). There were 7 original members: Austria, France, Great Britain, the Netherlands, USSR, Poland, and Czechoslovakia. By 1973, the members (national participants from a specific country) were expanded to 14; the board of directors included, inter alia, Adam Schaff and V. Vinogradov (Soviet Union). The objectives of the center were officially (and optimistically) defined as the following: (1) the sponsorship and coordination of comparative research projects; (2) the publication of results; (3) preparation and documentation relating to the selected field of research; and (4) the awarding of study grants. The latter two tasks have not been met, primarily because of limited financial and human resources, but the center's role as a clearinghouse has been institutionalized. That is, it organizes research and insures international cooperation on the administrative and scientific levels, helps maintain contact between the participating institutes, and is responsible for the final results.

Moreover, the research format sponsored by the center displays not only active Soviet participation, but its highly selective nature. Most research topics have placed emphasis on the comparative study of economic systems. By 1973, the center had sponsored 21 projects, of which 10 were still under way. One-third of these topics are sociological in nature, e.g., industrial sociology and the impact of automation on worker morale. Fourteen Soviet institutions participated in these projects 1963–1973. In 1968, the USSR Academy of Sciences proposed a comparative study to analyze the impact of modern technology on working conditions, the content of labor, and the attitudes of workers in different national contexts. The research design encompassed the most technologically advanced industrial societies—the United States, Japan, USSR, West Germany, Great Britain, France, East Germany, Sweden, and Denmark. At the October 1972 plenary conference held in Moscow, 54 experts from 16 participating countries, despite their disagreements concerning the impact of different political systems on social phenomena, hammered out a research program. Although their conclusions are not revolutionary, at least with respect to previous national studies, the international dimension of this project is important.

Another interesting research topic, given conspicuous Soviet noninvolvement, was "The Effect of Organizational Hierarchy on the Reaction of Organization Members." This project was coordinated by Professor Arnold Tannenbaum of the University of Michigan and the results were published in *Hierarchy in Organizations* (1974).[38] Tannenbaum examined the extent to which the attitudes of individuals vary according to their organizational position. The alleged universality of hierarchical phenomena, although providing interesting material for comparative study, has apparently discouraged Soviet participation. The objectives (and conclusions) of this study should be noted:

> The project proposes to verify whether members at higher levels in a given organization's hierarchy are more motivated, have greater interest in and dedication to work, a greater feeling of loyalty towards the organization, are more self-satisfied than those at lower levels in the hierarchy, *regardless of the size of the organization and its socio-economic framework* [emphasis added].[39]

Despite the gingerly Soviet treatment of this theme, the possible clash with Marxist–Leninist doctrine has not discouraged East European participation in the hierarchy project; Bulgaria, Hungary, Poland and Rumania have taken part.

IIASA

The most significant multinational endeavor for the USSR has been the International Institute of Applied Systems Analysis (IIASA) in Vienna.[40] Although the possibilities for establishing such a center originated in joint American–Soviet talks in 1967, lengthy negotiations were required before IIASA commenced operations toward the end of 1972. This was to be a nongovernmental, interdisciplinary institute organized into various collaborative, international research teams (the mix of international participation would vary from project to project). There were 12 original member countries (since expanded to 17). Prestigious scientific organizations from the member states sent scientists to IIASA for an extended research visit, perhaps a year or more. The scholars would conduct research, lecture, participate in conferences and symposia, or pursue other kinds of methodological or theoretical questions subject to approval by the director. IIASA has a distinctly international flavor, but the United States and Soviet Union are the dominant and coequal financial contributors and have the largest scientific delegations. The institute's official language is English, but key adminstrative posts are distributed between the United States and the USSR: Howard Raiffa (Harvard) was the first director, Alexander Letov (USSR) was deputy director, and D.M. Gvishiani was, and remains, council chairman. Indeed, during preliminary negotiations, Gvishiani appears to have played a key role in promoting this international project.

The Soviets have taken this institute quite seriously; for them, it has been a major conduit into the international management community. Prior to the establishment of the first institute of systems analysis (1976) in the USSR, there was a *Pravda* article describing and praising the collaborative efforts of the international community at IIASA.[41] In addition, Gvishiani has publically praised the research contribution of IIASA and its new director, Roger Levien (formerly of the Rand Corporation).[42] Both the Soviet Academy of Sciences and the MGU Management Center maintain contact with IIASA. Furthermore, Soviet specialists like Abel Aganbegian, Gatam Dzhavadov, Boris Mil'ner, and G.Kh. Popov have made short-term visits to the institute.

As utilized by IIASA, applied systems analysis is not a mere technique or group of techniques like probability theory or mathematical programing. Rather, it is a broad research strategy involving the use of techniques, concepts, and systematic approaches to problem solving. It represents an analytic framework designed to help decision makers choose a desirable, if not "best," course of action. In this sense, applied systems analysis is an umbrella term, incorporating such specific fields as operations research and management science; cost effectiveness and cost–benefit analysis; planning, programing, and budgeting (PPB); decision analysis; many aspects of cybernetics; information theory and artificial intelligence; control systems; behavioral decision theory; and organization theory. As stipulated in the IIASA charter, the institute shall initiate and support collaborative and individual research in relation to "global" problems—energy resources, environmental problems, food production, the management of large organizations, etc.

IIASA has quickly emerged as a prominent research and publishing center. In addition to methodological questions of systems analysis, the energy crisis dominated (quantitatively speaking) the institute's scholarly output. In these respects, the Soviet contingent has a noticeably weak publication record. For instance, in the first two years of operation, there were 115 published reports; 9 were Soviet works (8 percent), of which 5 represented studies by the prize-winning mathematician Iu.A. Rosanov. In 1976, there were 187 published reports and research memoranda; 16 were authorized by Soviet scholars (9 percent). Reasons for the modest number of these contributions are unclear; the relative inexperience of Soviet researchers in applied systems analysis may be the cause. Given the weakly developed infrastructure of systems methodolgy in the USSR, IIASA may be more important, in its formative period, as a learning experience, rather than as a research establishment. The Soviet penchant to reproduce (read: photocopy) the Western administrative literature has been noted by IIASA personnel.[43] In addition, this relative inexperience with systems analysis may explain the slow development and fruition of Soviet-directed research programs, e.g., integrated industrial systems (headed by A. Butrimenko), and large organizations.

Two specific IIASA projects may have considerable impact on Soviet developments in management science: (1) the state-of-the art survey and handbook, and (2) the management of large organizations. The former project is intended to produce timely publications which systemitize and generalize the current status of systems analysis.[44] These publications are directed to a wide audience, including pactititoners in government, industry, education, and research applications. The suvey project's editorial board was initially headed by Levien (USA); the deputy executive editor was V. Rakhmankulov (USSR). Because of the international character of the state-of-the-art publications, there is an obvious need for contributions from a wide range of experts in many different countries. For this reason, participating scholars will be chosen mainly from outside IIASA, based on recommendations by members of the editorial board, experts in appropriate topical areas, and direct proposals from prospective authors. Moreover, these publications are to be distributed worldwide through national member organizations, which, in turn, have established liaison committees in their countries to work with the survey project. These committees are expected to (1) distribute tentative outlines of certain publications to select audiences, (2) arrange for publication in national languages, (3) facilitate English-language translation, and (4) contribute to an international glossary and other references.

The project on planning and management in large organizations ("organizations") is of particular importance; it emphasizes retrospective case studies and the relevance of American experience.[45] Indeed, this project could provide the framework whereby Soviet administrative studies broaden into nonindustrial settings, with attention to issues like decision making under conditions of uncertainty, the impact of "environment" on organizational effectiveness, and the process of goal setting. IIASA research teams have examined the organizational experience of specific large-scale projects—the Tennessee Valley Authority and the Bratsk–Ilimsk Territorial Production Complex (BITPC) in Siberia. In 1975, IIASA specialists visited Tennessee in order to gather materials and prepare reports on various aspects of TVA. Shortly thereafter, a two-volume study of the organizations project appeared. This analysis examined specific issues: goal identification, environmental impacts, performance indicators, managerial methods.

The BITPC was the second case study. There was a field visit by a select team of researchers to Siberia, followed by the second conference on the organizations project (22–25 March 1976). The conference was devoted to assessing Soviet experience in managing large-scale complexes. Unfortunately, the Soviet papers revealed no new information or "critical" evaluation of the BITPC project. Instead, they were mainly normative studies: how *should* planning take place in large-scale development projects? Only the V. Gukov and N. Perevalov paper, "Problems of Management of the Bratsk–Ilimsk Territorial-Industrial Complex," represented a critical examination of management topics. The modest fruition of the organizations project notwithstanding, IIASA anticipates at least one additional case study, the Shin-kan-sen railway system in Japan.

Thus, multiple communication channels—exchange programs, joint ventures, international institutes—have provided Soviet administrative specialists with vastly expanded information sources. Despite the growing scope and diversity of these channels, their impact on Soviet management science has been uneven and highly differentiated. One of the important factors limiting the adoption of "foreign" concepts has been Marxist–Leninist doctrine, i.e., the necessity to develop a distinctly *socialist* theory of management.

This constraint warrants closer attention, especially as management science in the United States has had very recent developments that could not, for ideological reasons, enter the Soviet dialogue. This new American approach, known as the "organized anarchy" school, will be the subject of the next chapter. In addition, we will look at the leading Soviet theorists in administrative science who might be described as "Americanizers."

7

Organized Anarchies in the United States and "Americanizers" in the Soviet Union

> *Unhappy is the society that has run out of words to describe what is going on.*
>
> —*Daniel Bell*

> *Ours is an unhappy society.*
>
> —*John Gerard Ruggie*

Introduction

The central tenet of administrative science, which emerged early in the development of the field, is that it is possible to develop a management control system that will allow administrators to tightly direct the routines of the organization and the behavior of individuals in it. This is at the core of the dominant paradigms of management in both the United States and the Soviet Union, which are based on the rational assumption that techniques can be developed that will allow for the integration of value trade-offs. (We use the term paradigms in the plural because there is no single dominant paradigm in either country. As we have seen, there are several major approaches in the United States and dozens of techniques. And as we shall see, administrative science is also a "jungle" in the Soviet Union.) In the late 1970s and early 1980s, some Americans have begun to question this assumption of rationality. And while some Americans were introducing the notion that it may not be possible to fine-tune administrative science, Soviet management was being substantially influenced by the Americans who had developed many of the techniques of the rational approach, such as decision making, organizational design, case methods, and business gaming. As these techniques grew out of the decision-analysis and political models of organizations, as administrative science moved into an open (rather than closed) system perspective in the 1940s, 1950s, and 1960s, they were widely adopted throughout the government and business bureaucracies. In the 1970s, the Soviet "Americanizers" began to selectively emulate some of them.

The Dominant Paradigm: Rational Choice in Organizations

Despite the differences in decision analysis, open systems, political models, human relations, and the other approaches in administrative science, these approaches share a common underlying assumption. To put it simply, it is that people know what they are doing; that is, they act with the objective of maximizing values and minimizing perceived costs, however those values and costs may be defined. To many, this statement would appear to be a tautology: it would be inherent in the definition of a value. As we have seen, the long development of administrative science is rooted in this assumption, and Karl Marx and Max Weber would subscribe to the notion that once values are set, people proceed in a rational manner. As John Steinbrunner has noted, there are three forces that contribute to the momentum of growth of this idea.[1] The logic of rationality is spelled out in mathematical modeling and games, from which sets of axioms and inferences have emerged. This basic logic has been developed in economics and applied mathematics in such areas as the theory of the firm and the behavior of individual consumers. The statistical decision theories growing out of these disciplines permit quantitative analysis of the decision-making process. Explicit applications of the assumption of rationality are found in nearly all of the techniques in management-control systems such as the case method, games, and modeling.

The assumption of rationality begins with the individual decision maker faced with a problem involving the trade-off of values. Since there is no universal set of utility values, the decision maker makes the utility preference on an individual basis. Cost-benefit analysis is a technique useful to the solution of the utility preference. Uncertainty is dealt with through statistical means. Cost-benefit and statistical techniques have introduced the ideas of limited value integration and subjective probability on the part of the individual. It is not possible to treat all values in a trade-off because of the impossible numbers of variables, and because different individuals will have subjective notions on the value of items.[2]

As Herbert Simon has pointed out,[3] the rational decision maker requires "as complete understanding as possible of the causal forces which determine outcomes. He seeks to predict the flow of events and, where he has leverage, to manipulate them to his advantage. The processing of information while making decisions is all done for the purpose of constructing and improving the blueprint from which the optimal choice emerges."[4]

When one moves from the level of the decision maker to the level of a government agency, the rational model is confronted with some difficulties. In a collective decision, for example, different individuals may have different utility preferences. If those utility preferences are diametrically opposed, a collective decision either could not be made or would require the addition of other utility preferences of individuals such as acceptance by the group or other small group norms.[5] Nevertheless, the rational paradigm treats collective decisions *as if they were the product of an individual.* The rational paradigm works out of this dilemma by including additional assumptions about the rationality of the behavior and motivation of individuals. That is, collective decisions, according to the rational paradigm, are made through a process of debate in which the argument with the best "facts" wins and is adopted by the group as its decision. The problem here is similar to Taylor's scientific management. Taylor argued that no one could (or should) rationally object to scientific management because it was based on "scientific facts." Of course, to Taylor, the "facts" led, as we have seen, to the dehumanization of the worker. Stripped of its assumptions, Taylorism was a statement containing numerous social, political, and economic values. And when we strip away from the rational paradigm the assumption that people will accept the argument with the "best" facts, we find values at war.

This is the central difficulty with the techniques used in the rational model, such as PPBS, MBO, ZBB, games, and models. These techniques are the systemization of political choices in the form of budget and planning decisions. And they assume a causal learning process, in which new information generated from experience and change in the environment external to the organization are fed into the process of continuous calculation. In theory, this leads to a deeper understanding of the nature of the problem, its parameters, and alternatives.[6] But the "real-world" problems that plague these techniques persist (thus accounting for their fad-like nature). As Robert Coulam has demonstrated, the system can be loaded so as to favor outcomes.[7] As Franklin Spinney has argued, these techniques contain assumptions never seen in the operational world (such as an extended period of five to eight years of stable budgetary growth).[8] As Morton Halperin has shown, bureaucratic noncompliance and foot-dragging can ruin the forecasts of systems analysts.[9] And as Coulam has also argued, the prospects for reform of these deficiencies are not high, despite the rational argument that the "best" decision is the one that should be made after "the facts are in."[10] What modern techniques do promise, however, is the transfer of the power to make value choices in a society from one group (old power brokers such as politicians or elected representatives) to another (new power brokers such as technicians and management specialists). Therefore, it is not surprising to find proponents of these techniques among management specialists in both the Soviet Union and the United States.

It is not fair, however, to imply that these modern administrative techniques are so flawed that they should simply be discarded. They have indeed produced technical miracles in limited areas of management, such as accounting and inventory control. Rather, our argument is that they contain flaws because they are part of the rational paradigm. It is the rational paradigm itself that we wish to suggest has reached the limits of its analytical power and needs to be supplanted.

Challenge to the Dominant Paradigm

In *The Structure of Scientific Revolutions*, Thomas S. Kuhn forcefully demonstrated the power of assumptions in paradigms.[11] Working assumptions define problems, direct research to collect data, and structure explanations. By providing a framework for explanation, a dominant paradigm anchors views of the world. And it is clear that in American and Soviet administrative science, the dominant paradigm is the rational one. Yet, as Kuhn also shows, dominant paradigms are transitional. They are replaced by new paradigms during violent intellectual revolutions. Revolutions occur when anomalies appear that the dominant paradigm cannot explain. As the number of anomalies grows, there is a period of intellectual ferment in which defenders of the old paradigm and proponents of newer paradigms clash. The process of paradigm replacement is not one in which defenders of the old paradigm suddenly see "the facts" in a kind of "ah-ha!" phenomenon, and then take a new paradigm as their own. The acquisition of knowledge is not a series of objective progressions moving step by step to truth. Rather, many nonrational things happen during the struggle.

It is our contention that this is now happening in administrative science in the United States, while the process has not yet started in the Soviet Union. A growing body of administrative science in the United States is now directly challenging the rational paradigm, while in the Soviet Union, "Americanizers" are introducing techniques of "rational" American administrative science.

In the United States, the first challenge to the dominant paradigm came with the development of the bureaucratic politics or conflict approach to understanding decision making. American culture holds strong normative views against conflict in organizations; a vast body of literature supports

that view.[12] However, bureaucratic politics contends that conflict in organization is inherent in complex hierarchies and that policy making is as
strongly influenced by these considerations as it is by disagreements over
"wise policy." Thus, bureaucratic politics deals with one of the critical
assumptions of the rational paradigm, in which it is assumed that the organization acts as an individual. Rather, in bureaucratic politics policy
output is seen as "distinct from what any person or group intended"[13]
because of compromises, logrolling, pulling and hauling, and other political
processes.

Yet the bureaucratic-politics approach still has the rational assumption
that people are making value trade-offs in the sense that they know what
they want and they know what they are doing when they engage in bureaucratic politics. When a person compromises on an objective, for example,
that person is seen as rationally calculating that "half a loaf is better than
none." There is still a relationship between what happens and the desires
of people in the organization—bureaucratic politics is another form of the
value trade off view of organizational decision making.

To be sure, bureaucratic-politics models produce more satisfying explanations than do purely rational approaches. Indeed, in the Cuban missile
crisis, for example, the central questions about that event cannot be understood without those models.[14]

But anomalies to the rational model in any of its forms (and, to reiterate
our point, we contend that the bureaucratic-politics model *is* a form of the
rational model) continue to mount. It is impossible to reconcile U.S. involvement in Vietnam with any of the rational models since massive U.S.
involvement and then loss of the war were events and outcomes that cannot
be seen as any kind of value trade-off. Furthermore, the war had vast
unintended consequences, such as the inflation in the United States that
triggered the OPEC price raises, which, in turn, played an important role
in the continued inflation and recession in the United States lasting on and
off, for almost a decade and nearly ruining major parts of the U.S. economy.

The basic premise of the organized-anarchy theory is that, when analysts
produce explanations for events, the explanations reflect the ability of the
analysts to create post factum theories of behavior rather than the actual
decision-making process in complex hierarchies.[15] Almost all of the post-hoc
explanations produced in U.S. and Soviet studies of bureaucracy are
grounded in the rational theory, in which the analyst starts from the premise
of value trade-offs. But the organized-anarchy approach is most useful under
conditions that are frequently faced by policy-makers in bureaucracies.
Those conditions involve "a situation where both activation and definition
of the situation are changing, where several participants are activated. . . .,
where the definition of the situation is complex, involving many values and
decision-making variables, so that the situation is difficult to analyze and

it is difficult to see and compare the consequences of existing alternatives."[16] In short, organized anarchies must operate under conditions where people are able only to see through a glass, darkly. The rational paradigm requires that clear alternatives and consequences be visible, so that value trade-offs can be made. Organized anarchy does not assume that this is possible in the tumult of actual decision making at high levels. Value trade-offs may be easier to accomplish far down the hierarchy, where problems and solutions are more manageable, probably because they are more familiar. In the day-to-day operations of a large-scale hierarchy, the solutions generated to microproblems may indeed be amenable to simple trade-offs. But at high policy levels, competing demands pose unanswerable difficulties not soluble by traditional (rational) methods.

Modern organizations in the United States and USSR are large, complex, organized systems with members of the systems interacting with one another. They also must deal with a wide variety of problems and are therefore highly differentiated into specialized subsystems. Todd LaPorte's working definition of complexity (Q) is derived from the number of components in the system (C_i), their variety or differentiation (D_j) and their degree of interdependence (I_k). The greater the C_i, D_j, and I_k, the greater the Q.[17] John Gerard Ruggie then modifies this formula to include the rate of charge $(\triangle)$ in the C_i, D_j, and I_k, so that the complexity of any environment (X) in which public policies must be made is defined as $Q_x = f[C_i, D_j, I_k \triangle (C_i, D_j, I_k)]$.[18] This definition is required, according to Ruggie, because of four factors. First, demands made on government are increasing steadily, so that the number of targets for public policy has been increasing. Second, in the current international system, advanced societies are increasingly interpenetrated, thus increasing the variety of actors whose behavior must be regulated to affect coherent policy. Third, the interdependence among targets, actors, and instruments increases the uncertainty for decision makers, already described. Finally, the rate of charge in all of these developments has been increased by the modern communication and transportation systems.[19] Thus, as bureaucracies have grown in size, their scope and interdependence have also grown.

Because of these factors, a variety of poorly defined and inconsistent preferences confront the policy makers. There is little consensus, other than in the broadest sense, about what should be done. The lack of agreement at the operational level where programs are developed and implemented has many obvious consequences.

Lack of agreement is confounded by ambiguity in the external environment to any organization. As noted earlier, in formulating policy or evaluating programs, evidence about their success or failure is difficult to obtain and even harder to interpret. Advocates and opponents of any program frequently use the same evidence to argue their cases. Program evaluation indicators (depended upon in the rational paradigm) are subject to numerous intentional and unintentional errors.[20]

With a lack of agreement over objectives and ambiguity in the environment, members of the organization are also confronted by dozens of issues simultaneously, all of which require "immediate" attention. Yet only a few can be attended to at any one time by any individual. The decision system is overloaded, which means that many "decisions" are made in fact by *flight* (in the sense of an avoidance reaction by the decision maker, hoping that the problem will go away), and by *oversight*. The crush of issues means that participation of individuals will be varied according to the issue and the time available to them; when more time is available, more people will become involved. If little time is available, fewer people can be activated in the search for solutions. When the decision concerns a problem with multiple value trade-offs (e.g., the external environment is ambiguous), and time is available, the decision may become the work of a committee. In the committee, opposing viewpoints may be condensed into the lowest common denominator, which means that the issues actually at stake will not rise in the hierarchy. Thus, the structural channels that direct the flow of problems to choices or the flow of participants to choices will also influence the decision and may serve to hide unpleasant choices or information from senior personnel. As the complexity of organizations increases, "the bureaucratic maze may simply be too confusing for the rat,"[21] as information gets lost or is sent to the wrong people.

These are the characteristics of an organized anarchy. In the United States, the dominant paradigm is under challenge because the number of anomalies that it cannot explain is growing. The results of this intellectual ferment will be interesting to observe, and administrative science may finally burst the bonds of the rational paradigm's limits.

"Americanizers" in the Soviet Union[22]

In the Soviet Union, no such challenge to the rational paradigm has emerged. The "organizational search" for relevant Western concepts, however, has without doubt effectively ended the international isolation of Soviet studies of organization and management. Certain theorists in the USSR have become active Americanizers, and have either described important concepts, methods, business practices, and the like, or have actually adopted certain ideas in their research and theorizing. Americanizers can be found throughout the Soviet Union, although Moscow is the indisputable center of their activities. Despite the plethora of new ideas and wealth of information, however, there has been no headlong rush to "Americanize" the Soviet discipline. Most centers have shown an uneven, and partially isolated, adoption of new concepts. Opposition still exists to "uncritical" borrowing of capitalist experience, and Americanizers naturally concentrate on nuts-and-bolts technical issues. The areas where American concepts have been most readily accepted can be identified with relative ease: decision making, organization design, case methods, and business games. Each of these areas is, however, clearly within the confines of the rational paradigm. For a Soviet administrative specialist to attempt to borrow ideas from the organized anarchies approach would cause difficult theoretical problems to a management science aimed at rational management of a socialist economy. Thus, it is doubtful (at the moment) that any challenge to the rational paradigm will appear in the USSR.

DECISION MAKING *(PRINIATIE RESHENIIA)*

Decision making does not constitute a strongly developed theoretical tradition in the Soviet management-science community. Indeed, studies that address issues like the impact of uncertainty and risk on decision making and organizational behavior are exceptional. To the extent that such questions have been raised, however, a relatively small number of Americanizers in the Institute of the USA and Canada and the Tallinn Polytechnical Institute are responsible. Despite the proclivity to cite from and refer to leading American decision theorists (e.g., James March, Herbert Simon, Richard Cyert, and Stanford Optner), the organizing concepts of the Carnegie School have not achieved wide currency in the USSR. Nevertheless, certain decision-making concepts from the American repertoire have reappeared in Soviet studies of management. This is most conspicuous in the theorizing of Leonid Evenko (USA Institute) and Madis Khabakuk (Tallinn); relevant literature from each specialist will be reviewed briefly.

Leonid I. Evenko heads a section in the Institute of the United States and Canada; he has visited America (1976) and spent some time at the Graduate School of Industrial Administration, Carnegie Mellon University (Pittsburgh). His research work has involved the analysis of American corporate management as well as public administration. In addition, he is a frequent reviewer of American developments in systems analysis and applications (e.g., PPBS) in the federal bureaucracy.[23] While his advocacy of satisficing (*udovletvorenie*) and bounded rationality (*ogranichennaia ratsional'nost'*) as useful analytic constructs has met with little ostensible support in the Soviet management-science community, certain ideas drawn from American referents have appeared in the Soviet literature. For instance, in a work edited by B.Z. Mil'ner, *Organizatsionnye Formy i Metody Upraveleniia Promyshlennymi Korporatsiiami [Organizational Forms and Methods of Management of Industrial Corporations]*, Evenko reviewed several contemporary decision-making approaches in the United States. The recognition that conditions like the degree of uncertainty impinge not only on the nature

of decision-making problems, but on the capacity of analytic tools to over
come such constraints, was developed in a subsequent publication of
Mil'ner's research team, which examined Soviet organizations.[24]

In his review of decision making in American corporations, Evenko noted
the following:

> It would appear that problems like the formulation of long-term pro-
> duction plans, the exploitation of new products, the diversification of
> the firm, the elaboration of corporate policy with regard to market sales
> and price-setting, the assessment of expedient capital expenditures . .
> . and a series of other problems, are impossible to strictly formalize and
> precisely "resolve" with the help of algorithmic programmed computer
> procedures. *Such a class of "strategic" problems, as noted by I. Ansoff,
> inevitably are subject to significant influence from external environ-
> mental factors . . . and ultimately they contain a significant element
> of subjective judgments in all of their links* [emphasis added].[25]

In such a situation, managers are faced with poorly structured problems
(*slabo strukturizovannye problemy*); these involve significant ambiguities of
goals, means, expenses, environmental conditions, and performance indicators. Poorly structured problems create conditions for suboptimization
(*suboptimizatsiia*), in which solutions may be optimal for particular subunits, but not for the organization as a whole. The task of management,
therefore, is to secure the "rooting in" (*vrastanie*) of analytic methods in
corporate-level decisions. According to Evenko, American theorists have
elaborated two distinct, but closely interrelated, approaches: (1) variants
of systems analysis, and (2) applied models and methods of "decision-making." Advocates of the latter approach (presumably decision theorists of the
Carnegie School are not hostile to applications of systems analysis and operations research (*issledovanie operatsii*); but, in light of certain "constraints" (e.g., the nature of the decision situation), they assess those
opportunities modestly.

Following American theorists, Evenko argues that formal systems analysis
is useful in well to poorly structured situations, regardless of the (relative)
uncertainty of the latter. Since Herbert Simon notes that the problem situation can significantly influence organizational decision making, certain
Soviet theorists have drawn appropriate conclusions. In particular, uncertainty (*neopredelënnost'*) impinges on decision making: "The uncertainty
of the market, supply, activities of stockholders, the behavior of competitors,
the future activity of government bureaus characterize those conditions in
which the business firm operates."[26] Referring to Cyert and March's Behavioral theory of the firm, Evenko's linkage of uncertainty and decision
making bears an explicit relevance for socialist conditions:

> . . . With the solution of any problem, clarity and certainty are on hand
> only when the situation is repetitive, well-known and standard. In con-

trast to this, *any decision in a new situation demands research and comprehension of the problems and circumstances, in which . . . a large portion of information about objective processes are unknown to the manager, who is making the decision, these decisions inevitably will not be "objectively optimal"* [emphasis added].[27]

This is an important insight. Under conditions of "bounded rationality" the meaning of optimal solutions is dubious. Despite the limited utility of traditional analytic techniques in such conditions, Evenko shows that American administrative theorists have successfully applied imitation models like business games (*delovye igry*) and role playing (*razygryvanie rolei*). As Evenko notes, "an imitation model helps to reveal, while not the best, then a 'good' decision for a wide set of conditions which can change under the influence of uncontrollable external factors."[28]

The American examination of decision making and concepts like satisficing and bounded rationality have been replicated in a very limited manner in the Soviet literature. Thus, in *Organizatsionnye Struktury Upravleniia Proizvodstvom [Organizational Structures of Production Management]*,[29] two general classes of decision problems are identified: (1) those which are routine, programed, and repetitive, and (2) those which are nonroutine, nonprogramed, and nonrepetitive. The latter class describes the realm of creative decision making and requires individual judgment, experience, and other "subjective" attributes. The criteria which separate routine from non-routine problems are the fullness (*polnota*) and clarity (*iasnost'*) of information. With respect to the degree of uncertainty, the authors suggest a typology of decision-making situations. Each category lists the defining characteristics of these problems as well as the analytic models required for their solution. Accordingly, managers face three basic types of problem solutions. First, well structured problems (*khorosho strukturizovannye problemy*) are well known and can be expressed in quantitative fashion. With the help of operations research and economic-mathematical modeling, optimal solutions can be found. Techniques like mathematical programing, probability statistics, and simulation can also be applied successfully. Second, poorly structured problems (*slabo strukturizovannye problemy*), as a rule, are connected with the elaboration of long-term courses of action, each of which touches upon many aspects of enterprise behavior. Along with quantitative elements, these problems consist of numerous unknown and/or dynamic components, which ensure a high degree of uncertainty. Systems analysis and various quantitative methods are the most appropriate methodology, the significance of human judgments and experienced leadership notwithstanding. Unstructured problems (*nestrukturizovannye problemy*) constitute the third category. They are characterized by great uncertainty and are impossible to formalize. These problems include the formation of long-term plans, the planning of social and cultural measures, etc. Their solution depends on the experience, intuition, and qualification of managerial personnel. While the systems approach (*sistemnyi podkhod*) should provide the framework for analysis, there is no substitute for the creative leadership of experienced managers.

Given the prescriptive orientation of the Soviet literature, most studies of decision making are not concerned with describing actual decision processes or their impact on organizational behavior. An important exception is the work of Madis Khabakuk. Acknowledging his debt to Herbert Simon and James March,[30] Khabakuk considers decision making largely as a problem of choice. Despite earlier (and futile) efforts to popularize behavioral concepts, his current theorizing draws heavily from American ideas like management by objectives (MBO) and the optimal-decision techniques PATTERN and FAME. These techniques warrant brief review.

FROM MBO TO SEKOR

Management by objectives is perhaps more a philosophical approach than a concrete method of problem solving.[31] Unlike the traditional attention to tasks and functions, MBO is not concerned with "how one gets there," but rather with the final outcome. According to S.K. Chakraborty, MBO is "management of objectives, for objectives, and by objectives."[32] Khabakuk has promoted such an approach in his "*Upravlenie na Osnove Tselei*" ["Management on the Basis of Goals"].[33] While the author proclaims that the MBO tradition and philosophy have historical roots in the USSR, current approaches are determined by the wholeness (*tselostnost'*) and systemness (*sistemnost'*) of these views. The essential idea of "management on the basis of goals" is that managers should allocate their time to important activities that produce measurable results. Hence, at each hierarchical level in the organization, there should be a concrete (preferably quantifiable) goal governing specified activities, e.g.), a certain percentage increase in labor productivity. Progress toward the stipulated goal, not the activity itself, is the indicator of managerial success. While an MBO philosophy requires an attention to goal specificity, Khabakuk expects other benefits as well. For instance, it will encourage a nonauthoritarian style of management and raise the qualifications of managerial personnel.[34]

Moreover, Khabakuk suggests ways in which MBO can be implemented in the Soviet Union. With respect to concrete measures, there should be (1) seminars and meetings to familiarize executives with MBO, (2) problem-oriented analyses of those enterprises in question, (3) a scenario of long-range goals, (4) a disaggregation of enterprise-level goals among relevant subunits, and (5) a map of completed tasks.[35]

Khabakuk has liberally, but selectively, borrowed from the American repertoire to develop SEKOR, an optimal decision technique. For his more doctrinaire colleagues, worried about the "uncritical" study and "mechanical" application of bourgeois administrative ideas, Khabakuk notes:

> SEKOR was based on already established management systems. *From these systems everything was taken which, in our opinion, was most appropriate for socialist production organizations, and everything was expunged which was alien to them.* The basic, fundamental systems of management on which SEKOR is based are management by objectives, the systems PATTERN, FAME, QUEST, NAIKOR, and PROFAIT and also certain materials applicable to the planning of scientific research [emphasis added].[36]

While acknowledging that managers with different functional responsibilities have dissimilar priorities and preferences, SEKOR allegedly provides a technique for making "optimal" decisions. Hence, a "decision tree" is constructed in the following sequence: (1) the long-range goals (five–ten years) of the enterprise are elaborated (Khabakuk sees this as the most important and difficult task); (2) criteria and corresponding weight coefficients (three are used) are fixed for evaluating the elements at each level of the "decision tree"; and (3) weight coefficients are introduced for each element of the "tree" in relation to the criteria at each level. Khabakuk regards SEKOR as a general means (i.e., equally relevant for socialist and capitalist conditions) for making decisions; it is particularly helpful in rationalizing managerial functions.

ORGANIZATIONAL DESIGN (ORGPROEKTIROVANIE)

The design of organizations involves more than questions of structure; it includes the establishment of organizational goals, the identification of the ways in which the organization can achieve such goals, and the specification of internal roles and relationships.[37] While questions of organizational structure, particularly the optimal degree of centralization–decentralization, have always been salient issues with Soviet administrators,[38] it was not until the early 1970s that serious studies of organizational design were undertaken. On the level of management practice, this attention to design corresponded with Soviet efforts to turn the production association into the "enterprise of the future."[39] Moreover, the recognition that there are "objective similarities" between large-scale production units irrespective of social system led Soviet theorists to seriously examine the American organizational practice. With respect to the technical and organizational aspects of design, important concepts and lessons might be learned from American experience. To be sure, "learning" appears to have occurred in select areas: the functioning of research bureaus, intrafirm planning, project designs, program goal planning, and the application of information-processing systems.

The most innovative studies of organizational design have been undertaken by B.Z. Mil'ner's research team at the Institute of the USA and Canada: V.P. Averchevyi, I.K. Bykov, A.B. Tsybulevskii, A. S. Mironov, T.N. Kalinovskaia, L.I. Evenko, R.A. Perelet, E.A. Chizhov, V.N. Churmanteeva, and others. Not only has this team extensively examined American experience, but certain managerial concepts (note Evenko's treatment of decision making) have reappeared in a purely Soviet context. We suggest that American experience has provided relevant practical and theoretical "lessons" for Soviet theorists. In this respect, consider the Russian-language translation of articles from select U.S. business journals (e.g., *Harvard Business Review, Business Management*)—*Novoe v Teorii i Praktiki Upravleniia Proizvodstvom v SShA (New ideas in the Theory and Practice of Production Management in the USA)* (1971). In the introduction, Mil'ner makes it clear that certain American ideas are worthy of serious consideration by the Soviets. For instance, in order to utilize computers more effectively, U.S. specialists have turned to time sharing (*razdelenie vremeni*). Mil'ner encouages Soviet experts to critically examine this technique. Simmilarly, given today's dynamic technology, American corporations have been adopting program-goal planning and so-called matrix structures. These concepts, according to Mil'ner, are also relevant under socialist conditions.

American experience has, to a degree, structured the expectations of certain administrative specialists in the USSR. To the extent that inadequate domestic experience has warranted decision by analogy (*reshenie po analogii*), theorists at the USA Institute have adopted an "American mode." Hence, in various published works, not only is it difficult for the reader to determine whether the object of inquiry is Soviet or American, but—most importantly—certain ideas have been taken from the managerial vocabulary in the United States. For instance, while Evenko examined concepts like multigoal systems, life cycles, and matrix structures as illustrated by American referents, these subsequently have reappeared, albeit in modest circulation, in the Soviet literature.[40] Given our interest in substantive emulation, we will examine (1) Soviet learning from the analysis of American experience, and (2) the adoption of specific organizational design concepts.

Theorists at the USA Institute have made rather cautious assessments (given the technological bias and optimism of most Soviet specialists) regarding the capacity of data processing to simplify the manager's task environment. These relatively sober views or expectations may have been influenced, in part, by the analysis of American experience. Although it is not possible to establish a causal link, the similarity of perceptions as well as the timing sequence—i.e., U.S. views were analyzed prior to development of Soviet materials[41]—suggest the possibility that "vicarious learning" has taken place. For instance, in the Institute's 1971 publication *SShA: Sovremennye Metody Upravleniia [USA: Contemporary Methods of Management]*, B.Z. Mil'ner examines certain contending views on computer applications in the United States.[42] The salience of information-processing technology reflects the objective needs of modern, large-scale production (i.e., it is equally relevant under socialist conditions), and has led to the growing prominence of computer experts in the organizational hierarchy. However, in the United States, there are administrative theorists (Peter Drucker, Herbert Simon, and Igor Ansoff) who minimize the impact of information-processing systems on the manager's basic task environment. That is, certain American specialists have raised a more specific inquiry: in what particular managerial functions are major changes likely to occur? They suggest that only those repetitive and/or potentially routinized tasks will be substantially affected by computerization.

While warning against "electronic romanticism," American experts recommend a sober approach to "automatic systems"; indeed, the future holds the greatest potentialities in areas like market research, long-term planning, and the regulation of production. Similar views have been adopted by Soviet specialists in the USA Institute.[43] Hence, according to the Mil'ner group, the lessons of "Soviet and foreign experience" take issue with the one-sided technical approach of certain specialists. They suggest that the higher the level of organizational activity, the greater the role of creative, human activities in management. Those elements which are amenable to formalization and mathematical expression are confined to accounting, payroll, bookkeeping, etc. While data processing can expedite intra-organizational planning, goal setting, and decision making, these activities nonetheless remain the function of creative leadership, i.e., management.

SIMILARITY OF THEORY OF INTRA-ORGANIZATIONAL CONFLICT AND OTHER ASPECTS

The study of intra-organizational conflict is treated similarly in both American and Soviet contexts. In addition to personal disagreements among managers, the parochialism of functionally structured organizations can encourage interdepartmental conflict. This is commonly found in American firms where "separate subdivisions, paying too much attention to their particular tasks, have a tendency to self-preservation, organizational conservatism, and resistance to change."[44] Such conflicts often encourage suboptimization and can inhibit innovation (*novatorstvo*) in the organization. These functional conflicts are attributable to two causes: (1) the interdepartmental competition for resources, which, in turn, is seriously exacerbated by the emergence of new groups—usually from technological developments—and the resulting clash with traditional interests; (2) the competition involving new products and/or the modification of existing output.

The tendency for organizational subunits to overestimate their importance also occurs in the USSR. While Soviet analysts seldom dwell on the dynamics of these conflicts or their impact on organizational behavior and decision making, the Mil'ner team describes organizational conflict in a manner similar to previous treatment of American corporations. Conflict can occur among workers and managers, and:

> [i]n an organization, there can also emerge certain tensions and disagreements between separate subdivisions or employees who carry out joint labor (e.g., between the planning-economic section which is responsible for the date of filling orders and the production-control services, for which the main task is uniform work capabilities; between designers striving for the most modern design solutions and also technologists whose job is to guarantee the technical capacity of new products, etc.) [emphasis added].[45]

These conflicts involve, according to Mil'ner, particular economic goals, the manner of their realization, the failure of line personnel to fulfill staff instructions, the insufficient sensitivity of managers to the needs of workers, and so on. The task of management in creative leadership is to resolve them in order to insure the smooth functioning of the entire system.

In addition to structuring expectations and/or providing relevant lessons to Soviet specialists, certain American ideas have reappeared in the Soviet management literature. This is again evident from publications of the USA Institute—*Organizatsionnye Struktury Upravleniia Proizvodstvom*—which is depicted as the first comprehensive Soviet effort to examine organizational design. Thus, several novel concepts were introduced to Soviet readers: the complex analysis of the external environment, the life-cycle (*zhiznennyi tsikl*) approach to development, and the multigoal nature of organizations. With respect to the latter, four general classes of organizational goals can be identified: technical, production, economic, and social. Mil'ner notes that it would be a serious error to underestimate the importance of social goals; unfortunately, this has been a long-standing tradition in the Soviet management literature.

Despite the modest impression these concepts have made on Soviet therorizing,[46] serious attention has been given to program-goal planning (matrix designs) and project mangement. These ideas are favorably reviewed in the American context, and Mil'ner himself has actively promoted their adoption in the USSR. Project management, in particular, appears to have been implemented with varying measures of success in the industrial association *Uralelektrotiazhmash*.[47] Soviet fascination (at least in the USA Institute) with matrix structures and project management reflects a positive assessment of American experience; the analysis and promotion of these managerial structures found in *Organizatsionnye Strucktury Upraveleniia Proizvodstvom* closely follows from previous studies of American corporate design.

Soviet Responses to the Inadequacy of Present Organizational Structures

Functional structures have not provided corporate mangement with sufficient flexibility to deal with dynamic technology, complex interactions with the environment, or rapid product obsolescence. Not only do contemporary problems cut across departmental and functional lines (thus increasing interdependence and the demands of coordination), but innovation itself has become an important function of management. These factors have important consequences for organizational design. According to one American expert, future organizations will be (1) multidimensional in function and structure, (2) complex and instrumentally interdependent, and (3) professionally and personally specialized (as contrasted to the maximum of task specialization).[49] These considerations have promoted a growing interest in matrix models and specific features of project management:

> Unlike the traditional monocratic organization, which is built along vertical lines, the matrix or mixed organization bifurcates the management system into functional and project roles and structures. It has a formal functional hierarchy for normal routine decision-making. Superimposed on this primary authority structure is a secondary authority network, which focuses on accomplishing specific projects. The latter cuts horizontally across vertical functional and departmental lines. Its purpose is to ensure the achievement of interorganizational objectives.[50]

Soviet efforts to form industrial associations (obëdineniia), particularly since 1973, have encouraged experimentation with matrix structures, project management, program-goal approaches, and the like. Thus, specialists in the USA Institute suggest that the program-goal approach is the most significant innovation in organizational design in recent years.[51] These same specialists note that program-goal planning and project management were first applied in the U.S. aerospace industry in the late 1950s; by the mid-1960s they had spread throughout the American business community. The combination of functional and project structures reputedly permits the utilization of the positive sides of each; the interrelationships of horizontal and diagonal ties and communication create the matrix structure (matrichnaia struktura). The traditional functional structure—production, quality control, and research bureaus—exist alongside temporal project groups, which are created for a particular task. The advantage of project management (proektnoe upravlenie) is flexibility. It permits a concentration of material and human resources on a specified task, which changes as old projects are terminated and new ones started. In this manner, not only is the introduction of innovations (vnedrenie novovendnii) given institutional expression (i.e., as project groups), but the psychological barriers to such innovation are putatively reduced. Similar principles involve product management *(upravlenie po otdel'nym produktom)*. Thus, if large corporations have a great variety of product lines, then special managerial bodies can be created for planning, distribution, research and development, and control over the specified output. Moreover, these organizational structures have distinctive authority relations. For instance, project managers normally do not have direct control over those involved with the project. They do determine *what* and *when* things should be done; functional managers, on the other hand, decide *who* and *in what manner* the task should be fulfilled.[52]

Theorists at the USA Institute have done much to promote and utilize ideas like program-goal planning and project management. While the American referent has given them a solid peg on which to hang their case, certain "objective" conditions must also be considered: *"The emergence and development of program-goal structures* which guarantee the interconnected and directed activity on various elements of the object of management both vertically and horizontally *is historically appropriate at the contemporary stage of development of production"* (emphasis added.)[53]

CASE METHODS (KEIS-METODY OR METOD KONKRETYNKH SITUATSII)

Despite the Soviet penchant for quantitative analysis, the art of management has also received considerable attention. This has been the domain of management empiricists. In addition to their analysis of leading experience, empiricists deal with the personal qualities of managers and the contents of education and training programs required under developed socialism. Not only has the idealized imagery of the socialist manager evolved from technical specialist to managerial generalist (e.g., *organizator planirovaniia narodnogo khoziaistva*),[54] but certain innovations in educational curricula and teaching techniques have been adopted. While these changes reflect institutional developments and the establishment of separate departments *(Kafedry)* of management (largely since 1970), the attention to and emulation of American experience is also much in evidence. Thus, business education in the United States has been carefully analyzed by Soviet experts, e.g., curricula materials and development, sensitivity training, business games, computer applications, modern educational techniques, "active" (case) methods of instruction, etc. Moreover, the notion that management is a separate professional activity, a fact consistently noted by Soviet reviewers of the American system, is now accepted in broad segments of the management-science community. While great differences in the Soviet and American approach to management training remain (e.g., advanced training normally occurs *after* managers have been identified through work experience in the Soviet Union), a certain confluence in perspectives has occured. In this light, the adoption of case methods requires closer attention. This innovation can be attributed to the efforts of Americanizers like Vitaly Ozira and exchange programs between the United States and Soviet Union.

Case methods of instruction are an integral part of the repertoire of American business education. These involve the active analysis by participants of specific problem-situations likely to occur in the business world, as well as prescriptions concerning the probable manner of their resolution. Virtually all graduate business schools in the United States employ such methods, but it is at Harvard that they are most prominently displayed. It is not surprising, therefore, that Ozira—who spent ten months at the Harvard Business School (1966–1967)—has been the most persistent advocate of such methods in the USSR. Ozira has utilized the Soviet media to promote case methods. For example, not only was the Harvard program positively reviewed by *Literaturnaia Gazeta*,[55] but specific features of the case method were favorably described in other journals as well.[56] Centralized planning, specific accounting procedures, and "rules of the game" that depict Soviet reality will obviously affect problem-situations; however, the general orientation of American cases (e.g., corporate strategy, long-range planning) is considered appropriate under socialist conditions. More substantive problems have been encountered in overcoming the traditional roles and expectations of students and instructors alike. That is, given the traditional lecture or seminar format in Soviet universities, the more active requirements of student participation and student interaction with teachers—the bases of the case approach—have not been satisfactorily achieved in the Soviet Union. Indeed, for the case method to be successfully applied, there must be not only a reserve of situations and exciting examples (in considerable detail) to analyze, but properly trained instructors. By the late 1960s, Ozira had prepared several concrete cases for use in the management lab of Moscow State University.[57] When he later assumed the leadership of the department of planning and industrial production at the Plekhanov Institute, the case method became an integral part of the course curricula. While Ozira continues to promote case methods in the face of considerable lethargy within the management-science community (their diffusion has been restricted to Moscow universities), he has recently examined, in explicitly favorable terms, the role and functioning of American consulting firms.[58] In fact, a large conference on management consulting was scheduled at the Plekhanov Institute in 1977, and several publications on this theme were to follow in 1978.[59]

Given Ozira's efforts and the 1972 Soviet–American agreement, how widely diffused are techniques like the case method in Soviet management education? In which particular institutes are they most actively utilized? Have case methods substantially influenced the educational programs of Soviet management centers, or has their impact been marginal? Since by all indications case methods have received considerable attention from Soviet specialists since the mid-1960s, this is virtually a test case in miniature of the substantive emulation of American ideas in the Soviet management community. If their application is considered a measure of the adaptability of traditional structures to new ideas, then, and not surprisingly, the results are mixed. That is, despite considerable attention from Soviet Americanizers, the concrete application of case methods has been limited to Moscow institutes and universities. Even in these centers their utilization has been modest. Moreover, Professor B.M. Mochalov, a colleague of Ozira's at the Plekhanov Institute, while noting the growing popularity of case methods in the USSR, lists only the training center of the Latvian Republic as a non-Moscow center employing this teaching technique.[60] While Ozira has noted that "all [Soviet] authors agree that more case methods should be included in management education,"[61] others have been significantly less enthusiastic. For instance, V.G. Shorin, the director of the Institute of Management of the National Economy, is not excited about the case method and considers it "static."[62] John Austin, an American participating in the 1972 Agreement on Scientific and Technical Cooperation, has corroborated the limited use of such techniques in the Soviet Union and the constraints on future developments.

BUSINESS GAMES (DELOVYE IRGY OR IGROVOE MODELIROVANIE)

Since the American Management Association's first use of business games ("top management decision simulation") in 1956, the acceptance and diffusion of such games have been spectacular. Thus, surveys revealed that within ten years, of the 90 responding major schools of business, over two-thirds were experimenting with gaming techniques.[64] This prominence can be attributed to several interconnected factors: (1) a general recognition in the management profession of the need to acquire better and shorter methods of learning managerial skills; (2) the emergence of related fields like operations research and game theory; and (3) the educational use of role playing and case studies.[65] Despite the heterogeneity concealed by the rubric "business games" and the fact that their purposes and/or functions can vary, they are simply techniques of providing vicarious experience. The presumption is made that managerial skills can be learned and that such "learning" is best facilitated by the experience of games, rather than by lectures or similar didactic methods.

Soviet developments in business gaming reflect more than a recognition of the relevance of active educational methods. To a significant extent, motivation and concrete theorizing have liberally drawn from the American experience. For example, V.I. Marshev and A.K. Popov suggest that the gaming method is appropriate for the three major tasks of perfecting management in the USSR; the rationalization of leadership, the training of management personnel, and the formulation of theory. With respect to foreign experience:

> ... the gaming method is a technique for the formation of a theory of
> management and can successfully be utilized for the analysis of problems
> like ... influence methods on the object of management; the explication
> of general principles of constructing the subject of management and its
> functioning; the division of functions ... decision-making ... the
> structure and process of management.[66]

The leading Soviet authority in business gaming, Ivan M. Syroezhin, spent
1963–1964 at Stanford and Cornell. He has published several articles in
Management Science and was actively involved with the 1972 Agreement
with the United States. Syroezhin is collaborating closely with Myron Uretsky
of the New York University Business School; Uretsky is one of the leading
American specialists on business gaming. In a manner reminiscent of other
prominent Americanizers (e.g., the Iuksviarav–Khabakuk group in Tallinn
and Vitaly Ozira at the Plekhanov Institute), Syroezhin is chairman of the
department of economic cybernetics of the Leningrad Finance Economics
Institute and heads a team of specialists including Iu.Iu. Kurochkin and
Svetlana Gidrovich. His conception of economic cybernetics purports to be
not only the utilization of gaming techniques for the training and/or retraining of managerial cadres, but a theory of the socialist production organizations as well. Indeed, the theory of the production organization (the
"theory of the firm" under socialism) deals with the structure and internal
processes of socialist organizations. It explicitly takes into account the economic interests of various organizational subunits (i.e., the participants in
the game), which, in their mutual interaction, determine the functioning and
effectiveness of those organizations. Syroezhin's theoretical treatment of the
socialist production organization can be found in *Ocherki Teorii Proizvod-
stvennykh Organizatsii (Essays on the Theory of Economic Systems)* (1970).
Furthermore, a recent English-language translation, *Simulated Game
Models as a Means of Management Training and a Form of Collective
Decision-Making (1976)*, reviews the basic theoretical elements of this "system" as well as the purposes and characteristics of specific games.[67] Although
a detailed review of this theory does not belong in our study, two important
issues will subsequently be examined: (1) the basic language of analysis, and
(2) the purposes of business gaming.

In Syroezhin's theoretical formulation, certain analytic concepts (e.g.,
economic interests, responsibility, management centers, cohesion, property)
not only receive concrete, operational expression, but suggest a redefinition
of certain traditional categories of political economy. These redefinitions
facilitate the examination of organizational processes (thus, conflict and
parochialism become standard "facts" of organizational life) and reorient
Soviet management studies toward a more descriptive mode of analysis.
Furthermore, the role of management cannot be confused with mere information processing (as in technical systems); management is concerned with

the effectiveness in realizing certain basic systemic functions. In this light, the Syroezhin group views the socialist economy, although unified by collective ownership, as structurally divided into separate management centers (MC). Every MC, at least for analytic purposes, is a separate organization uniting production resources with managerial personnel. The latter insure purposive, goal-oriented behavior in every link of the economic system. Any particular MC, however, does not necessarily concur with juridical regulators of its boundaries. It may include several "businesses" and/or institutions. Not only do such MCs delimit separate economic systems, but they can exist on different scales within the national economy. According to Syroezhin, the level of concurrence between the economic interests in systems existing on different scales, and the relative independence of the processes of their differentiation and agreement are the most significant points for game modeling.[68]

In its most general expression, the task of management (i.e., each MC) is to raise the organization level *(organizovannost')* of the system or to increase its "manageability" *(upravliaemost')*. On the level of practical activity, however, the *organizovannost'* of the system reflects concrete managerial efforts (decision making) to economize on time and production resources. Thus, managers utilize the distinguishing characteristic of their profession—the resource of power. If the "art of management" plays a decisive role, then

> . . . to overcome the continuous contradictions between the conservatism
> of the structure and the dynamics of the environment . . . [it] is not
> only . . . the natural right of the HLM [high level manager] to make
> authoritative decisions, but the real reserves and resources of subor-
> dinates which are the material conditions of effectiveness in the resources
> of power . . .[69]

While managers posses the knwoledge by which the economic system operates (such knowledge is 'automatically" acquired as managers function in the system, the activity of any MC is expressed through decision making and is realized only when ""positive results" (emphasis in original) are obtained. The multitutde of positive results garnered from the resource base available to a given MC is not only the *economic responsibility* within that (micro-) system, but the domain of its participation in carrying out the (macro-) system's functions, i.e., raising the level of *organizovannost'*. *The objective conditions buttressing such views are the material and technical base of thesystem and its administrative structure. In thsi contect:*

> The managers' material stimulus, their professional readiness and social
> awareness act as the internal conditions for the formulation of these
> views. These three conditions form together the managers' economic-
> self-interest in the MC. *Then their subjective perception of economic
> responsibility is the essence of economic interest, since only on the basis*

of this perception do they compare possible forms of action and make economic decisions. [emphasis added].

"Responsibility" and "economic interests" are key terms in Syroezhin's analytic language. In turn, these are closely related to important elements in the political economy of socialism—property and cohesion. Assuming that the material and technical base of a given economic system is the motor force of tis development, then not only do organizational factors play a secondary role, but property relations assume paramount importance in any social formation. While property relations can be expressed in terms of ownership, distribution, and utilization—in a socialist economy (as opposed to all presocialist systems—the influence of property relations on the econmic structure is "multi-facted." Similarly, the manifestations as well as the influence of economic interests are "multi-facted." The socialist economy, then, is aunity of *various* economic systems differing in both scale and cohesion. There isa definite difference in socioeconomic interests not only between public and cooperative secotrs (under socialism), but within the latter as well. These conflicting interests are not delimited according to the socioeconomic conditions of ownership. Under socialism:

> [in]n the conditions of a general form of appropriation, the function of distribution by an object of property from a purely legal standpoint becomes an independent economic phenomenon and gives birth to an independent class of interests—to economic interests. *Differing from socio-economic interests, they are not unified and cannot be unified as long as they are defined, first fo all, by the difference and interdependence of material-technological conditions in the economy in various elements of a given economic system* . . .[emphasis added].

Given the foregoing analysis, it follows that games simulate organizational economic interactions within and/or between various management centers or—on the macrolevel—the economic system in its entiretyl. In this manner, business games represent a unique way of reproducing existent economic processes and structures; they not only model the interaction among real economic interests, but they can differ among themselves as whole systems differ from various functions. There are certain elements in any gaming model: (1) *people*, i.e., the participants in the game who possess the interests being modeled; (2) those *laws*, corresponding tot the constructor's understanding of the object being modeled, which define economic interests; and (3) the *information mass*, which reflects the movement of resources in the examined economic system and, furthermore, which stimulates the phenomena of economic interests.

TRAINING WITH GAMING MODELS

Business games are constructed with various purposes in mind; these condition the "rules of the game" (*pravila igry*), its structure, the form for regulting decision making, and the algorithms for data processing. For instance, gaming models can be an important component in the training process for managerial personnel. Second, gaming techniques can be used in assessing the competency of previously trained cadres (certification games). The necessary condition for the success of such games is a certain level of skills and/or experience among the participants who play against the test group; however, the interactions are directed toward revealing the participant'sknowledge of a set of questions. Third, games can be constructed for investigatory aims. In this instance, the game's players and their interests are the background against which various experiemnts (e.g., the "laws" of interaction) are conducted. In this type of game it is possibel to test various management princples or recipes. This can only provide subsrantive results when the people who participate in the game are the same workers who will use the tested suppositions in practice.

The entire training process for high-level managers can be constrcted on simulated game models which reflect the important traits of economic activity of a given contingent of trainees. In fact, two specific game models, e.g., ASTRA (administrative structural analysis) and IMPULSE (simulated model of plannin nd mangment by localized means), have been used ro some time in the Soviet management community. While ASTRA is not used at the Voznesenskii Institute, Syroezhin considers it a (potential) basis for comparative projects involving Soviet and American approaches to decision making. It has already proven useful in structural analysis of the enterprise and has found application in the Center for Scientific Organization of Labor and Management of the Estonian Ministry of Light Industry. IMPULSE is a higly complex game, which involves managing the Soviet economy. More specifically, three branches and nine enterprises are involved in the simulation. Relevant factors include raw materials, industrial tools, and consumer goods. Group interactions have not been examined in this game, but such analyses are planned in the future. Another set of games, EPOS, has been created by Svetlana Gidrovich. EPOS models the administrative structive of a "business" with an overall coordinator and administrator of resources. The three versions of this game are based on the bidding process. The objective of the game, as explained to American specialists, is to illustrate the ways in which a coordinator might "sell" a plan to subordinates. For instance, when an enterprise attempts to introduce new products, this gaming model can be utilized as a method exploring and evaluating alternatives.

Syroezhin's team has firmly established its reputation in the Soviet management-science community and has good working relations with American counterparts. Nevertheless, the "Leningrad approach" is not without opposition. There are competive notions of business gaming in the USSR, which—their noticeably lower profile notwhstanding—have gained a modest following. Thus, V.I. Marshev, a senior research fellow and head of the theoretical section of MGU's management center, takes issue with the conflict orientation of Syroezhin's "collective decision games." Marshev suggests that modeling can have great utility as a teaching device when there is no ineraction and/or conflict among the participants in the game. Considering himself a proponent of Martin Shubik's approach, Marshev is less interested in formulating a theory of the socialist production organization than using games in the management education process. Like the Syroezhin team, Marshev closely follows American developments in business gaming. In fact, the MGU management center uses a Russian-language translation of the well-known text *Business Games Handbook* (1969), and receives the quarterly journal *Simulation and Games: An International Journal of Theory, Design, and Research.*

As with the diffusion of case methods, there are only a few major gaming centers in the USSR. In addition to the In addition to the Voznesenskii Institute (Leningrad) and the MGU Center, the Institute of Management Problems *(IPU)* and Novosibirsk University are most active. The publication list of *IPU*, given the modest Soviet literature on the topic, is quite impressive. Prominent researchers include M.M. Birshtein, V.N. Bukov, A.A. Galos, A.N. Nemtseva, V.D. Solokov, A.G. Ivanovskii, .a.V. Shchepkin, and several others. Moreover, N.V. Syskina heads a group of game theorists at the Novosibirsk University. Among her publications are *The Business Game SAYANY* (1976) and *The Business Game Enterprise-Ministry* (1974). There is, however, evidnece of growing interest in gaming techniques. For instance, in November 1975, the first all-union school on business games was held in a suburb of Moscow. Over 65 specialists participated and numerous papers were delivered. Given the fact that *tsemi was one of the chief sponsors of the school, increasing attention to this time theme can be expected.*

Conclusion

Four areas in Soviet mangemtn studies—decision making, organizational design, case methods, and business gaming—appear to have been substantially influenced by American research and theorizing. Although in some cases it si difficult to identify the manifestations of this "Americanization" or trace the influence flows between mangment specialists in each country, our assessment, based on published Soviet materials and interviews with various experts (both Soviet and American), lends credence to the emulative posutre of the Soviet discipline *in these particular areas.* This does not suggest that other relevant lessons (particularly in data processing) from the American experience have been inconsequential. On the contrary, many have probably made a significant impression on Soviet theorists, regardless of the observational problems in uncovering such influence. It is not inconceibalbe that Soviet research may exert a corresponding fascination and possible emulation in the American management-science community. This has already occurred to some extent in mathematical economics; in "business management," however, such "reverse emulation" awaits future developments in the USSR.

It is also clear that the Soviet emulation will not include the concept of large-scale complex systems as organized anarchies. This recent American development simply will not fit in the Soviet perspective. Thus, in the next chapter we summarize the current Soviet approaches, noting that, like U.S. theory, Soviet mangement theory is a jungle. However, what concepts *are not* in the Soviet jungle (but *are* in the American one) make the comparative perspective particularly worthwhile.

8

The Current "Jungle" in Soviet Management Theory[1]

> *[T]he scientific and technological revolution is a fundamental qualitative transformation of productive forces and, accordingly, [it] means that a revolutionary change in the material and technical basis of social production has taken place. . . .* Management is becoming one of the basic types of activity, one that is closely connected with all other spheres of social life *[emphasis added]*.
>
> —D. M. Gvishiani

> *If one view considers the theory of socialists management as primarily a juridical science, then others regard [it] as . . . a special branch of cybernetics . . . optimal planning . . . Marxist–Leninist political economy . . . [or] a synthesis of many social and natural sciences. All of this [confusion] raises the question*—whether there can be in principle several theories . . . of socialist production management that *[deal with]* Communist construction? *[emphasis added]*.
>
> —V. C. Usenko

Introduction

The USSR has entered a new, qualitatively higher stage in constructing a Communist society: "mature" or "developed" socialism.[2] Although it remains unclear whether this stage has already been reached or is still in formation, most Soviet commentators regard the scientific–technological revolution (STR) as one of its defining traits. Reflecting objective changes that have occurred in development of society's production forces, the STR poses an unprecedented challenge to the political leadership: "to integrate complexity and manage change through advances in organization and technology."[3] Because the "knowledge explosion" has greatly expanded the value

130

of managerial skills in the STR, politicians cannot meet this challenge successfully without the active support and participation of administrative specialists. Occasional setbacks and even agonizing reappraisals have not dissuaded politicians from sharing a common reference point with their academic and administrative brethren, namely, that socialism provides the optimal framework for organizing societal development. But those same specialists begrudgingly recognize that the reputed advantages of the socialist economy—national planning, public property, class solidarity—do not manifest themselves automatically; rather, they must be brought to life through the creative application of scientific knowledge and the organizational skills of human beings.[4]

"Mature socialism" also requires "intensive development"—the effective utilization of scarce labor and capital reserves. The days have long since passed when shock labor, storming, trail-and-error planning methods, socialist emulation, and simple increments of manpower were sufficient to raise output. And the preoccupation with gross output targets—a defining trait of the Stalinist economy—has given way to other, sometimes competing, success indicators: raising labor productivity *(proizvoditel'nost' truda)*, the effectiveness of production *(effektivnost' proizvodstva)*, and the quality *(kachestvo)* of goods and services. These remain elusive goals for Soviet planners and administrators, however, particularly because substantial cognitive, psychological, and behavioral adjustments are required.[5] But the present leadership confidently maintains, at least publically, that development will continue, and even speed up, in the STR due to the qualitative transformation of science into a direct production force.[6] Consequently, economic cadres are urged to sharpen their skills; planners to learn and apply new procedures; data analysts to adopt the latest Western computing techniques; and theorists to articulate a distinctive theory of management under socialism.

The nature of "developed socialism" and the impact of the STR on all facets of socioeconomic life have been widely examined by both Soviet and Western analysts.[7] Although an official Soviet view has yet to emerge, there is little doubt that administrative specialists in the USSR are elaborating—really for the first time—a concept of the directed society.[8] Politically, this view props up the cautious, conservative ethos in Kremlin leadership circles. It also discourages any changes, save those designed to "rationalize" the system, that could undermine the party's preeminence in the Soviet hierarchy. Economically, developed socialism points to management *(upravlenie)* not only as an instrument to improve organizational performance, but as a general philosophy of social life.[9] Thus, it is commonly regarded "as the binding, cementing link [which] . . . ensures the effective functioning of production, science, technology, and education."[10]

The burgeoning Soviet literature on the science of management, or *uprav-*

lenie, has been carefully charted by Western observers.[11] And their studies reveal that *upravlenie* has no direct English-language equivalent. Depending on context or nuance, it can refer to *steering* of an automobile, airplane, or guided missile; *management* of production or military operations; *regulation or control* of social, biological, or technical systems; *governance* of state or society; *administration* of things, complex organizations, business firms, or the national economy; or even *management* of one's own feelings.[12] Thus, it comes as no surprise to find theorists talking past one another. They routinely examine dissimilar phenomena and do so from the perspective of competing research traditions—cybernetics, administrative law, political economy, systems engineering, and the like. Some have tried to order this confusion. For instance, I. Tikhomirov identifies three basic types *(vidy)* of *upravlenie:* the administration of society, of the socialist state, and of socialist social production.[13] His scheme has enjoyed widespread circulation in the community of specialists, but it has done little to order the disarray in Soviet administrative studies.

Since *upravlenie* constitutes such a diffuse, impenetrable thicket in the Soviet literature, analysts are well advised to restrict their inquiry to manageable dimensions. Hence, this study examines *upravlenie* in primarily one applied sphere, that of industrial production, and it draws from recent Soviet works on theoretical as well as practical issues.[14] To be sure, there is great confusion and diversity even in this relatively narrow domain: theorists do not use key concepts in similar ways, they do not pose similar questions, and they seldom arrive at similar conclusions.[15] Such disarray represents an important, albeit largely neglected, scholarly tasks, that of classifying the major contrasting approaches to industrial management in the USSR. By ordering the present chaos, we expect not only to gain valuable insights into the complex realm of an emerging social science, but also to tentatively assess the impact of socialist doctrine and/or Western concepts on the field. If we can isolate parochial views, actors, and communications channels, then we have taken a modest first step in describing a recurrent pattern of group interactions.

To shed light on these issues, several specific objectives are pursued in this chapter. First, the tension inherent in borrowing Western "techniques" and, simultaneously, in elaborating a distinctive socialist theory is briefly traced from the advent of Soviet power through the Brezhnev era. Such a perspective illustrates the doctrinal and political constraints on inquiry and establishes criteria whereby separate approaches to the field can be identified. Second, the major competing schools of thought in the Soviet Union are examined, including their basic organizing concepts and leading institutes, journals, spokesmen, etc. Special attention is given to the clash of political interests between and among these schools. Finally, the prospects for untangling the jungle in Soviet management science are assessed, and certain conclusions are drawn regarding the likely paths of future evolution in the field.

"Techniques" vs "System": A Historical Sketch

Leonid Brezhnev's call for an *organic fusion* of the achievements of the worldwide scientific and technological revolution and the distinctive traits of socialism has struck a responsive chord among Soviet administrative specialists as well as among Marxist–Leninist philosophers and political economists.[16] Virtually every interest in Soviet society has been able to find what it seeks in the general secretary's vague phraseology. Thus, orthodox forces stress the incompatibility of socialism and capitalism, especially regarding fundamental socioeconomic principles and institutions. But what they ignore—namely, the organizational forms, industrial technology, and administrative techniques that exist irrespective of social system—are precisely the phenomena most relevant to management specialists. To be sure, this fascination with capitalist "techniques" has strong roots in Soviet history and even sanction in Marxist–Leninist doctrine. Good socialists never doubted the ability of the capitalist system to organize and manage large-scale production. And by their own admission, it was in the realm of industrial "techniques" that Soviet administrators and scientists had much to learn from their bourgeois predecessors. Those "techniques" would fit into an organizational framework not radically different from that which existed under capitalism, despite the greater centralization and more comprehensive planning implied by proletarian rule.[17] But even Engels's prediction that the "governance of men" would become the "administration of things" did not mean that management would disappear as a separate command function. Consequently, Lenin was acting in consistent Marxist fashion when he insisted that specialists adopt "all that is progressive" in Taylorism but, at the same time, reject the universal nature and/or capitalist application of Taylorism.[18]

Neither Lenin nor his followers have adequately shown where administrative "techniques" leave off and the capitalist "system" begins. Thus, it has been inherently difficult to neatly detach acceptable from unacceptable Western ideas and/or to separate allegedly positive bourgeois attitudes (e.g., the work ethic) from negative ones (e.g., acquisitiveness). Marxist–Leninist doctrine has provided managers, not to mention organization theorists, with little policy guidance. As a result, the precise manner in which *socialist* administrative science should take shape—particularly in light of the massive and largely haphazard diffusion of Western management concepts into the USSR—has always remained unclear. Such ambiguity has allowed CPSU officials, economic cadres, ideologues, and bourgeois specialists to adopt dissimilar stances on pressing theoretical and practical questions. Justifiable doctrinal grounds have always been found to prop up those different positions. Nevertheless, one can observe certain political constraints on the content as well as conduct of Soviet administrative theorizing. Specialists have not been permitted to blindly follow Western experience, much less focus *exclusively* on the practice of management under socialism. They have not been allowed to isolate themselves, and their studies, from the politics of class struggle, dictatorship of the proletariat, and the USSR's relationship to the outside world. Theoretical works have been expected to account for the distinctive features of the socialist system and, consequently, could not focus on industrial technology and/or administrative "techniques," at the expense of broader socioeconomic phenomena. Administrative theorists have had to identify criteria whereby socialist management could be differentiated from that existing under capitalism. And only people, not things, could meet such a requirement for conceptual analysis.

VARIABILITY OF SOVIET RESPONSE

Even within these parameters, however, the Soviet response to Western concepts and methods has varied, and has sometimes resulted in disastrous consequences for specialists, their institutional standard bearers, as well as their political patrons. In the 1920s, for example, Bolshevik theorists did not shirk from canvasing the West for relevant ideas on how to order the growing administrative malaise they themselves had helped to create. Attempts to gather and disseminate information about Western "techniques" were not only officially sanctioned, but vigorously promoted and enthusiastically received by the community of specialists. The Bureau of Foreign S ience and Technology *(BINT)* was formed in March 1921, and began to publish a reference collection shortly thereafter.[19] Soviet administrative specialists from prestigious institutes in Moscow, Kazan, Kharkov, and elsewhere routinely visited their counterparts abroad. The Central Institute of Labor was particularly active in exchanging information and experience with Western management centers. (Unfortunately, most of this correspondence and related records were later destroyed by Stalin's order.) Soviet research and theorizing in the 1920s thus fell under the heavy influence of Western schools of public administration, industrial management, and their leading spokesmen—Taylor, Fayol, and Henry Ford.[20] This emulative posture was strong medicine indeed for doctrinal purists, but evoked little soul searching among professional specialists dedicated to building a more efficient state machine in the USSR.

Along with the flourishing of scientific studies came "erroneous views on the substance, methods, and possibilities of NOT [the scientific organization of labor] under conditions of the dictatorship of the proletariat."[21] Self-serving statements about *NOT*'s focus on the worker, his health, working conditions, and fatigue (*utomlenie*) could not hide the basic similarities of approach and subject matter between *NOT* and Taylorism.[22] And spirited defenders of Taylorism in the USSR found no social obstacles to spreading this "system" throughout the country. To be sure, they considered it the legitimate property of socialism, and stressed this point at the first conference on *NOT* in 1921. Vigilant Bolsheviks, however, rejected such assertions. Instead, they found the indiscriminate use of bourgeois concepts and were able to identify those specialists who interpreted *NOT* as a *universal* system of labor organization.[23] These conclusions were sufficiently compromising on strict doctrinal grounds to give political leaders cause for alarm, but they could be tolerated, if only grudgingly, as long as the New Economic Policy remained the official line. If NEP should "wither away," however (it was always seen as a temporary measure), then certain views and their political expression could drastically part company with socialist orthodoxy.

By 1928, a consensus had emerged that NEP should be terminated, agriculture collectivized, class enemies routed, and maximum effort placed on rapid industiral growth. Not only did the first five-year plan concentrate on gross output targets, but it did so by ignoring, and actually overturning, many of the goals and methods of economic rationalization.[24] Nothing would be permitted to stand in the way of Stalin's all-out drive to catch up and surpass the advanced capitalist states, least of all research centers "mechanically" copying bourgeois "techniques." Consequently, management institutes were shut down, their staffs dispersed, publications suspended, and leading scientists put under the pall of suspicion. Most of the 558 Soviet journals dealing with administrative questions met their demise in the early 1930s.[25] Others passed from the control of rationalizers into establishments committed to rapid industrialization.[26] And management theorists, especially those with bourgeois credentials, would find themselves linked to the "right deviation" in politics and, hence, subject to severe repression and even liquidation.[27]

BOLSHEVIK ÉLAN AS A SUBSTITUTE FOR THEORY

Bolshevik élan almost completely displaced scientific management and technical rationality as leadership values in the 1930s. For Stalin and his entourage, there could be no technical expertise apart from the "correct" political line. Thus, administrative science suffered near total demise, except for a badly truncated branch of technical and engineering knowledge. By pursuing short-range policy benefits, scholars gingerly avoided theoretical analysis and, instead, concentrated on microlevel questions like intrafirm planning, control, accounting, and bookkeeping.[28] Their neglect of theory was, in Soviet lexicon, "not accidental." In a practice now recognized as disastrous for the field, Stalin had consciously divorced theory from practice and pronounced the latter the sole criterion of theoretical truth. From this doctrinal standpoint, "[to] foist upon political economy problems of economic policy is to kill it as a science.[29] What survived of theoretical inquiry remained safely tucked away in administrative law (for analysis of the state apparatus) and did no more than provide ex-post-facto justification for policy choices made on other grounds.[30] Henceforth, until the mid-1950s, administrative specialists would engage in agitprop and were completely replaced by economic practitioners (mainly engineers) who made decisions on a "five-fingers-plus-abacus" basis.[31] And the relevance of Western "techniques"—a central issue in the previous decade—was carefully avoided by specialists concerned with their own personal safety and, hence, content to restate "eternal truths." They could no longer apply the rhetorical device of separating "techniques" from the capitalist "system." The whole package, so to speak, was out of step with political and psychological needs of the Stalinist system. Only the rich, albeit poorly mastered, experience of constructing socialism in the USSR could provide the theoretical basis of Soviet management science.

Stalinism had obviously been a nightmare for analytical economics and administrative science. But by Stalin's death on 5 March 1953, the massive Soviet economic machine was foundering badly: growth was down, shortages increasing, supply irregular, and many were losing faith that the economy could be controlled from a single administrative center. While policy-makers were clearly in need of a theoretical framework as well as analytical principles, specialists somberly concluded that they had no conceptual language to adequately describe the economic malady, much less prescribe a cure.

From an objective standpoint, this situation called for nothing less than a revolution in those sciences dealing with every facet of organization, management, and planning in the national economy. But economists themselves were in no position to launch such a revolution. Indeed, no individual or group dared to press the political leadership to adopt new policies or even to "agitate" for innovative research and theorizing without clear signals that the changes were, in fact, desired by at least some faction in high political circles. Those purposive signals were forthcoming at the July 1955 plenum, when leading political and scientific officials began to seriously criticize the moribund state of the art in Soviet economic science.[32] Such prodding from the top hit its mark. Finally scholars were urged to concentrate on studies that could improve the practice of management and economic planning under socialism. And the leadership's message to upgrade analytical disciplines was vigorously reasserted by Khrushchev, Mikoyan, and others at the historic Twentieth Party Congress in 1956.

Post-Stalinist Developments

The props supporting Stalinist political economy began to crumble, and competent specialists needed little additional encouragement to challenge their orthodox foes openly and in the professional literature. Initially clustering around V.S. Nemchinov, L.V. Kantorovich, and V.V. Novozhilov, an identifiable grouping of specialists emerged and started to promote linear programming, input–output analysis, and application of mathematical techniques to policy-relevant studies. By stressing the Russian roots of these ideas and the promise of improved managerial performance, economic-mathematical methods found an enthusiastic response in certain segments of the scientific community.[33] Some even pointed to the successful application of similar techniques in the United States to buttress their case.[34]

Other trends emerged in administrative science and quickly took root. Thus, after several articles openly attacked cybernetics (the science of communication and control), leading scientists in 1954–1958 gradually shifted over to a defense of the field.[35] The major organizing concepts of cybernetics—information, control, feedback, regulation—reinforced planners' sagging faith in their own ability to conceptualize real economic problems and, hence, to deal in optimal fashion with the immensely complex Soviet economy. After a lengthy haitus, the *NOT* movement resurfaced in 1957 when, according to M.G. Babin, "the State Committee on Labor and Wages made a decision about utilizing the experience and methods of the Central Institute of Labor."[36] While *NOT*ists would continue to argue about the scope and content of micromanagement, their retrospective analysis of the 1920s contained many important lessons, especially regarding the utility of borrowing select Western "techniques" that could be adapted to socialist goals.[37] Such a message was officially promoted by D.M. Gvishiani's appeal to adopt "all that is progressive" in American management science.[38] His seminal *Sotsiologiia Biznesa* (1962) stressed that large-scale production organizations have certain *objective* features, which exist irrespective of social system. Those uniformities indicate that administrative concepts and methods relevant for one system can, in turn, be usefully applied to another.

These changes represent, in toto, a fundamental shift in the strategic balance away from Stalinist orthodoxy and toward various "moden" approaches to management science. They have taken place in spite of bureaucratic lethargy and even fierce resistance from conservative forces in the Soviet establishment.[39] Although the latter have tried on numerous occasions, with some success, to reverse that balance, their efforts have proven to be no more than tactically significant. The revolution has continued and actually speeded up under Brezhnev–Kosygin, as the USSR has rapidly moved into the mainstream of international developments.[40] Not only have political leaders defended leading theorists, especially mathematical economists,[41] but they have made firm institutional commitments to advance innovative research and theorizing. Thus, several management centers have been staffed with "Americanizers," Soviet change agents who deal predominantly with U.S. business concepts and methods. Their strategy seems clear:

to scan the American literature, study relevant organizational experience, and filter out leading examples and useful administrative ideas.[42]

CONTINUITY OF ORTHODOX CONSTRAINTS ON WESTERNIZATION

But there have always been doctrinal and political constraints on outright Westernization in Soviet management science. Hence, the internal debate in the USSR continues to reveal certain special, if not unique, elements, which have not withered away in the post-Stalinist era. Soviet analysts now believe that it is both possible and necessary to elaborate a distinctive science and theory of management under socialism.[43] Despite the good standing in the field of cybernetics, EMM, and systems analysis, orhoox specialists insist that such approaches are incapable of meeting the conceptual needs of socialist theory, that they simply fail to provide a sound basis (much less an analytical language) for differentiating between social systems. From this doctrinal perspective, political economists can always deal their foes a stern rebuff: "the specifics of socialist production disappear in their analysis."[44]

To render the borrowing of capitalist "techniques" more palatable to ideologues, Soviet specialists often resort to dichotomies that detach (1) socialist from general theory and (2) socioeconomic from organizational-technical aspects of management.[45] General theory includes any framework that ignores the specific features of a given social system, but nonetheless still provides insights as well as useful ideas with which to improve socialist management. Cybernetics would be an example of such a theory. Socialist theory, on the other hand, must deal with the defining traits of socialism—national planning, public property, class solidarity—and then demonstrate their *objective* connection to the managerial structure in the USSR. Although such a theory remains an aspiration, rather than a concrete achievement, political economy lays the strongest claim to being its methodological base. Socioeconomic aspects constitute the defining characteristics, or essence, of the society in question and cannot be transferred between systems. However, organizational-technical aspects of management (e.g., industrial technology) represent uniformities that exist irrespective of social system and, hence, can be consciously exchanged with a minimum of hazard.

Such dichotomies permit Americanizers and others to defend their studies, which, although not designed to meet the needs of socialist theory, can provide "techniques" to improve the practice of management under social-ism. And they also delineate criteria whereby the observer can identify as well as differentiate between and among various schools of thought in Soviet administrative science.[46] These relationships are illustrated in Figure 1. The horizontal axis separates general from socialist views; the vertical axis does so for organizational-technical and socioeconomic aspects of management. An identifiable school can be found within each quadrant. For example,

Organizational–Technical Aspects

	Planning	Cybernetics	
Socialist			General
Theory	———————————		Theory
	Political	Empiricism	
	Economy		

Socioeconomic Aspects

Fig. 1. Relationships between General and Socialist Theory

cybernetics and the empirical approach are both general analytical frameworks. Each can make important contributions to socialist and capitalist management science, but they differ in that cybernetics deals with "things" (e.g., technical control processes), whereas management empiricists concentrate on leadership in human collectives. The quadrants on the left side of Figure 1 focus on socialist management. Political economy has traditionally examined socioeconomic principles and has tried to demonstrate an objective linkage between economic laws *(zakonomernosti)* and the purposive nature of economic developments in the Soviet Union. Planning *(planirovanie)* on the scale of the entire national economy not only represents a distinctive feature of the socialist economy, but its major reputed advantage over market systems. In comparison with political economy, however, planning contends with narrower, more technical issues.

Despite the prominence of these schools, it would be highly misleading to speak of a dominant theme, much less an officially sanctioned theory or general line, in the Soviet Union. In stark contrast to the Stalinist era, the Brezhnev regime has strongly promoted an unusual measure of conceptual innovation and international contacts in administrative science. Thus, management specialists have been generally free to pursue divergent lines of inquiry. And they have not been reticent to attack and/or downgrade what others in the field have said, thought, or done. If they so choose, specialists can safely ignore the entire domain of socialist theory, and instead concentrate on improving managerial practice. The current jungle in studies of organization and management reflects more than leadership preferences. Although there is basic agreement that management should play a key role in the 1980s, there is no consensus, and even outright conflict, on the most fruitful lines of advance.

Contemporary Soviet Schools of Management Science[47]

Our task is now to untangle the jungle in Soviet studies of organization and management by examining each major approach to management science.

Although any attempt to classify such a complex and confusing topic is bound to overlook certain views, misclassify others, and ignore subtle nuances within each, our conceptualization of four basic schools has been restated, albeit using different categories, by Soviet theorists themselves.[48] Table 1, summarizing our findings, lists important concepts, institutes, scholarly journals, and theorists representing each view. Efforts to sharpen these distinctions are, unfortunately, seriously hampered by the virtual absence of studies that review the state of the art and/or classify divergent perspectives.[49] The discontent and exasperation resulting from ambiguous terminology, bitter jurisdictional disputes, and viciously argumentative theses, has nonetheless led to few efforts to order the turmoil.[50] Instead, we find rival groupings scrambling to find support in political circles, which might enhance their own clout in the field.

THE POLITICAL-ECONOMY INTERPRETATION OF MANAGEMENT

Political economy is an official part of ruling orthodoxy in the USSR, and it provides the basic texts and common reference points taught to all Soviet administrative theorists. By formulating "correct" analytical tools, political economy uncovers "the laws which govern production, distribution, exchange, and the consumption of material wealth in socialist society."[51] It constitutes the methodological core of the economic sciences, including those fields that examine socialist management. The language of political economy—*nauchnost'*, democratic centralism, *planomernost'*—creates an imagery and expectation of optimal organizational performance and makes no conceptual allowance for various administrative dysfunctions. And its normative bent has made an enduring impression on the field. Subsequent views like cybernetics, operations research, and systems analysis can be seen as instruments designed to achieve the aspirations of political economy. Thus, I.M. Syroezhin, a powerful voice in Soviet management science, regards his own work as largely a concretization of political-economic categories.[52]

While *partiinost'* has been a defining trait of political economy, its relation to applied fields and/or the practice of management has been a dependent, rather than an independent, variable. Its role under Stalin—to justify the dictator's policy choices theoretically—has evoked harsh retrospective criticism: "political economy could not serve as the methodological basis of management science . . . and the leadership of the national economy was deprived of a scientific foundation."[53] Since the reemergence of scientific analysis in the mid-1950s, political economists have tried to carve out a policy-relevant niche for their field, while reconfirming its leading role in theoretical studies. And they have undertaken the strictly ideological task of giving management an acceptable Marxist–Leninist interpretation. (To date, however, this has proven to be no mean task; and no definitive treat-

Table 1 Soviet "Schools" of Management Science

	Concepts	Institutes	Journals	Theorists	Locations
Political Economy	Planomernost' "Principles" Democratic Centralism Nauchnost' Optimization Objectivity Proportsional 'nost'	Leningrad State University Leningrad Engineering Economics Institute	Kommunist Organizatsiia Upravleniia	A. Godunov I. Signov A. Erëmin D. Kruk I. Lavrikov A. Rumiantsev N. Noiseenko V. Cherkovets	Centered in Leningrad
Empiricism	Case Methods Business games Rukovodstvo Consulting Management education Organizational design Rationalization Functions	Moscow State University Tallinn Polytechnical Institute Moscow Institute of the National Economy Moscow Institute of Management	Vestnik Moskovskogo Univ-ersiteta Organizatsiia Upravleniia Ekonomika i Organizatsiia Promyshlennogo Proizvodstva	O. Deineko G. Popov R. Iuksviarav M. Khabakuk S. Kamenitser B. Mil'ner V. Ozira G. Dzavadov	Centered in Moscow and Tallinn
Cybernetics	Automated systems System Feedback Regulation Control Information Environment Programming	Institute of Cybernetics Institute of Systems Research Institute of Management Problems	Kibernetika Avtomatika i Telemekhan-ika Mekhanizatsiia i Avtomatizatsiia Upravleniia	A. Berg V. Shorin V. Glushkov V. Trapeznikov I. Syroezhin V. Marshev S. Dumler I. Novik	Widely Dispersed
Planning	Input-output Linear programing Modeling Planirovanie Optimal Planning Mathematical economics	TsEMI Institute of Economics and Organization of Industrial Production	Ekonomika i Matematiches-kie Metody Planovoe Khoziaistvo	N. Drogichinskii N. Fedorenko V. Dadaian J. Kantorovich R. Raiatskas A. Modin A. Aganbegian V. Kossov	Moscow and Novosibirsk

ment has yet appeared.) This has assumed two specific directions, although consensual positions on each have yet to be achieved. First, orthodox theorists have tried to show that managerial relations *(upravlencheskie otnosheniia)* under socialism are distinctly different from those existing in capitalist systems. Thus, conservative theorists have been preoccupied with uncovering the objectivity *(ob"ektivnost')* of management and its organic connection to the economic laws of socialism. From this standpoint, David Kruk regards *upravlenie* as a basic social relationship between owner and means of production: "the goals of production management, its content, form and methods depend on the form of property."[54] Some see *upravlenie* as a complex intermingling of base and superstructural elements;[55] and still others regard it as "secondary production relations" under socialism.[56] Second, political economists have tried to dominate, if not to monopolize, the major theoretical departures in administrative science. Most continue to argue dogmatically that their field defines the theoretical core, basic principles, and analytical categories of management science. But Albert Erëmin and other moderates separate political economy from the science of management. [57] To be sure, the latter "puts in concrete" the theoretical concepts of a more general and abstract field. Finally, certain theorists (e.g., I. Signov, A. Godunov) in the political-economy school regard *upravlenie* as a distinctive phenomena, complete with its own economic laws. Thus, it represents an autonomous science, even though political economy remains it methodological base.

Orthodox political forces can be identified standing behind the political-economy interpretation of management. They can be found in certain academic-research institutes as well as in the conservative wing of the party apparatus. The geographical center of this school remains Leningrad, where leading theorists publish vigorously and play important roles in organizing conferences, seminars, and other relevant forums. And some, including I. Lavrikov, have successfully frustrated efforts by empiricists to publish a separate management-science journal.[58] Prepared to accept disciplines that can improve managerial practice, political economists nonetheless insist that only their field can elaborate the theoretical basis of the regime's economic policy. From this vantage point, they envision scientific management *(nauchnoe upravlenie)* under socialism, but not an autonomous, interdisciplinary, social science of management *(nauka upravleniia)*, because "what would [then] be the role of political economy . . . in mastering the economic laws of socialism?"[59] Of course, political economists can be counted on to back up conservative politicians who oppose even moderate reforms in the central planning institutions. For example, N.A. Moiseenko considers socialism and centralism indivisible, the very soul of the Soviet economy.[60] Similar views have been insistently maintained since the ill-fated Sik economic reforms in Czechoslovakia (1968). Political economists are also becoming increasingly apprehensive over the "mechanical" imitation of bourgeois techniques by

certain less vigilant specialists. They see a dangerous trend toward the pro-
fessionalization of management in the USSR. And together with their allies
in high political circles, orthodox theorists uncover the "groundless thesis
about the separation of management activities into some kind of . . . priv-
ileged sphere of a certain social stratum [which] is erroneous . . . and in
contradiction with the entire way of life in our society."[61]

THE EMPIRICAL SCHOOL

Unlike political economy, the "empirical" school[62] is a general, rather
than socialist, approach to *upravlenie*; i.e., it can improve managerial practice in both socialist and capitalist systems. Instead of examining the "objective" features of management, however, Soviet empiricists concentrate
on various subjective elements of creative human leadership at various levels
in the national economy. They also seek to generalize and make systematic
the inductive principles drawn from analysis of real administrative experience. This view is based on the premise that, if the experiences of successful
managers and consultants—or their mistakes—are thoroughly examined,
the analyst will learn to apply the most effective techniques in a given
situation. This approach is closely related to that popularized by Ernest
Dale in *The Great Organizers*.[63] However, during the 1960s, Soviet theorists
somberly noted the lack of studies reviewing the industrial experience of
outstanding managers like I.A. Likachëv and A.I. Efremov.[64] Of course, the
aim of this approach is to train managers so that they can make better
decisions and apply useful principles. Most empiricists attempt to transfer,
in vicarious fashion, the experience and know-how of real managers to the
practitioner and/or student. To be sure, they are less concerned with describing how large organizations actually function than with prescribing how
to improve their effectiveness by raising the qualifications of high-level man-
gers.[65] Consequently, great attention is paid to the training and retraining
of administrative personnel, which has been accomplished, in part, by borrowing and adapting techniques (e.g., case methods, business games, sensitivity training) from the repertoire of U.S. business administration.

This school is centered in Moscow and has an important branch in Tallinn.
While there is broad agreement among empiricists that the leadership role
constitutes its major analytical focus, certain specialists concentrate their
efforts elsewhere. For instance, B.Z. Mil'ner and his colleagues at the Institute of USA and Canada are organization-design theorists. They have
championed notions like project management and program-goal planning in
the USSR by reviewing American corporate experience.[66] Madis Khabakuk,
R. Iuksviarav, and others at the Tallinn Polytechnic Institute have ex-
perimented modestly with descriptive theory and have examined decision
making in the organizational context.[67] Moreover, various centers (e.g., the

Ordzhonikidze Management Institute) focus primarily on narrow, enterprise-level phenomena and/or problems occurring *within* separate industrial sectors—machine building, steel, chemicals, petroleum, etc. By contrast, some deal with interbranch (*mezhotraslevye*) problems and/or issues bearing on the national economy as a whole. And still others (e.g., Plekhanov Institute of the National Economy) train "students" (actually successful managers who have qualified for retraining) in various skills prior to reassignment to a variety of industrial or nonindustrial areas.

These differences have not stopped empiricists from demarcating the boundaries of an *autonomous* management science, which borrows and then synthesizes the contributions of numerous sciences, including biology, economics, cybernetics, sociology, administrative law, and mathematics.[68] To be sure, the issue of disciplinary independence has been a crucial one. Empiricists have consistently argued (1) that *upravlenie* cannot be simplistically reduced to data processing, and (2) against the application of computers to administrative problems. And they have made great efforts to detach *upravlenie* from *planirovanie*, the reputed heart (*serdtsevina*) of the Soviet economy.[69] Concluding that *upravlenie* is the broader, more inclusive, concept, empiricists contend that it involves different goals as well as problems, and thus, as a separate field, has distinctive theoretical needs. From this perspective, research and theoretical analysis in each field can proceed with minimal conceptual overlap and institutional conflict.

Although empiricists have had their jurisdictional disputes with cybernetics and the planning school, they reserve special scorn for political economists, whom they regard as incapable of improving the practice of management. Led by G.Kh. Popov, they have even assaulted political economy's theoretical primacy in the field. By relating his version of *socialist* theory to *rukovodstvo*[70] and the art (*isskustvo*) of management, Popov has arrived at a devastating conclusion for orthodox theorists: " . . . theoretical generalization is the result of practical experience. The work on rationalizing management [along with] its planning and execution, will serve as a basis for further development of a theory of management."[71] This establishes the unity of theory and practice of management under socialism, but certainly not on the basis of conventional wisdom. And empiricists have exerted considerable political muscle in the field, particularly regarding resource allocation questions—the funding of new research institutes, joint ventures, international contacts with Western specialists, and the like. They actively seek economic contracts (*khoziaistvennye dogovory*) and want to play a leading role in rationalizing the gigantic Soviet economy.[72]

For their part, political economists have not stood idly by while others attack them. They regard empiricists as technicians who deal solely with the trifles of management and flirt dangerously with bourgeois concepts. But despite its strong institutional fortress in Leningrad, political economy's influence in the field has waned noticeably since the late 1950s, and its theoretical concepts remain in splendid isolation from modern thinking. Notwithstanding fierce and persistent rearguard actions, orthodox theorists have neither stopped nor even slowed down the forced march of Soviet management science into the mainstream of international developments.

THE PLANNING SCHOOL *(PLANIROVANIE)*

The planning school equates *planirovanie* with *upravlenie*, or, at a minimum regards the former as the major element in socialist management. Although certain bourgeois techniques can upgrade planning practices in the USSR, Soviet theorists insist that only socialism permits their full, creative application on a country-wide scale. Thus, *planirovanie* is considered a defining trait of socialism and a prerequisite for purposive, systematic economic development. According to N. Drogichinskii, *"planirovanie* fulfills every function in the production-administrative complex . . . [and] coordinates all technical, organizational, and material aspects of production."[73] It is the basis not only of a broad system of knowledge, but also of practical activities that regulate virtually every element of social life.[74] It finds its highest conceptual expression in the application of mathematical methods and data processing to economic planning. Building on ideas pioneered by L.V. Kantorovich and other mathematical economists (e.g., linear programming, input–output analysis, systems engineering) as well as on the concrete historical experience of the Soviet Union, specialists at the Central Mathematical Economics Institute *(TsEMI)* have advanced a "theory of the optimally functioning socialist economy."[75] Such a view and the panoply of mathematical techniques buttressing it have rapidly moved into the forefront of economic-managerial thinking in the USSR. This can be attributed to several interrelated factors, including the traditional Russian genius in mathematics, the political acumen of economists like V.S. Nemchinov, and the growing availability of high-speed computers.[76] Moreover, *planirovanie* finds its greatest practical and political expression in Gosplan, an institution representing over 60 years of Soviet planning experience. Defining *planirovanie* broadly, and organizationally committed to enhancing its own power and prerogatives in the economic system, Gosplan has largely renounced the trial-and-error methods that typified its earlier operations.

The application of mathematical techniques promises to improve the hierarchical planning apparatus in the Soviet Union without risking the adverse political consequences of economic decentralization. But while champions of this school envision optimal planning, there are substantial differences among those who approach optimality from the perspective of linear programing, general equilibrium theory, technical systems, or the problems of an administrative economy.[77] Sharp disagreements have also surfaced between mathematical economists in *TsEMI* and practitioners in Gosplan, especially regarding what the latter consider *TsEMI*'s periodic lapses into abstract theorizing far removed from real economic problems. Political leaders have echoed similar comments, which, on occasion, have resulted in significant changes on the editorial board of *Economics and Mathematical Methods*.[78] Consequently, theorists who can shed light on pressing economic problems, like Abel Aganbegian, have gained considerable prestige and clout in the field.[79] Recently, a certain disenchantment with the notion of optimality has surfaced within the planning school. Led by V.S. Dadaian and R.L. Raiatskas, theorists are now attempting to cope with uncertainties in human behavior as well as with rigidities in the bureaucratic environment.[80] And in response, various novel institutional arrangements have emerged, portending greater cooperation between research and line agencies.[81]

The planning school is entangled in severe jurisdictional battles as well as in seemingly endless semantic disputes with rival views. Indeed, it is extremely difficult to ascertain precisely where *planirovanie* leaves off and *upravlenie* begins.[82] However, both political economists and empiricists define planirovanie narrowly; it is either an applied discipline taught to future planners (for political economists), or the most important function in the broader managerial system (for empiricists).[83] And while there is great overlap between *planirovanie* and cybernetics, particularly in terms of mathematical modeling and data processing, substantial differences nonetheless remain. As Ellman points out, these two schools differ in organization, in personnel, and in mental set.[84] Those dealing with cybernetics are often computer specialists and operations researchers. Their major task, the development of automated systems, is a state matter. By contrast, optimal planning is a field of academic research; most specialists are mathematical economists; and *TsEMI* is the leading institute.

Optimal planners skilled in quantitative methods have not only modernized *planirovanie*, but they have functioned as a powerful reform movement in Soviet economic science. To be sure, the challenge mounted by leading mathematical economists to orthodox views in 1960–1968 has represented

> . . . an attempt to replace one doctrine, political economy, which provides the ideological legitimization for rule by the bosses, by another doctrine, optimal planning, which legitimizes the rule of the white-collar intellegentsia (which both calculates the optimal plans and manages the optimally functioning socialist economy), as the theoretical basis of the economic policy of the Soviet state.[85]

However, their success had ostensible limits. Although bureaucratic lethargy and orthodox protests could not stop the legitimization of mathematical techniques per se, conservative theorists and their political patrons have successfully thwarted attempts to displace political economy as the methodological core of the regime's economic policy. And with the Soviet-led invasion of Czechoslovakia, the challenge presented by optimal planners began a rapid decline. Since then, specialists at *TsEMI* have withdrawn their extreme claims. They have subsequently initiated few attacks against the theoretical primacy of political economy. For their part, orthodox theorists have accepted the utility of linking quantitative methods to planning problems, but they interpret this connection as an analytical tool or applied sphere, rather than an independent school of thought. They do not hesitate to blast less vigilant planners for their fascination with, and even "mechanical" borrowing of, capitalist techniques. By finally accepting an instrumental role, that of rationalizer and not basic change agent, members of the planning school have become an important component of today's conventional wisdom in the USSR.

THE CYBERNETIC SCHOOL

The observer can find no more popular treatment of administrative phenomena in the USSR than that of cybernetics. This comes as no surprise. As the science of communication and control, cybernetics deals with major problems facing Soviet planners and administrators, e.g., the control of dynamic processes and the prevention of increasing disorder within them.[86] It reinforces the Marxist vision of a society amenable to rational direction as well as the Leninist preoccupation with purposive human activity. Thus, not only does cybernetics prop up doctrinal imagery, but it rekindles the expectation that the Soviet economy can, in fact, be managed from a single administrative center.[87] Despite initial misgivings among socialist ideologues, cybernetics now has greater prestige in the Soviet Union than perhaps anywhere else in the world. Indeed, if specialists regard political economy as the theoretical core of socialist management science, then they are also likely to conclude that cybernetics represents the field's practical orientation.[88]

Most typically, the cybernetic school views *upravlenie* as "the processing of information into signals which correct the activities of machines and organisms,"[89] or, according to A.I. Berg, it is the "transferring of a complex dynamic system from one state to a new [higher] one by influencing its variables."[90] Such definitions not only stress certain organizing concepts— system, information, regulation, feedback—but set forth a distinctive interpretation of administrative processes. To be sure, the cybernetic-systems approach faces no serious rival in the Soviet literature, not even among those theorists who emphasize its limitations, but who nonetheless often resort to cybernetic ideas to describe the process of management.[91] Cybernetic theorists look at the administrative mechanism at all hierarchical levels—the shop, production section, enterprise, industrial branch—as a *system* of interconnected elements. A change in one naturally affects all others. In each system the observer can identify a subject (*sub"ekt*) and object (*ob"ekt*) of management. And there is a purposive relationship between them: the subject (usually a state or party organ) leads and manages the object in a certain direction for specified purposes. By continuously processing information about the system's performance over time, and then feeding it back into the system, the subject can transform a given state of affairs into a higher level or organizational development (*organizovannost'*). Since the system monitors and adjusts its own behavior to take such feedback into account, it is self-managing (*samoupravliaiushchaia*) and can maintain equilibrium in the face of internal and external disturbances.

Moreover, cybernetic concepts have not been confined to narrow technical-engineering problems or even to the non-human milieu. On the contrary, they have been given broad application to societal as well as economic questions. For example, V.G. Shorin uncovers important analogies between cybernetic and administrative systems.[92] A.S. Petrov finds that basic managerial functions like planning, organizing, regulating, etc., correspond to cybernetic laws that embrace virtually all aspects of social production.[93] Although the descriptive power of cybernetics when applied to social phenomena has been severely criticized,[94] I.M. Syroezhin has tried to elaborate a theory of the firm under socialism.[95] His conception of "economic cybernetics" not only takes into account human activities, but advances a noteworthy reinterpretation of traditional economic categories.[96]

The most significant practical thrust of the cybernetic school has been the development and application of "automated management systems" (*avtomaticheskie sistemy upravleniia* or *ASU*).[97] This of course is intended to upgrade administrative efficiency and has led to the establishment of a large number of research institutes dealing with problems of ASU. In contrast to the empirical school or even optimal planning, relevant cybernetic institutes are not widely dispersed throughout the country, but are attached to either the Academy of Sciences or to state committees. For instance, the All-Union Scientific Research Institute for Problems of Organization and Management—the agency responsible for implementing the nation-wide computer network—reports directly to the State Committee on Science and Technology.[98] Officially sanctioned by CPSU directives in 1971, the institute is empowered to conduct research, plan and design new projects, and coordinate the entire system. But there are other agencies in the Soviet Union, which stand behind parochial, and competing, views of ASU. For example, the Institute of Cybernetics (Ukrainian Academy of Sciences) regards ASU as little more the processing of primary economic data by means of modern computing techniques.[99] Its most prominent spokesman, V.M. Glushkov, argues that by automating routine accounting operations, managerial personnel are relieved of mundane tasks and thus can focus their attention on decision-making problems. In this view, ASU fosters basic changes in neither organizational structure nor interpersonal relations. Consequently, planners and administrators do not have to contend with *qualitative* changes in the practice of management due to ASU. This conclusion is challenged, however, by V.A. Trapeznikov and others at the Institute of Management Problems (*IPU*). They base their ideas on cybernetic control. That is, *upravlenie* is a process of incessant struggle against a system's natural tendency toward entropy. Nevertheless, by processing information and learning through feedback, a control center can maintain the system's viability, but not without potentially significant changes in structure and process.[100]

The cybernetic school is not without vocal opponents in the Soviet management science community. These opponents are motivated by practical as well as parochial interests. Thus, political economists and doctrinaire specialists insistently warn against displacing Marxist–Leninist ideology with that of systems theory. They emphasize that dialectical materialism and the concepts of traditional economic analysis represent a more general, and distinctly *socialist*, approach to organization and management.[101] Administrative lawyers and others attack the vague, abstract nature of cybernetic categories; they find ideas like "system," "information," and "feedback" ill-equipped to deal with the social aspects of management.[102] Finally, empiricists take the cybernetic school to task for its inattention to leadership in the production collective. Coupled with major hard- and soft-ware developmental problems, these criticisms have done much to discredit the naive faith in some sort of cybernetic utopia that was evident in the 1960s. To be sure, the successful introduction (*vnedrenie*) of modern computing techniques not only lags far behind that already accomplished in the West, but it remains the greatest challenge today for Soviet cyberneticists.

Untangling the Jungle

These four schools of thought—political economy, the empirical approach, planning, and cybernetics—represent the major lines of progress in Soviet management science. Revealing the gross and general contours in the field, our classification identifies its major actors as well as points of contention.[103] Like their counterparts in the United States, Soviet administrative theorists have apparently run smack into irreconcilable semantic entanglements, bitter jurisdictional disputes, and even fundamental differences over the content and boundaries of management as a field of scientific inquiry. The unwillingness of specialists to engage in meaningful dialogue with rivals—a trait of the American managerial debate uncovered by Koontz some twenty years ago—also pertains to the Soviet jungle.[104] In fact, theorists in the USSR today often appear more content to downgrade, if not misrepresent, what others in the field have said, written, or done.

However, the diversity, ambiguity, and competition in Soviet studies of organization and management reflect much more than simply typical disputes among rival specialists. And the relatively free inquiry tolerated under the Brezhnev regime is still only a partial explanation. At bottom, the current jungle in Soviet management science has resulted from the gradual diffusion of authority throughout the administrative hierarchy since the demise of Stalin's personality cult. Consequently, specialists can now disagree substantially on matters of organizational technique without provoking official displeasure and/or political reprisals. Encouraged by leading politicians to develop a socialist science of management, analysts have been able and willing to find what they seek. Behavioral treatments aside, they have advanced numerous ideas and techniques designed to improve managerial practice. And those same specialists also want a piece of the political action.[105] The severe competition in the field resembles a genre of resource allocation politics—the distribution of *tangible* benefits has proven to be *asymmetrical*.[106] To be sure, there have been ostensible winners and losers: political economists have been largely kicked upstairs whereas "Americanizers"— Gvishiani, Popov, Mil'ner, and others—have made dramatic advancements. But the situation remains sufficiently ambiguous so that it is usually difficult to ascertain who does *not* speak for the regime on questions of management.

The disputes in Soviet management science will neither disappear nor even abate in the immediate future. The persistence of this jungle can be attributed to certain doctrinal as well as political factors. Thus, if developed socialism and the entire thrust of the STR literature in the USSR point to a greater awareness of complexity, to constraints on rational choice, and to unintended consequences, then the current political leadership has taken these lessons into account by purposively renouncing the "hare-brained scheming" of its predecessor. To be sure, under Brezhnev, the Soviet Union moved forward cautiously and incrementally, according to the "politics of marginal adjustments," rather than epoch-making changes.[107] This has entailed charting a moderate political path, and by modernizing administrative techniques, the regime has given expression and legitimacy to competing centers of administrative expertise.[108] Assuming they can contribute to the rationalization of the system, various schools and their institutional bastions will find support in at least some faction of the leadership. But while their techniques can only offer partial remedies to the USSR's pressing difficulties, specialists and their political patrons increasingly recognize that total solutions in the modern era are illusory. Should techniques fail or greater demands overload the system, however, then stronger medicine might be in order, specifically, that of a *krepkii khoziain* and a return to a "political ideology of administration."[109] Thus the systems of managing complex organizations in the United States and the USSR remain quite different, yet certain concepts are shared. It is to these that we turn in the Epilogue.

9

Epilogue: Convergence, Divergence, and Other Possibilities

Introduction

Soviet and American theories of administration and techniques of management are neither converging nor diverging in the broad sense. Rather, as we have tried to show, the Soviets are selectively emulating those American concepts and techniques which they believe are applicable to a developed socialist society. And those concepts and techniques are rooted in the American dominant paradigm, which contains the contention that it is possible to manage a highly complex society in a rational manner. This contention is the central issue in both societies. However, this similarity does not mean that administrative science will be similar in both countries, somewhere down the road. Rather, administrative science will continue to reflect the basic social, political, and economic values of each society. This means that in the United States, administrative science will continue to contain a welter of concepts and approaches. And if the organized-anarchy view gains wider acceptance in the United States, there will probably be a future divergence between the literature of the two nations, since the assumptions of the organized-anarchy approach flatly contradict a critical (if not *the* critical) idea of socialism: that capitalism is inherently unstable—that a complex industrial society must eventually either turn into a socialist one, centrally directed and rationally managed, or collapse under its contradictions. Thus, while some analysts in the United States question the notion that it is possible to fine-tune a highly complicated society, the Soviets continue to work toward a socialist theory of management. In this epilogue, we will review that effort, noting the differences and commonalities with the dominant American paradigm.

Toward a Socialist Theory of Management

The influx of information about Western administrative science and actual adoption of select U.S. business concepts has effectively ended the international isolation of Soviet studies of organization and management. Although orthodox specialists have tried on many occasions, some successful, to turn back the clock to Stalinist uniformity, their efforts have proven to be little more than tactically significant. From the Brezhnev era onwards, Soviet management science has moved forward, with few interruptions, into systems analysis, mathematical economics, business gaming, and the like. Although most innovative research and theorizing has remained concentrated in a small number of key institutes and among a relatively small number of specialists, this work has led to a dramatic transformation of how analysts in the USSR study management. Orthodox forces have continued to battle against "bourgeois" contamination, and political economists have reasserted their right to formulate the doctrinal basis of the regime's economic policy.[1] Aided by the conservative tide after the ill-fated "Prague spring," orthodox theorists have reasserted the primacy of central direction and control over the economic mechanism. To be sure, one seldom hears serious discussions of decentralization and other heretical ideas in the Soviet literature.

As mathematical economists defended the Marxist credentials of their field, so management specialists tried to demonstrate that *upravlenie* did not violate essential doctrinal givens—democratic centralism, *planomernost'*, and faith in purposive organizational leadership. In addition, specialists were determined to show that the wholesale borrowing of U.S. concepts was not, in principle, inconsistent with the needs of a socialist theory of management. Thus, a major task of theoretical analysis in the USSR has been to formulate a distinctive science of management under socialism, one that can be differentiated from its Western counterpart. In this regard, the theorizing of G.K. Popov warrants closer scrutiny.

The first comprehensive treatment of socialist theory (*Problemy Teorii Upravleniia*, 1970) adopted an "empirical" persuasion and demonstrated that the emulation of Western theorizing was consistent with the needs of socialist theory. The author of this work, G.K. Popov, outlined the basic terminology and contours of a science (theory) of socialist management and linked them directly to the practice of socialist management economic rationalization and the training of managerial personnel. *Problemy Teorii Upravleniia* was formulated in the center of management problems at Moscow State University (MGU), which was headed by D.M. Gvishiani from 1961 to 1964, author of the seminal *Sotsiologiia Biznesa*.[2] In the early 1960s Gvishiani and Popov developed university management-course materials ("Nauchnye Osnovy Upravleniia Proizvodstvom"—"The Scientific Bases of

Production Management" that have become widely used in the USSR. Popov is familiar with the American conceptual repertoire and draws freely from it to buttress the major arguments of *Problemy Teorii Upravleniia*.[3] For instance, he suggests that Western "techniques" like business schools, training programs, and consulting firms are useful (and potentially adoptable) in improving the "art of socialist management."

By the time Popov assumed leadership of the MGU center in 1965, he had already published several articles in *pravda* as well as his book.[4] These articles familiarized a broader audience with the science of management and, simultaneously, propagandized a particular conception of the field. Hence, for Popov, management is an autonomous discipline, synthesizing the contributions of many fields. Despite the renowned achievements of Soviet industry under conditions of the scientific-technological revolution, socialism requires a science of management.[5] Moreover, this science has a direct bearing on practice, and, under the conditions of the economic reform, it is vitally important for continued economic growth and development. "The question is . . . about the creation of one state system which, in a complex way, resolves two problems: *the problems of the formation of the science of management and the practical problems of raising the qualifications of leadership cadres.* The resolution of those problems urgently requires a new managerial system in the modern scientific-technical revolution" (emphasis added).[6]

Given official endorsement and the manner in which it connects theory and practice, Popov's theorizing in *Problemy Teorii Upravleniia* warrants closer scrutiny. This is less an analytic theory—i.e., an attempt to explain or predict the relationship between posited variables—than a general conception of management science and the specification of paths for its future development. Theorizing will take place within this general framework: "the organization of scientific research in the sphere of management demands the elaboration of a conception of a theory of management."[7] One of Popov's major tasks is to adumbrate the system of knowledge about management and the place of theory in that system. He frequently quotes from and cites Western referents, but his purpose is to develop a distinctly socialist theory. According to Popov, a theory of socialist management should generalize the lessons of economic rationalization and training programs for managerial personnel. He also attempts to demonstrate that socialist theory cannot, in principle, be contradicted by the selective emulation of Western concepts and methods. Thus, several important points are emphasized in *Problemy Teorii Upravleniia*: (1) priority is accorded to the special (socialist) features of management, i.e., these are considered most important in defining systemic character; (2) the object of inquiry is production management rather than state administration; (3) the complex, multi-disciplinary character of management is recognized; (4) the system of knowledge about management and the role of theory in that system are examined; and (5) theory ignores particular functions in preference for the "synthetic" whole. The central concepts in Popov's formulation are the theory of leadership *(rukovodstvo)* and the art *(isskustvo)* of management of the national economy. These elements will be reviewed in turn.

Distinctive Features of Socialist Management

Are there specific features of management under socialism? If so, what do they have in common with general features of management, which exist irrespective of social formation? With respect to Leninist principles (e.g., democratic centralism, one-man management, the unity of economic and political leadership), what occurs when Western ideas are adopted into the socialist repertoire? Although Leninist principles determine the planned, proportional development of the socialist economy, certain general traits are held in common with other managerial systems. According to Popov, ". . . the management of socialist social production is a special object of research, possessing features held in common with other types of management, and its specific features. The concept of the management of socialist social production is a very complex and multi-faceted and it is impossible to define it in a simple manner."[8]

These general features are often subsumed under the rubric of cybernetic aspects of *upravlenie*. Indeed, cybernetics, systems theory, and operations research are specific disciplines that bear on general features of management. In contradistinction to Leninist principles, important concepts include systems; the dynamic characteristics of systems; the subject and object of management; the storage, retrieval, and processing of information; feedback; and purposiveness. Furthermore, Popov recognizes that certain disciplines (e.g., *prakseologiia*) examine the general features of management in the human collective. The relevance of these approaches notwithstanding, ". . . it is impossible to absolutize the conclusions drawn from the analysis of 'general leadership.' But at the same time the general principles of the management of collectives permit [us] to note a whole series of important features for understanding this or other concrete collectives, including socialist production."[9]

Popov and other analysts have warned, however, that the preoccupation with general features of management can blur the distinction between socialism and capitalism and thus have unintended political consequences (witness the Czech "counter revolution" in 1968). Therefore, in formulating a socialist theory, specifically socialist features of management must always assume greater importance. But this priority can be conceptualized in terms of a synthesis between general and specific features in which, by definition, the latter are accorded greater potency. Implications for borrowing capitalist techniques are obvious: they cannot, regardless of their specific content and/ or quantitative significance, affect the basic character of management under socialism.

Since Soviet theorists readily acknowledge that objective uniformities exist in large-scale production irrespective of social system, Popov emphasizes that socialist theory deals with phenomena on the level of the national economy. He repeatedly argues that particular subsystems (e.g., the enterprise, production association, or industrial branch) cannot reflect the distinctive features of management under socialism. In order to allay the fears of doctrinaire colleagues, he quotes Barry Richman, an American Sovietologist, whose own work has emphasized the different environmental conditions of the socialist enterprise vis-à-vis the competitive market firm.[10] Thus, Popov shows that capitalist management science and socialist management science have identifiable (and different) objects of inquiry: Western specialists attend to the private capitalist firm and Soviet specialists to the national economy considered as a holistic phenomenon.[11]

If during the personality cult there was always scientific management in the Soviet Union (according to Popov), then the science of management was conspicuously absent. In the modern era, however, "the complex process of management demands complex knowledge which synthesizes the achievements of the most varied disciplines which study every aspect in the process of management."[12] One of Popov's major achievements has been to synthesize the relevant branches of knowledge concerning *upravlenie*, e.g., (1) the managerial aspects of certain general sciences like political economy and scientific communism, and (2) concrete sciences about the separate aspects of management (planning, accounting, bookkeeping). These fields delimit Popov's two basic concepts, the theory of leadership and the art of management of the national economy. The idea of a synthesis is crucial. "The contemporary theory of systems reaffirms the great truth of the dialectic, that the whole has laws which cannot be reduced to the laws of the components of the whole."[13] It is precisely this synthesis that provides the subject matter for the science of socialist management. As a holistic phenomenon, "the subject matter *(predmet)* of the management of socialist social production is those laws of the management of socialist production which are peculiar to management as a whole, that is, not as separate functions or sides of management, but management examined as a whole, complex, and concrete social phenomena."[14]

The attention to a synthesis of the various sides of management separates this realm from other scientific disciplines. It becomes an autonomous field of inquiry:

> The theory of management does not study the process of planning, it
> studies it only as an element of the whole, it studies the connection with
> accounting, with control, etc., that is it studies precisely that which
> neither the theory of planning nor the theory of accounting can uncover.
> The theory of leadership shows the role of the state among other subjects
> of management in the economy, since only it analyzes the totality of
> subjects and the particulars of each of them.[15]

This system, or rather synthesis of knowledge, is concerned with leadership of the national economy. While it is based on deducing principles of
management at various levels of abstraction, Popov suggests four basic categories of analysis: (1) the mechanism of leadership—the goals, means, principles, and methods of leadership; (2) the managerial system in static, i.e.,
administrative functions, cadres, organs, techniques; (3) the managerial
system in dynamic, i.e., administrative processes, decision making on the
micro- and macro-levels;[16] and (4) rationalization of the managerial structure.

The art of Management

Herbert Simon pointed out over thirty years ago, however, that the principles of management are in fact proverbs, which are too abstract to be
operationally defined. To the extent that contradictory policy prescriptions
are likely to emerge from these principles, Popov complements the theory
of leadership with the art *(isskustvo)* of management. Although it deals with
identical subject matter, the art of management involves empirical generalizations drawn from actual experience. Its methodology is descriptive
rather than logical:

> The theory of leadership and the art of management are differentiated
> only by method. They have the same subject matter; they study the laws
> of management as a holistic, complex, concrete social phenomenon. One
> discipline expresses its subject as a system of principles, and the other—
> in the manner of examples. One examines management as a sphere
> [where] laws operate, the other—as a sphere of creative activity. The
> unity of subject is to introduce a general concept for the theory of
> leadership and art of management as theory (science) of management.[17]

With respect to managerial art, Popov positively evaluates American business schools and the case method of instruction. He notes that V.I. Ozira—
a fellow specialist at the MGU management center—is an advocate of case
methods and proposes their widespread application in the USSR. Furthermore, in order to improve the art of management, Popov considers it essential to collect, study, and preserve the experience of leading organizers
of the Soviet economy. Their methods constitute an important dimension of
socialist theory, at least to the extent that generalizations can be drawn.

American experience is relevant here. Businessmen and administrators have left an important legacy of published materials—memoirs, analyses, principles, personal experiences, etc. These are routinely studied by prospective managers in the United States. Unfortunately, as Popov notes, "in the Soviet literature only in the last few years has the idea been recognized that the system of knowledge about *upravlenie* should include the art of management."[18] To the extent that the generalization of practical experience constitutes the subject matter of socialist theory, then Western experience, particularly management training and methods of instruction, is applicable to socialist conditions.

While these two concepts—the theory of leadership and the art of management—represent the basis of Popov's theory, he poses a further query: what specific measures can hasten the development of socialist theory? Theory and practice, he argues, should be mutually related: theory generalizes practical experience and, on the other hand, it influences the practice of management. Popov suggests that this unity will occur from (1) the concrete experience gained in rationalization and (2) the training *(uchëba)* of management executives. Moreover, in the formulation of socialist theory, the scholar will play a special role: "for the development of a theory of management [there must be] a special mechanism whereby it is possible to unite the experience, the knowledge, and the skills of managers with scholars in order to analyze, generalize, evaluate, and formulate [such a theory] . . ."[19] He suggests that the careful analysis of Soviet and foreign experience will indicate where and how these contacts are most expedient.

POPOV'S PROPOSALS FOR SOCIALIST THEORY

Popov makes several proposals to improve the practice of management and develop a distinctly socialist theory. First, the publication base requires significant broadening, i.e., a special publishing house for questions of management should be established and foreign materials given greater attention.

Second, the manager, or *rukovoditel'*, should be considered a generalist and his activity a special profession. In this sense, the selection and training of executives assumes fundamental importance in rationalizing the economic apparatus. As Popov indicates, however, the situation in the USSR is seriously deficient and lags behind the training systems in advanced capitalist countries. Thus, in the Soviet Union, there are no special course curricula for "business" executives; there are no special methods of instruction; there are no separate, identifiable stages in executive training and development.[20] As a matter of illustration, Popov compares this somber picture with the situation in the United States where there are, he asserts, over 600 business schools with over 600,000 students, special course curricula, teaching methods and techniques, etc.[21]

Third, and most important, Popov proposes to establish a series of institutes headed by a "state Committee for Rationalization of the National Economy."[22] This system would include project branch and interbranch centers of management, departments for rationalization in various state organs, and republican and All-Union committees. These institutions, particularly the state committee, cannot be a blind copy of *Rabkrin* or a control agency; they should follow the general experience of analogous organizations in either Poland or the German Democratic Republic.[23] Popov, however, questions certain recommendations that a single major institute should lead rationalization. Instead of recognizing the theoretical primacy of this center, he suggests that conditions must be created whereby individuals at every level in the administrative hierarchy can work on and elaborate questions of (socialist) management theory. Such a system will ensure the unity of theory and practice: ". . . *theoretical generalization is the result of practical experience. The work on rationalization of management, its planning and realization will serve as a basis for further development of a theory of management*"(emphasis added).[24]

The first edition of *Problemy Teorii Upravleniia* was a remarkable book. If our interpretation is correct, then Popov's treatment not only addressed socialist priniciples (e.g., the priority of specific vs general traits of management), but demonstrated that (1) theory and practice can be linked through the experience gained in economic rationalization and management training programs, and (2) Western experience is closely related (by implication) to such theorizing. Indeed, the widespread emulation of American management concepts, methods, and analytic techniques is no contradiction to socialist principles; it cannot (by definition) affect the socialist character of management.

Notes

1. Introduction

1. Harold Brown, *Department of Defense Annual Report: Fiscal Year 1982* (Washington, D.C.: Defense Printing Service, 1981), pp. 19–20.

2. William Zimmerman, *Soviet Perspectives on International Relations, 1956–1967* (Princeton, N.J.: Princeton Univ. Press, 1969).

3. For a good illustration, see Urie Bronfenbrenner, *Two Worlds of Childhood: U.S. and U.S.S.R.* (New York: Russell Sage Foundation, 1970).

4. William Zimmerman, "The Soviet Union," in Stephen Spiegel and Kenneth Waltz, eds., *Conflict in World Politics* (Cambridge, Mass.: Winthrop, 1971), p. 50.

5. Paul Cocks, "Retooling the Directed Society: Administrative Modernization and Developed Socialism," in Jan Truka and Paul Cocks, eds., *Political Development in Eastern Europe* (New York: Praeger, 1977), p. 56. See also Ferrel Heady, *Public Administration: A Comparative Approach* (Englewood Cliffs, N.J.: Prentice-Hall, 1966).

6. The beginnings of this false dichotomy can be found in Woodrow Wilson, "The Study of Administration," *Political Science Quarterly* (June 1887); reprinted in Jay M. Shafritz and Albert C. Hyde, eds. *Classics of Public Administration* (Oak Park, Ill.: Moore, 1978), pp. 3–16.

7. Similar questions have been examined on the macro-societal level by Zbigniew Brezezinski and Samuel Huntington, *Political Power: USA/USSR* (New York: Viking, 1963).

8. See Douglas Kinnard, *The Secretary of Defense* (Lexington: Univ. Press of Kentucky, 1980), p. 77.

9. I. Kasitskii, "Problemy izucheniia navchnoi organizatsii upravlencheskogo trvda", *Sotsialisticheskii trud*, no. 8 (August 1964): 51.

2. The Emergence of Administrative Science

1. See Robert Merton, et al. *Reader in Bureaucracy*.

2. Ibid.; see also Reinhard Bendix, *Max Weber: An Intellectual Portrait*.

3. James March and Herbert Simon, *Organizations*, pp. 34–47.

4. Frederick Winslow Taylor, *The Principles of Scientific Management*. This seminal work has been reissued in paperback form and thus is available to contemporary readers at a modest price. See the 1967 edition by W. W. Norton.

5. March and Simon, *Organizations*; Richard Cyert and James March, *A Behavioral Theory of the Firm*.

6. See Sudhir Kakar, *Frederick Taylor: A Study in Personality and Innovation*.

7. See James L. Rowe, Jr., "Corporate American Wallowing in Debt," *Washington Post*, 18 Aug. 1980, p. D1; "Reviving Industry: The Search for a Policy", Clyde Farnsworth, Agis Salpukas, Peter Schuyten, Henry Scott Stokes and Edward Cowan, "Reviving Industry: The Search for a Policy," *New York Times*, 18 Aug. 1980, p. 1; 19 Aug. 1980, p. 1; 20 Aug. 1980, p. 1; 21 Aug. 1980, p. D1; 22 Aug. 1980, p. D1; William Abernathy and Robert Hayes, "Management Minus Invention," *New York Times*, 20 Aug. 1980, p. D2.

8. The biographical details are drawn from Kakar, *Frederick Taylor*.

9. Taylor, *Principles*, p. 5.

10. Ibid.

11. Ibid., pp. 46–54.

12. Jacob Bronowski, *The Ascent of Man*.

13. Martin Landau and Russell Stout, Jr., "To Manage Is Not To Control: Or the Folly of Type II Errors," *Public Administration Review*, *39* (March/April 1979): 148.

14. Richard Hofstadter, *Social Darwinism in American Thought*.

15. The extended quotation is from Taylor, *Principles*, pp. 40–47.

16. V.I. Lenin, *Collected Works*, 27: 259.

17. Anne Jardim, *The First Henry Ford: A Study in Personality and Business Leadership*, pp. 237, 246.

18. Robert Caro, *The Power Broker: Robert Moses and the Fall of New York City*.

19. Allan Nevins and Frank Ernest Hill, *Ford: The Times, the Man, and the Company*, vol. 1.

20. Alfred P. Sloan, Jr., *My Years with General Motors*, pp. 151–52.

21. Chris Argyris and Donald Schon, *Organizational Learning: A Theory of Action Perspective*, esp. chap. 4.

22. Charles E. Lindblom, *Politics and Markets: The World's Political-Economic Systems*, p. 298.

23. Ibid., p. 299.

24. Allan Nevins and Frank Ernest Hill, *Ford; Expansion and Challenge*, p. 673.

25. Jardim, *The First Henry Ford*, p. 87.

26. The preceding discussion was drawn from ibid., pp. 85–94.

27. Quoted in ibid., p. 122.

28. Henry Ford, *My Life and Work*, p. 92.

29. Jardim, *The First Henry Ford*, esp. chaps. 3, 7.

30. Luther Gulick and Lyndall Urwick, eds., *Papers on the Science of Administration*.

31. Luther Gulick, "Notes on the Theory of Organization," in Luther Gulick and Lyndall Urwick, *Papers*, pp. 3–13.

32. Herbert A. Simon, "The Proverbs of Administration," in *Public Administration Review*, 6 (Winter 1946): 53–67.

33. See Burleigh Gardner, "The Factory as a Social System," in W.F. Whyte, ed., *Industry and Society*, pp. 1–52; Chester Barnard, *The Functions of the Executive*.

34. Nicos Mouzelis, *Organization and Bureaucracy*, p. 201 n.

35. See, e.g., James Mooney and A.C. Reiley, *The Principles of Organization*, first published in 1939.

36. Robert Kahn and Daniel Katz, "Leadership in Relation to Productivity and Morale," in Robert Sutermesiter, *People and Productivity*, ed., pp. 131–45.

37. See Fritz Roethlisberger and William Dickson, *Management and the Worker*. Roethlisberger was one of the original experimenters. See also Fritz Roethlisberger, *Management and Morale*.

38. Robert Zajonc, *Social Psychology: An Experimental Approach*.

39. Alex Carey, "The Hawthorne Studies: A Radical Criticism," *American Sociological Review*, 33 (1968): 403–16; Richard Franke and James Kaub, "The Hawthorne Experiments: First Statistical Interpretation," *American Sociological Review*, 43 (1978): 623–43.

40. Muhmaud Wahba and Lawrence Bridwell, "A Review of Research on the Need Hierarchy Theory," in Kenneth Wexley and Gard Yukl, eds., *Organizational Behavior and Industrial Psychology: Readings with Commentary* (New York: Oxford Univ. Press, 1975), pp. 5–11; see also Wahba and Bridwell, "Maslow Reconsidered: A Review of Research on the Need Hierarchy Theory," *Organizational Behavior and Human Performance*, 15 (1976): 212–40.

3. Administrative Science and the Rise of Soviet Power

1. This theme is persuasively developed by Theodore H. Von Laue, *Why Lenin? Why Stalin?* (New York: J.B. Lippencott Co., 1964).

2. These changes represented an indisputably *liberal* direction, e.g., judicial and educational reforms, emancipation of the serfs, and establishment of local self-government councils (known as *zemstvo*). But liberal change agents ran up against formidable obstacles in old Russia. For example, the *zemstvos* stood off by themselves, entirely isolated from other administrative agencies. Indeed, it is not surprising that they were unable to play a major role in political life. See Paul Miliukov, *Russia and its Crisis* (London: Collier Books, 1962), esp. chap. 5.

3. Witte was a forerunner to Stalin in terms of his ruthless determination to industrialize Russia. Both men preached caution in foreign policy, at least until internal strength matched external ambition.

4. Pointing out that old Russia had always been beaten for her backwardness, Stalin warned in 1931 that the USSR had ten years to catch up with the advanced Western states or else be crushed. And on 22 June 1941, Hitler's armies crossed the frontier and were soon threatening Moscow.

5. Universal compulsory education became an official goal of Tsar Nicholas II.

Impressive gains were registered and, by 1913, 73 percent of all military recruits were literate.

6. There were certain noteworthy exceptions to the diffusion of "scientific management" eastward. Thus, in the late 1890s, various Russian ideas on organizing labor found their way into the American scientific literature. See *Nauchnaia Organizatsiia Truda Dvadtsatykh Godov: Sbornik Dokumentov I Materialov (The Scientific Organization of Labor in the 1920s: A Collection of Documents and Materials)* (Kazan, 1965), pp. 657–60.

7. It remains unclear just how effective these "scientific" principles were in raising production efficiency and/or the quality of output. While the scale of operations in certain Russian factories compared favorably to that achieved in the West, the tsarist regime could not match the aggregate production levels attained in Germany, France, England, or the United States.

8. More than national pride is involved here. By claiming technological equivalence, the Soviet writer emphasizes the *social* causes of revolution and thereby supports a Marxist treatment of history.

9. Soviet interpretations of Marxism can be categorized under three major headings: the materialist conception of history, political economy of capitalism, and nature of socialism and communism. Perhaps the most trenchant part of the entire theory examines the dynamics of capitalist society, particularly the inherently ambiguous role played by private property. See David Lane, *Politics and Society in the USSR* (New York: Random House, 1970), pp. 1–20.

10. This treatise, written by Lenin during World War I, pointedly rejects Marx's "exceptionalism," i.e., the idea that the working class might assume power in certain advanced bourgeois countries (for example, the United States and England) through peaceful means. Arguing vehemently that the proletariat could not be "bought off," Lenin insistently maintained that only violent revolution could resolve the fundamental class antagonisms of bourgeois society.

11. This conclusion has been reached by Jeremy Azrael, *Managerial Power and Soviet Politics* (Cambridge: Harvard Univ. Press, 1966), pp. 12–27.

12. Lenin's last published works focused on the administrative apparatus and ways to upgrade its performance. His two key articles on the subject—"How to Reorganize RABKRIN" and "Better Smaller, but Better"—suggest that two agencies, the workers and peasants inspection and the central control commission, should be merged into a single agency devoted to scientific research. Several leading Bolsheviks headed *RABKRIN*, including Felix Dzerzhinsky and V.V. Kuibyshev. For a good review of this agency and the rationalization movement in Soviet politics, see Paul Cocks, "The Rationalization of Party Control," in Chalmers Johnson, ed., *Change in Communist Systems* (Stanford: Stanford Univ. Press, 1970).

13. Philip Selznick, *The Organizational Weapon* (Glencoe, Ill.: Free Press, 1960).

14. This characterization has been suggested by Alfred Meyer. His now-classic *Leninism* (New York: Praeger, 1962) examines the complex (and sometimes contradictory) thoughts, ideas, and conditions that have shaped the theoretical heritage of Lenin.

15. Azrael, *Managerial Power and Soviet Politics*, p. 14.

16. Ibid., pp. 20–24.

17. Some confusion remains on this point; but in the main, Bolshevik theorists saw accounting and control as routine operations, whereas management remained "mental labor" and, hence, could only be performed by technically qualified specialists. Azrael suggests that Lenin consciously obfuscated his managerial views in order to capitalize on anarchist sentiments: "the principal tactic he adopted was to shift the focus of his discussion rapidly back and forth from the question of accounting and control *over* production to the question of the management *of* production, thereby creating the illusion that his remarks on the former function applied also to the latter." *Managerial power and Soviet Politics*, p. 19.

18. O.A. Pozdniakov, *O Problemakh Nauchnoi Organizatsii Truda I Upravleniia (On the Problems of the Scientific Organization of Labor and Management)* (Moscow: "Lenizdat," 1969), p. 19.

19. Cocks, "Rationalization of Party Control," pp. 159–161.

20. Virtually all elements of the Stalinist command system were present under war communism. Major differences involved methods by which resources were expropriated from the peasantry as well as the purposes of economic organization. Thus, priorities imposed in 1918–1921 were current ones—how to wage war successfully—while those existing under Stalin pointed to long-term developmental goals.

21. For a good historical survey of economic organization and reform in the USSR, see Abraham Katz, *The Politics of Economic Reform in the Soviet Union* (New York: Praeger, 1972).

22. The spontaneous rebellion of the Kronstadt sailors, Trotsky's most reliable shock troops during the civil war, struck at the very foundations of Soviet power. It bore a sobering message: that radical policy changes were urgently required. And Kronstadt proved indispensible in helping Lenin sell NEP to the party.

23. M.G. Babin, "Problema Nauchnoi Organizatsii Truda V Sovetskoi Ekonomicheskoi Literature Dvadtsatykh Godov" ["The Problem of the Scientific Organization of Labor in the Soviet Economic Literature of the 1920s"], Ph.D. dis., Moscow State Univ., 1966), p. 5.

24. The class standing and professional orientation of administrative specialists present at the second conference on *NOT* in 1924 would tend to support a generally favorable review of Taylor's ideas. For example, 87 percent of those attending were from the intelligentsia; 72 percent had received higher education; 70 percent were not party members; and a modest 10 percent were representatives of the working class. See P.F. Petrochenko, *Nauchnaia Organizatsiia Truda: Materialy Vtoroi Vsesouznoi Konferentsii Po Nauchnoi Organizatsii Truda (The Scientific Organization of Labor: Materials from the Second All-Union Conference on the Scientific Organization of Labor)* (Moscow: "Mysl'," 1965), pp. 6–7.

25. O.A. Ermanskii stressed this point at the first conference on *NOT* in 1921. See *Nauchnaia Organizatsiia Truda Dvadtsatykh Godov*, p. 68.

26. To be sure, it was not uncommon for "bourgeois specialists" to call Taylor a "genius." However, for Lenin and other Bolsheviks, an individual's class standing was more important than his ideas per se. Thus, since Ermanskii had shown an obvious sympathy for Menshevism, his highly acclaimed book on *NOT* could not serve as a text on the subject, despite a critical assessment of Taylorism.

27. This point was emphasized by N.A. Gredeskul in a speech at the First Con-

ference on *NOT*. See *Trudy I Vserossiiskoi Initsiativnoi Konferentsii Po Nauchnoi Organizatsii Truda I Proizvodstva (Works of the First All-Russian Conference on the Scientific Organization of Labor and Production)* (Moscow, 1921), p. 11.

28. That first bibliography contained 76 works completed in the first three years of Soviet power. Three years later I.P. Elets listed 763 Soviet books and articles on *NOT*. An official index appeared in 1924, containing 2400 Russian-language citations. One year later, that number rose to 4400.

29. Aleksei Kapitonovich Gastev, 1882–1941, was one of the few management theorists who displayed genuine Bolshevik credentials. He was active in the revolutionary movement beginning in the early 1900s and even spent several years with the emigree community abroad (Paris, Geneva). Returning to Petersburg in 1905, Gastev played an instrumental role in helping to organize Bolshevik party cells in that city. His background made him an ideal choice to head the prestigious Central Institute of Labor formed in 1921. He also led numerous Soviet delegations to Europe and edited several major journals in the period between the wars. His important publications included *Norm-setting and the Organization of Labor, Industrial Peace, Our Tasks, Reconstruction of Industry*, and the widely acclaimed *How One Should Work* (1924). But Gastev's organizational skills, revolutionary ardor, and scientific reputation could not save him from the Great Terror.

30. *SOVNOT*, formed in 1921, consisted of workers from important research institutes and other scientific agencies. Its own research format included laboratory experiments as well as the generalization of leading experience. And *SOVNOT* actively encouraged useful interchanges between industrial enterprises and public organizations. For a brief overview of key scientific, party, and state agencies in the 1920s, see D.M. Berkovich, *Formirovanie Nauki Upravleniia Proizvodstvom (Formation of the Science of Production Management)* (Moscow: "Nauka," 1973), pp. 80–143.

31. *Referativnyi Ukazatel' Tekhnicheskoi Literatury (Reference Guide to Technical Literature)* was widely distributed throughout the Soviet Union.

32. S.I. Ikonnikov, *Sozdanie I Deiatel'nost' Ob''edinennykh Organov Tskk-Rki V 1923–1934 gg (The Creation and Activity of the Combined Organs/Tskk-Rki in 1923–1934)* (Moscow: "Nauka," 1971), p. 171.

33. The Soviets showed great interest in advanced German research. Prominent specialists like A.K. Gastev, O.A. Ermanskii, N.A. Semashko, F. R. Dunaevskii, I.M. Burdianskii, and many others visited that country in the early 1920s.

34. F.R. Baumgarten, a Polish citizen, sent the central institute information on American literature as well as on activities of the Masurak Institute in Czechoslovakia.

35. From 1925 onwards, perhaps no Western specialist exerted greater influence on Soviet administrative thinking than Henry Ford. His autobiography, *My Life, My Accomplishments*, was translated and reprinted nine times. By decade's end, the term "fordism" was commonly used in the Soviet literature.

36. Acrimonious disputes broke out at the 1924 conference between advocates of a narrow inductive approach and those stressing broader organizational perspectives. And party spokesmen strongly discredited the idea that *NOT* could be a general system of labor organization. However, in retrospect, current analysts find that conclusion premature: "It is...impossible to understand why the notion of creating a whole system for the organization of labor is anti-Marxist. Declarations about the

perils of theorizing as such were injurious and discouraged specialists from attempting to elaborate a theory of [socialist management]." Berkovich, *Formirovanie Nauki Upravleniia Proizvodstvom*, pp. 117–18.

37. P.M. Kerzhentsev (1881–1940) emerged as a strong rival of Gastev's at the second conference. He favored a "broad base" (*shirokaia baza*) approach to the organization of labor; i.e., the enterprise as a whole should be analyzed prior to rationalizing a particular operation. His own research dealt with developing organizational principles based on systematic observation of existing managerial procedures. His most famous work, *Prinstsipy Organizatsii (Principles of Organization)*, resembles the classical American approach to public administration.

38. A.N. Shcherban', ed., *Nauchnaia Organizatsiia Truda I Upravleniia (The Scientific Organization of Labor and Management)*, 2d ed. (Moscow, 1966), p. 41.

39. M.G. Babin reaches such a conclusion without excessively praising Soviet accomplishments in the years between the wars.

40. Babin, "Problema Nauchnoi Organizatsii Truda v Sovetskoi Ekonomicheskoi Literature Dvadtsatykh Godov," esp. chap. 4. Soviet historians who uncover purpossive efforts to develop *socialist* management theory assume that which needs to be proven. However, many specialists found themselves in serious political difficulties because they ignored the reputedly distinctive traits of socialism in their published works.

41. N.F. Charnovskii, *Tekhniko-Ekonomicheskie Printsipy V Metallopromyshlennosti (Technical Economic Principles in the Metal Industry* (Moscow: "Orgmetall," 1927), p. 17.

42. E.F. Rozmirovich, *Metodologiia I Praktika Tekhnika Upravleniia (Methodology and the Practice of Administrative Techniques)* (Moscow: "Tekhnika Upravleniia," 1927).

43. E.F. Rozmirovich, "K Itogam Raboty RKI po *NOT*," ("On the Results of *RKI*'s Work on *NOT*"), *Voprosy Sovetskogo Khoziaistva I Upravleniia*, 45 (1924): 277.

44. See E. Drezin, *Rukovodstvo Po Organizatsii Upravlenscheskogo Apparata Sovetskikh Uchrezhdenii (Leadership of Organizations in the Administrative Apparatus of Soviet Institutions)* (Moscow: "NKRKI," 1927). In this work's introduction, Rozmirovich points out that Russian Fayolists typically overestimate the importance of psychological factors in management. And she reminds the reader that this tendency represents a serious "theoretical distortion" in the Soviet literature.

45. Drezen, *Rukovodstvo Po Organizatsii Upravlenscheskogo Apparata*, p. 198.

46. For a brief review of Bogdanov's work, see Robert F. Miller, "The New Science of Administration in the USSR," *Administrative Science Quarterly*, 18 (September 1971): 248–50.

47. A.A. Bogdanov, *Ykazatel' Proizvedeniia (An Index of Works)* (Moscow, 1925), as quoted in David Kruk, *Razvitie Teorii I Praktiki Upravleniia Proizvodstvom V SSSR(The Development of Theory and the Practice of Production Management in the USSR)* (Moscow, 1974), p. 90.

48. Bogdanov's name is no longer anathema in the Soviet Union. In fact, many have come to admit that he made important contributions to administrative theory and perhaps even laid the groundwork for the science of communication and con-

trol—cybernetics. See V.P. Bogolepov, "O Sostoianii i Zadachakh Razvitiia Ob-shchei Teorii Organizatsii" ("On the Status and Tasks of Developing a General Theory of Organization"), in A.I. Berg, ed., *Organizatsiia I Upravlenie: Voprosy Teorii I Praktiki* (Moscow: "Nauka," 1968).

49. Berkovich, *Formirovanie Nauki Upravleniia Proizvodstvom*, pp. 123–26.

50. Vigorous debates arose among Soviet economists in the 1920s about problems of industrialization in a backward country. For an excellent review of the arguments presented by various factions, including bourgeois specialists, former Mensheviks, and Communist planners, see Nicolas Spulber, ed., *Foundations of Soviet Strategy for Economic Growth: Selected Soviet Essays, 1924–1930* (Bloomington: Indiana Univ. Press, 1964).

51. These problems involved many aspects of a traditional market economy (e.g., unemployment, uneven terms of exchange between agriculture and industry), as well as some that were distinctly socialist (e.g., an oversupply of poor quality goods). But perhaps most depressing for dedicated Bolsheviks was the lagging growth rate in heavy industry.

52. Katz, *Politics of Economic Reform*, p. 12.

53. The question of leadership succession loomed behind every substantive policy issue in the 1920s. Following Lenin's death, senior Bolsheviks were united in their opposition to Trotsky, although he made no real leadership bid. By 1925, a "left" faction headed by G. Zinoviev and L. Kamenev was defeated in the Politburo by Stalin and the so-called right. Although they subsequently ended all criticism of NEP and "socialism in one country," Zinoviev and Kamenev led a precarious existence in the party. Both were imprisoned and ultimately executed during the purges. By 1928, however, Stalin turned on the right: he ended NEP, collectivized agriculture, and initiated the first five-year plan. By 1930, he commanded a unified, disciplined political entity from which he soon weeded out all remaining vestiges of *potential* opposition.

54. See J.P. Nettl, *The Soviet Achievement* (New York: Harcourt, Brace & World, 1967), p. 101.

55. The chief difference between Stalin and the left (e.g., E.I. Preobrazhensky) was that the emergent dictator wanted to force heavy industry far beyond the calculation envisioned by others. And to do so, he was prepared to adopt a military solution to the peasant question and to apply unpredictable and arbitrary political terror to achieve policy objectives.

56. Leonard Schapiro, *The Communist Party of the Soviet Union* (New York: Random House, 1959), p. 364.

57. Petrochenko, *Nauchnaia Organizatsiia Truda*, p. 15.

58. See O.A. Deineko, "Izuchat' i Obobshchat' Organizatsionnyi Opyt Proshlogo" ("Study and Generalize the Organizational Experience of the Past"), in A.I. Berg, ed., *Organizatsiia I Upravlenie: Voprosy Teorii I Praktike* (Moscow: "Nauka," 1968).

59. Cocks, "Rationalization of Party Control," p. 161.

60. This phrase typified Bolshevik attitudes in the 1930s. Indeed, careful scientific analysis was less important than correct political values and/or the willpower of economic cadres. Thus, organizational complexity and limited resources were bar-

riers to storm, rather than objective constraints on behavioral change. And failure meant insufficient will, not inadequate knowledge.

61. For an outstanding review of theoretical and practical developments in management science during the 1930s, see Kruk, *Razvitie Teorii I Praktiki Upravleniia Proizvodstvom V SSSR.*

62. Joseph Stalin, *Economic Problems of Socialism in the USSR* (New York: International Publishers, 1952), p. 72.

63. This badly truncated research format should not obscure an essential development: all-out industrialization created the organizational framework for the Soviet economy and, hence, the subject matter of future theorizing.

64. Kruk, *Razvitie Teorii I Praktiki Upravleniia Proizvodstvom,* p. 130.

65. The text referred to by I.O. Liubovich is *Organizatsiia Proizvodstva V Mashinostroenii: Uchebnoe Posobie (Organizing Production in Machine Building: Educational Textbook)* (Moscow, 1937).

66. *Tekhpromfinplan* represents the industrial enterprise's technical-industrial-financial plan in a given year. Its formulation represents not only the general economic goals of the political leadership, but complex bargaining between the enterprise itself and various higher-level agencies. For an insightful description of how this process works, see Barry Richman, *Soviet Management: With Significant American Comparisons* (Englewood Cliffs, N. J.: Prentice-Hall, 1965).

67. The central committee's resolution—"On the Organization of Industrial Academies in Regions, Districts, and Republics"—was endorsed on 17 July 1931. It stipulated that industrial academies would be consolidated into autonomous educational establishments.

68. Katz, *Politics of Economic Reform,* pp. 26–40.

69. Although Kantorovich's brilliant work in linear programing actually preceded that done by G.B. Dantzig in the United States, American specialists first applied the ideas in administrative practice.

70. Work on this science was conducted by two scholars, I.O. Liubovich at the Ordzhonikidze Engineering-Economics Institute and B.I. Katsenbogen at the Central Scientific Research Institute. Their ability to publish theoretical studies in the 1930s demonstrates that administrative science survived even the most repressive era of high Stalinism.

71. I.O. Liubovich, *Metody Khoziaistvennogo I Tekhnicheskogo Rukovodstva Proizvodstvom*(The *Methods of Economic and Technical Production Leadership*) (Moscow, 1938), p. 86.

72. B.I. Katsenbogen, "K Voprosy o Teorii Sotsialisticheskoi Organizatsii Proizvodstva" ("On the Question of a Theory of Socialist Production Organization"), *Organizatsiia Upravleniia,* 3 (1936): 6.

73. I.O. Liubovich, *Sotsialisticheskaia Organizatsiia Proizvodstva Kak Predmet Prepodavaniia (Socialist Organization of Production as the Subject Matter of Teaching)* (Moscow, "Moskovskii Rabochii," 1938), p. 50.

74. Today, many analysts detach management science from political economy in a similar manner. Political economy is the more abstract, theoretical field.

75. Liubovich, *Sotsialisticheskaia Organizatsiia Proizvodstva Kak Predmet Prepodavaniia,* p. 75.

76. The essence of political terror involves its arbitrary nature. Thus, individuals have no criteria by which to judge the acceptability of their actions. See Alexander Dallin and George Breslauer, "Political Terror in the Post-Mobilization Stage," in Chalmers Johnson, ed., *Change in Communist Systems* (Stanford, Cal.: Stanford Univ. Press, 1970).

77. Nevertheless, there was some reassessment of how the labor theory of value functions under socialism. See Katz, *Politics of Economic Reform*, p. 27.

78. D. F. Ustinov has recently been named minister of defense and added to the politburo.

4. The Revitalization of Administrative Science

1. See James D. Thompson, *Organizations in Action*

2. Talcott Parsons, *Structure and Process in Modern Societies*.

3. The environment external to the organization can be defined as organizations, cultures, or other factors external to the organization that decision makers within the organization take into consideration. See Gerald Zaltman, Robert Duncan, and Jonny Holbek, *Innovations and Organizations*, p. 114; Merlin B. Brinkehoff and Philip R. Kunz, eds., *Complex Organizations and Their Environments*, p. xix. This definition ignores an extraordinarily sticky problem of definitions of organizational boundaries: where does the oganization end and the external environment begin? This question has serious implications for the functioning of the organization and has yet to be resolved in a satisfactory manner by organizational theorists. In this sense, it is similar to the problem faced by physicists as they try to define light as either a particle or a wave. Contemporary theory says that it may be either, depending on the problem at hand. Thus, in administrative science the boundary problem must be resolved at this time by saying that the boundary of the organization changes depending on the situation, and that the definition is an operational one. See William Dill, "Environment as an Influence on Managerial Autonomy"; R.E. Emery and E. Trist, "The Causal Texture of Organizational Environments"; and D.S. Pugh, D.J. Hickson, C.R. Hinings, and C. Turner, "Dimensions of Organizational Structure."

4. See Zaltman, Duncan, and Holbek, *Innovations*, p. 106.

5. This discussion is drawn from Thompson, *Organizations in Action*.

6. Alvin Gouldner, "Organizational Analysis," in Robert K. Merton, Leonard Broom, and Leonard S. Cottrell, Jr., eds., *Sociology Today* (New York: Basic Books, 1959), pp. 400–428; Charles Perrow, *Complex Organizations: A Critical Essay* (Glenview, Ill.: Scott, Foresman, 1972).

7. Robert L. Kahn, "Organizational Development: Some Problems and Proposals," *Journal of Applied Behavioral Science*, 10 (1974): 485–502.

8. Robert A. Ulrich and George F. Wieland, *Organization Theory and Design*, (Georgetown, Ont.: Irwin-Dorsey, 1980), p. 28; see also Daniel Katz and Robert Kahn, *The Social Psychology of Organizations*, 2d ed. (New York: Wiley, 1978).

9. Daniel Katz and Robert Kahn, *The Social Psychology of Organizations*, 1st ed., 1968.

10. Karl Deutsch, *The Nerves of Government* (New York: Free Press, 1966).

11. Nicos Mouzelis, *Organisation and Bureaucracy* (Chicago: Aldine, 1967), p. 149.

12. Heinz Eulau, *Micro-Macro Political Analysis* (Chicago: Aldine, 1969), p. 5.

13. Deutsch, *Nerves of Government.*

14. The term "adaptively rational" is borrowed from Richard Cyert and James March, *A Behavioral Theory of the Firm* (Englewood Cliffs, N.J.: Prentice-Hall, 1963).

15. Deutsch, *Nerves of Government*, p. 111.

16. Ulrich and Wieland, *Organization Theory and Design*, p. 34.

17. See David McClelland, *Personality* (New York: Holt, Rinehart & Winston, 1951); and Robert White, "Motivation Reconsidered: The Concept of Competence," *Psychological Review*, 66 (1959): 297–333.

18. Some of the visions of heaven offered by fundamentalist religious leaders— in which harmony and bliss were valued so highly—led Mark Twain to remark that while he might prefer heaven for the climate, he would certainly prefer hell for the conversation.

19. James Clay Thompson, *Rolling Thunder.*

20. Joseph Daughen and Penter Binzen, *The Wreck of the Penn Central* (Boston: Little, Brown, 1971).

21. Mouzelis, *Organisation and Bureaucracy*, pp. 158–62.

22. Graham T. Allison, *Essence of Decision: Explaining the Cuban Missile Crisis* (Boston: Little, Brown, 1971), p. 146.

23. Ibid., p. 145.

24. Samuel Huntington, *The Common Defense* (New York: Columbia Univ. Press, 1961).

25. Allison, *Essence*, p. 145.

26. Melville Dalton, *Men Who Manage* (New York: Wiley, 1959).

27. Morton Halperin, *Bureaucratic Politics and Foreign Policy* (Washington, D.C.: Brookings Institution, 1974), p. 28.

28. Arnold Kanter, *Defense Politics: A Budgetary Perspective* (Chicago, Ill.: Univ. of Chicago, 1980).

29. Dalton, *Men Who Manage.*

30. James Fallows, *National Defense* (New York: Random House, 1981).

31. Michel Crozier, *The Bureaucratic Phenomenon* (Chicago: Univ. of Chicago, 1964).

32. The sad history of the M-6 rifle is contained in Fallows, *National Defense*, pp. 77–95; for the organizational decay in the army as a result of combat in Vietnam, see Cincinnatus, *Self-Destruction* (New York: Norton, 1981).

33. Victor Thompson labels this "bureaupathic behavior" in his *Modern Organizations* (New York: Knopf, 1961), pp. 152–77.

34. Morton Halperin, *Bureaucratic Politics*, pp. 235–60.

35. Cyert and March, *Behavioral Theory.*

36. Lawrence Mohr, "The Concept of Organizational Goal," in *American Political Science Review*, 67 (1973): 470–81.

37. Herbert A. Simon, *Models of Man* (New York: Wiley, 1957); *Administrative Behavior* (New York: Macmillan, 1961); *The Shape of Automation for Men and*

Management (New York: Harper & Row, 1965); and *The Sciences of the Artificial* (Cambridge, Mass.: MIT Press, 1969).

38. James March and Herbert A. Simon, *Organizations* (New York: Wiley, 1958).

39. Charles Lindblom, "The Science of Muddling Through," *Public Administration Review*, 19 (Spring 1958): 79–88.

40. Muzafer Sherif, *The Psychology of Social Norms* (New York: Harper & Bros., 1936); Solomon Asch, *Social Psychology* (Boston: Little, Brown, 1951).

41. Robert Zajonc, *Social Psychology: An Experimental Approach* (Belmont, Cal.: Wadsworth, 1966), p. 37.

42. Ibid.

43. Patrick Suppes and M. Schlag-Rey, "Analysis of Social Conformity in Terms of Generalized Conditioning Models," in Joan Criswell, Herbert Solomon and Patrick Suppes, eds., *Mathematical Models in Small Group Processes* (Palo Alto, Cal.: Stanford Univ. Press, 1962), pp. 56–94; Ole R. Holsti, "Individual Differences in 'Definition of the Situation,' " *Journal of Conflict Resolution*, 13 (1970):303–11.

44. Zajonc, *Social Psychology*.

45. Burleigh B. Gardner, "The Factory as a Social System," in W.F. White, ed., *Industry and Society*, (New York: McGraw-Hill, 1946), pp. 1–52.

46. Irving Janis, *Victims of Groupthink* (Boston: Houghton-Miflin, 1972).

47. See J. Patrick Wright, *On a Clear Day You Can See General Motors* (New York: Avon, 1979); Ed Cray, *Chrome Colossus: General Motors and Its Times* (San Francisco: McGraw-Hill, 1979).

48. Thompson, *Rolling Thunder*, p. 53; Janis, *Victims of Groupthink*.

49. Harold Wilensky, *Organizational Intelligence* (New York: Basic Books, 1967).

50. Roland McKean, "Criteria of Efficiency in Government Expenditures," in Robert T. Golembiewski, ed., *Public Budgeting and Finance*, (Itasca, Ill.: F.E. Peacock, 1968), pp. 516–21.

51. Wilensky, *Organizational Intelligence*, p. 45.

52. Robert Presthus, *The Organizational Society* (New York: Vantage, 1962), p. 43.

53. Herbert Simon, George Kozmetsk, Harold Guetzkow, and Gordon Tyndall, "Management Uses of Figures," in Robert T. Golembiewski, ed., *Public Budgeting and Finance* (Itasca, Ill.: F.E. Peacock, 1968), pp. 15–23.

54. Quoted in Art Pine, "Reagan's August Guns: Critics Shout Their Warning Cries," *Washington Post*, 7 June 1981, p. H1.

55. Frank Levy and Edwin Truman, "Toward a Rational Theory of Decentralization: Another View," in *American Political Science Review*, 65 (June 1971): 177.

56. Cyert and March, *Behavioral Theory*, p. 82.

57. Roland N. McKean, "Criteria of Efficiency," p. 516.

58. Thompson, *Rolling Thunder*, p. 116.

59. Robert Merton, "Bureaucratic Structure and Personality," in Robert Merton, Ailsa P. Gray, Barbara Hockey, and Hanon Selvin, eds., *Reader in Bureaucracy* (Glencoe, Ill.: Free Press, 1952), pp. 361–71.

60. Arthur Ross, "The Data Game," in *Washington Monthly*, 1 (February 1969): 64.

61. Anthony Downs, *Inside Bureaucracy* (Boston: Little, Brown, 1967), p. 191.

62. Thompson, *Rolling Thunder*.

5. From Stalin to Kosygin: The Reemergence of Administrative Science

1. Katz, *The Politics of Economic Reform in the Soviet Union*, p. 36.

2. Perhaps more than any other actions, the Great Purges occurring under Stalin's rule symbolized political terror. There was, however, a rational element or motivation in the purge mentality—creating a mechanism whereby bureaucratic leaders could be circulated and/or replaced. Thus, the purge becomes a way to prevent social arthritis and it provides social mobility to junior officials in the organization's hierarchy. Even the expectation (and fear) of replacement can be a way to "keep things moving" and thereby guard against bureaucratic immobility.

3. The term "unpravlenie" itself virtually disappears from the scientific literature in 1930-1953. In an atypical work, however, A. Arakelian concludes that it ". . . coordinates numerous production elements [and] transforms labor by means of the purposive work of man." *Upravlenie Sotsialisticheskoi Promyshlennost'iu (The Management of Socialist Industry)* (Moscow: "Moskovskii Ravochii," 1947), p. 4. While such a treatment ran dangerously close to voluntarism—by stressing management's historical task of securing Soviet economic independence from the imperialist bloc—attacks were not forthcoming against the author.

4. Although most treatments of micro-management were mundane as well as conceptually barren, analysts could and did examine questions like intra-firm planning, production control, and accounting. And a tradition of "scientific management" did remain alive in machine building, where the Society of Machine-Building (*Vintomash*) published several reference books, including *Organizatsiia I Ekonomika Mashinostroitei 'nogo Proizvokstva (The Organization and Economics of Machine-building Production)*, (Moscow: "Mashgiz," 1951).

5. Robert Conquest reviews this episode, *Power and Policy in the USSR: The Struggle for Stalin's Succession, 1945–1960* (New York: Harper & Row, 1961), pp. 88–111.

6. Ibid., pp. 88–89.

7. Richard Judy points to the significance of this omission, in "The Economists," in H. Gordon Skilling and Franklyn Griffiths (eds.), *Interest Groups In Soviet Politics*, (Princeton: Princeton University Press, 1971), p. 221.

8. For a good review of this work, see Katz, *The Politics Of Economic Reform In The Soviet Union*, pp. 35–40.

9. Ibid., pp. 30–34.

10. Initially, the Dictator was so impressed with this book that he awarded it the Stalin prize. But after receiving lavish praise, *The War Economy* was suddenly withdrawn from circulation and Voznesensky condemned for paying tribute to dead dogmas.

11. Voznesensky was probably purged less for the content of his economic ideas than for the perceived political threat he posed for Stalin.

12. Katz, *Politics of Economic Reform*, p. 35.

13. This "affair" involved the purge of Zhdanov's coterie in Leningrad. While much remains obscure, Georgi Malenkov—aspiring to bigger and better things in the Politburo power struggle—played a major role.

14. In 1953, several prominent doctors, many of them Jewish, were arrested for

allegedly plotting to kill members of the Party and government. Since Israel had become an independent state in 1948, Stalin probably envisioned sinister foreign ties to a disloyal national minority.

15. "Kto-kogo" has been the classic approach to political struggle in Kremlin high politics. Unfortunately, observers sometimes undervalue the stakes in political conflict—the right to pursue certain policies.

16. Beria was arrested *after* the ill-fated Berlin uprising (June 17, 1953). He was thought to favor some sort of "neutrality' for a reunited Germany and was reputedly preparing to play such a foreign policy card in his own campaign for political leadership.

17. Katz, *Politics Of Economic Reform*, pp. 55–60.

18. For the classic statement on the totalitarian model of Soviet politics, see Carl J. Friedrich and Zbigniew K. Brzezinski, *Totalitarian Dictatorship And Autocracy*, (New York: Praeger, 1966).

19. Recognizing a gap between aspiration and performance is commonly thought to be a powerful inducement to innovation in the organizational setting. For an excellent survey of the literature on organizational innovation, see Gerald Zaltman, Robert Duncan, and Jonny Holbek, *Innovations And Organizations* (New York: John Wiley, 1973).

20. Katz, *Politics of Economic Reform*, pp. 54–56.

21. Judy, "Economists," p. 225.

22. Judy uncovers such a leader-follower relationship in the editorial commentary of *Vestnik Akademii Nauk SSSR*, No. 3 (1956). See "The Economists," p. 226.

23. At bottom, the leadership's critique at the Twentieth Congress focused on the utter separation of economic theory and research from the practical work of communist construction.

24. Judy, "Economists," p. 232.

25. Khruschev would fashion "de-Stalinization" into a formidable political tool in 1957–1964. But there were severe limitations in how far—and fast—he could proceed. Indeed, an inherently ambiguous line would always divide Stalin's henchmen from the mass of Party cadres who, in fact, profited from his reign.

26. The *sovnarkozy* reform proved to be a fiasco. Rather than improving the rationality of central planning, it created great pressures for local autarky and exacerbated regional conflicts over scarce resources.

27. I. Cherniak and I. Bitiukov, "Noveishie Napravleniia Razvitiia Nauki Upravleniia v Kapitalisticheskikh Starnakh" ["Latest Trends in the Development of Management Science in Capitalist Countries"] in D.M. Gvishiani (ed.), *Itogi Nauki: Seria Organizatsiia Upravleniia, Vypusk I*, (Moscow, 1971), p. 11.

28. Conservative Soviet economists (e.g., L. Gatovskii and K. Ostrovitianov) sharply attacked several East European specialists, particularly V. Brus of Poland, for suggesting that "equilibrium" prices ought to be shaped by forces of supply and demand.

29. Katz, *Politics of Economic Reform*, p. 80.

30. See Wassily Leontief, "The Decline and Rise of Soviet Economic Science," in W. Leontief (ed.), *Essays In Economics: Theories And Theorizing* (New York: Oxford, 1966), p. 227.

31. Kruk, *Razvitie Theorii i Praktiki Upravleniia Proizvodstvom V SSSR*, p. 287.

32. For example, after *Economics And Mathematical Methods* was charged with publishing "useless abstract theorizing," six members of its editorial board were replaced in early 1975.

33. The contributions to this volume, a genuine watershed in the development of mathematical economics, have been reviewed by L. Johansen, *The Economic Journal*, No. 303 (September 1966).

34. The All-Union Scientific Conference on the Application of Mathematical Methods to Economic Research and Planning was held on April 4–8, 1960, at the Academy of Sciences. Organized by various Academy institutes (e.g., Law, Economics, Philosophy), there were over 500 specialists in attendance and fifty-six papers were circulated. See "Mathematical Methods in Economics," *Management Science* 4 (July 1961).

35. See Loren Graham, "Cybernetics," in George Fisher (ed.), *Science And Ideology In Soviet Society* (New York: Atherton Press, 1967).

36. The fact that Berg, a world-renowned scholar, was placed in charge of the Council, signalled the importance of cybernetics to certain economic "rationalizers" in the political leadership.

37. A.N. Kolmogorov, *Kibernetika (Cybernetics)* (Moscow, 1958), p. 149.

38. A.I. Berg, *Kibernetika Na Sluzhbu Kommunizmu (Cybernetics In The Service Of Communism)*, (Moscow, 1961), p. 29.

39. Political economists typically argue that EMM is an applied discipline which—although taught to economic planners—is an inadequate *theoretical* basis for economic science or management.

40. While specialists often referred to doctrinal concepts and/or categories, their debate on economics and administrative science after 1957 began to focus on methods for improving managerial practice.

41. Political economists, as a rule, ask questions for which the answers are known in advance. They are determined to uncover how society's economic base determines socio-political as well as administrative trends. A necessary end point of their analyses is that the socialist economy develops "objectively," i.e., according to observable laws, in regularized, systematic fashion. Of course, this is in sharp contrast to the anarchy, class conflict, spontaneity, etc. inherent in capitalist society.

42. Administrative law specialists stress the voluntaristic nature of management. Consequently, it is more art than science, more form than content, and more amenable to conscious, purposive manipulation by human activity.

43. "The treatment of production management only as an attribute of the superstructure inevitably leads to the denial of the objectivity of . . . *planomernost'*. Thus, *planomernost'* does not appear as an inherent feature of socialist production, but rather as some kind of externally introduced trait by activities of the superstructure." E.P. Dunaev, "Mesto i Rol' Upravleniia Proizvodstvom v Sistem Obshchestvennykh Otnoshenii" ["The Place and Role of Production Management in the System of Social Relations"] *Vestnik Moskovskogo Universiteta*, ser. VIII (ekonomika, filosofiia), no. 6 (1960): 5.

44. Dunaev, "Mesto i Rol' Upravleniia Proizvodstvom," p. 6.

45. V.N. Volovich, *Mesto I Rol' upravlencheskikh Otnoshenii Proizvodstva V Ekonomicheskoi Strukture Sotsialisticheskogo Obshcestva (The Place And Role Of Administrative Relations of Production In The Economic Structure Of Socialist Society)* (Leningrad, 1975), p. 5.

46. I.N. Gal'perin and E.L. Lartikian, *Khoziaistvennoe Rukovodstvo I Planirovanie Sotsialisticheskoi Ekonomikoi (Managerial Leadership And Planning In The Socialist Economy)* (Kharkov, 1963), p. 4.

47. M.G. Babin, "Problema Nauchnoi Organizatsii Truda v Sovetskoi Ekonomicheskoi Literature Dvatsatykh Godov" ["The Problem of the Scientific Organization of Labor in the Soviet Economic Literature of the 1920's"] (Moscow: Ph.D. dissertation, 1966), p. 5.

48. In 1957, a bibliographical index of American and British sources appeared in the USSR containing citations from 33 different management journals, including *Administrative Science Quarterly, British Management Review, Management Science* and numerous others. See *Organizatsiia I Upravlenie Proizvodstvom V Kapitalishicheskikh Predpriiatiiakh Anglii I SSHA (The Organization And Management Of Production In Capitalist Factories In England And The USA)* (Moscow, 1957).

49. Soviet NOTists usually treat worker satisfaction as one factor in a long checklist of technological elements that influence production efficiency. For a typical view, see P. Serb, "Nauchnaia Organizatsiia Truda na Rabochem Meste" ["The Scientific Organization of Labor in the Workplace"]*Sotsialisticheskii Trud*, no. 8 (August 1964):33.

50. Attempts to link morale, satisfaction, and cohesiveness to productivity have consistently failed to reveal a simple, compelling relationship. Indeed, individuals can perceive rewards as unrelated, or even negatively correlated, to their own productivity. Part of the confusion in the organizational science literature stems from the analyst's failure to distinguish between *turnover* (i.e., the decision to participate) and *productivity* (i.e., the decision to produce at the rate demanded by the organization's leadership). See James March and Herbert Simon, *Organizations* (New York: John Wiley, 1958), pp. 47–82.

51. If conflict is idiosyncratic, then its resolution can occur without disturbing the systemic traits of socialism. To be sure, different individuals, rather than different organizational roles or a new macro-economic structure, are required to "rationalize" the system.

52. Estonian specialists told RV that in the early 1960's NOTists vigorously tried to raise production efficiency in several factories in the Republic. But their skills proved no match for their zeal and few organizational improvements were actually made. The scientific organization of labor failed, according to these specialists, because of the narrow technical-engineering background of the NOTists.

53. Initiated in the Leningrad "Svetlana" plant (1969), the social planning movement has since expanded to include factors like recreation facilities, leisure time, health care, etc. And it is now commonly recognized that factors existing within the enterprise are an inadequate basis for purposively directing social improvements in worker collectives.

54. N.S. Khrushchev, "Razvitie Ekonomiki SSSR i Partiinoe Rukovodstvo Narodnym Khoziaistvom" ["Development of the Economy in the USSR and Party Leadership of the National Economy"] *Pravda* 20 November 1962, p. 3.

55. Iu.N. Dubrovskii, "Problemy Teorii i Praktiki Nauchnoi Organizatsii Truda" ["Problems of the Theory and Practice of the Scientific Organization of Labor"] *Vestnik Moskovskogo Universiteta*, ser. VII (ekonomika), no. 6 (November-December, 1970), p. 51.

56. When Soviet theorists use the term "complex approach" to management, they usually mean one from an interdisciplinary perspective.

57. A.M. Birman, *Nekotorye Problemy Nauki O Sotsialisticheskom Khoziaist-Vovanii (Certain Problems On The Science Of Socialist)* (Moscow: "Ekonomicheskoi Literatury," 1963), pp. 10–11.

58. S. Kamenitser, "Upravleniiu Promyshlennym Proizvodstvom. Nauchnuiu Osnovu" ["Managing Industrial Production. The Scientific Bases"] *Sotsialisticheskii TTUD*, no. 11 (1965):48.

59. By stressing the socialist dimension of theory, specialists would examine phenomena at the level of the entire national economy. Since capitalism is incapable (by definition) of managing its affairs at the systems level, ideologues insist that the private capitalist firm remains the proper subject matter for the science of management.

60. N.V. Adfel'dt, "Problemy Organizatsiia Upravleniia Nauchnym Khoziaistvom" ["Problems of Organizing Management by Scientific Administration"] *Voprosy Filosofii*, no. 3 (1965): 15.

61. N. Adfel'dt, "Management Personnel and the Science of Administration," *Ekonomicheskaia Gazeta*, no. 40 (September 29, 1962), p. 7; translated in *Current Digest Of The Soviet Press*, 14, no. 40 [October 31, 1962]: p. 3).

62. Several crucial articles include: I.Ia. Kasitskii, "O Nauke Upravleniia Proizvodstvom" ["On the Science of Production Management"] *Kommunist*, no. 15 (1962); N.V. Adfel'dt, "Khoziaistvennye Kadry i Nauka Upravleniia"["Economic Cadres and the Science of Management"] *Ekonomicheskaia Gazeta*, 29 September 1962; D.M. Gvishaini, "Razvivat' Nauki Upravleniia" ["Develop the Science of Management"] *Ekonomicheskaia Gazeta*, 16 March 1963; V.N. Lititsyn, "Ot Oglavleniia—k Nauke" ["From the Table of Contents to Science"] *Ekonomicheskaia Gazeta*, 26 October 1963.

63. I. Kasitskii, "Problemy Izucheniia Nauchnoi Organizatsii Upravlenchskogo Truda" ["Problems of Studying the Scientific Organization of Managerial Labor"] *Sotsialisticheskii Trud*, no. 8 (August 1964):50.

64. For example, see D.M. Gvishiani, "The Organization of Management," *Izvestia*, 7 June 1966, p. 3 (Excerpted in SDSP 18, no. 23 [Jula 29, 1966]:).

65. L. Kachalina, "Problemy Nauchnoi Organizatsii Upravlencheskogo Truda" ["Problems of the Scientific Organization of Managerial Labor"] *Kommunist*, no. 15 (October 1964):45.

66. Kasitskii, "O Nauke Upravleniia Proizvodstvom," pp. 66–67.

67. For a strong promotion of PERT in the USSR, see V. Reskim, "Chto Takoe PERT?" ["What is PERT?"] *Sotsialisticheskii Trud*, no. 8 (August 1964).

68. Zygmunt Bauman has shown where and how Soviet specialists purposively used the idea of Polish sociology to promote an independent field in the USSR. See Zygmunt Bauman, "Eastern European and Soviet Social Science: A Case Study in Stimulus Diffusion," in R. Szporluk (ed.) *The Influence Of East Europe And The Soviet West On The USSR* (New York: Praeger, 1976).

69. For a distinction between *symbolic* and *substantive* emulation, see Richard F. Vidmer, "The Emergence of Administrative Science in the USSR: Toward a Theory of Organizational Emulation" *Policy Sciences* 11 (1979).

70. D.M. Gvishiani, *Sotsiologiia Biznesa (Sociology Of Business)* (Moscow: Sot-

sial'no-Ekonomicheskaia Literatury, 1962). Administrative specialists in Estonia told me that this book was a crucial message to move ahead with analyzing U.S. management techniques.

71. Change agents in large organizations often hold out new ideas as a *return* to orthodox practices, thereby hoping to undercut those favoring the status quo.

72. Gvishiani, *Sotsiologiia Biznesa*, p. 63.

73. See Barry Richman, *Management Development And Education In The Soviet Union* (East Lansing, Michigan: Michigan State University Press, 1967), p. 246.

74. Richman, *Management Development And Education*, p. 248.

75. Iuksviarav has also written widely on American management "schools" of thought and various analytical traditions in the U.S.

76. The Literary Gazette article appeared in June 22, 1965.

77. If both socialism and capitalism develop in similar fashion, then there would be no *objective* basis to differentiate them. Naturally, such a conclusion is anathema to Soviet ideologues.

78. For example, see M.V. Popov and N.A. *Moiseenko, Demokraticheskii Tsentralizm: Osnovnoi Printsip Upravlenii Sotsialisticheskoi Ekonomikoi (Democratic Centralism: Basic Principle of Managing The Socialist Economy)* (Leningrad: "Lenizdat," 1975). Of couse, to these authors, the only true science of management in socialist society is political economy.

79. E.G. Liberman's editorial in *Pravda* (September 1962) touched off a prolongued debate in management circles about the proper role of the socialist enterprise in socialist society. By stressing profitability as its main performance criteria, specialists favoring Lieberman's proposals saw dramatic repercussions throughout the entire economic system.

80. For a good view of the administrative law perspective on management, see Iu.A. Tikhomirov et al., "O Nauke Upravleniia" ["On the Science of Management"] *Sovetskoe Gosudarstva I Pravo*, no. 9 (1964).

81. D.M. Gvishiani, "Problemy Upravleniia Sotsialisticheskoi Promyshlennost'iiu" ("Problems Of Managing Socialist Industry") *Voprosy Pilosofii*, no. 11 (1966): 10.

6. The Brezhnev Period and "Collective Leadership"

1. See G.K. Popov, *Problemu Teorii Upravleniia*, p. 174.

2. Paul Cocks, "The Rationalization of Party Control."

3. Katz, *The Politics of Economic Reform in the Soviet Union*, esp. Chap. 7.

4. Gvishiani's capacity to play such a role was enhanced by his position as deputy chairman of the state committee on science and technology and his kinship ties with Premier Kosygin.

5. For an excellant analysis of power and politics under Khrushchev, see Carl Linden, *Khrushchev and the Soviet Leadership, 1957–1964* (Baltimore: Johns Hopkins Univ. Press, 1966).

6. Katz, *Politics of Economic Reform*, p. 130.

7. See Karl Ryavec, *Implementation of Soviet Economic Reforms: Political, Organizational, and Social Processes* (New York: Praeger, 1975).

8. For an examination of Gatovskii's promotion of mathematical economics, see

Aron Katsenelinboigen, *Soviet Economic Thought and Political Power in the USSR* (New York: Pergamon, 1980), pp. 71–74.

9. See Katz, *Politics of Economic Reform*, esp. chap. 8.

10. D. Kruk, *Razvitie Teorii I Praktiki Upravleniia Proizvodtvon V SSSR (Development of the Theory and Practice of Production Management in the USSR)* (Moscow, 1974), p. 190.

11. Ibid, p. 193.

12. See D.M. Gvishiani, et al., eds., *Materialy K Vsesoiuznoi Nauchno-Tekhnicheskoi Konferentsii (Materials on the All-Union Scientific-Technical Conference)* (Moscow, 1966).

13. Kruk, *Razvitie Teorii I Praktiki*, p. 191.

14. Indeed, being branded a mere "technician" is a severe rebuff to Soviet analysts.

15. For a good examination and criticism, see Jerman Gvishiani and Gavrill Popov, "Developments in the Theory of Management within the planned Socialist Economy," in Geert Hofstede and M. Sami Kassem, eds., *European Contributions to Organization Theory* (Amsterdam: Van Gorcum, 1976).

16. Ibid.

17. Ibid., p. 164.

18. R.K. Iuksviarav, "Nekotorye Vazheishie Voprosy Upravleniia Promyshlennost'iu i ikh Razrabotka" ("Certain Very Important Questions on the Management of Industry and their Elaboration"), in Gvishiani, et al. eds., *Materialy K Vsesoiuznoi Nauchno-Tekhnicheskoi Konferentsii*, p. 353.

19. To be sure, our judgment as to the status of modern techniques in the USSR today rests on our selection criteria. By standards of past Stalinist practices, progress has been impressive. In comparison to the achievements in advanced Western countries, however, the Soviets have a long way to go.

20. For example, there has been a review article—with virtually no critical commentary—on the work of Zaltman, Duncan, and Holbek, *Innovations and Organizations*.

21. L.V. Savel'ev, interview held in Tallinn, Estonian SSR, 27 April 1976

22. I. Cherniak and I. Bitukov, "Noveishie Napravleniia Razvitiia Nauki Upravleniia v Kapitalisticheskikh Stranakh," in D. M. Gvishiani, ed., *Itogi Nauki: Seriia Organizatsiia Upravleniia* (Moscow: VINITI, 1971), p. 11.

23. For example, consider the following analyses of American management: S.M. Men'shikov and N.E. Mnogolet, *SShA: Ekonomicheskie Rychagi v Upravlenii Firmami* (Moscow: "Nauka," 1971); S.M. Men'shikov, ed., *Noveishie Tendentsii v Organizatsii Upravleniia Krupnymi Firmami v SShA* (Moscow: "Nauka," 1966); I.P. Vasil'ev, *Novaia Tekhnika v Sisteme Upravleniia Proizvodstvom za Rubezhom* (Moscow: Progress, 1972); and I.I. Razumova, *SShA: Organizatsiia Upravleniia Zavodami* (Moscow: "Nauka," 1975).

24. Vadim Ivanovich Marshev, interview held at the Center of Management Problems, Moscow State University, 12 July 1976.

25. These specialists are usually involved with various adaptations of American approaches in their own research: R. Iuksviarav, I. Marshev, and L.I. Evenko.

26. Gvishiani, *Organization and Management*, p. 143.

27. Ibid, pp 144–45.

28. Ibid., p. 233.

29. Ibid., P. 249.

30. Ibid., p. 312.

31. Gvishiani reviewed the Leavitt-Whisler article, "Management in the 1980s," in considerable detail. In sum, it is an optimistic assessment of the capacity of modern information-gathering technology to promote the recentralization of corporate structures.

32. In an interview in Ann Arbor, Michigan, on 8 April 1977, Murray Feshback made this point.

33. The materials used in this section have been provided by D.D. Aufenkamp of the National Science Foundation. Aufenkamp is the U.S. chairman of the U.S.-USSR Joint Working Group in the Application of Computers to Management.

34. D.D. Aufenkamp, "Trip Report of the U.S. Delegation on 'Computer-Aided Refinement of Decision-Making and Education of High-Level Executives' to the USSR, September 18–30, 1975," National Science Foundation, 1976. Prior to this review, the only American-authored study of Soviet management education was Barry Richman, *Management Development and Education in the Soviet Union* (1976).

35. This was revealed to the authors by Professor Thomas Schreiber of the University of Michigan's Graduate Business School.

36. For a general review of these conferences, see Lyudmila Yenyutina, "Management: Exchange of Views," *Soviet Life* (April 1975): 54–56.

37. For a review of the history, structure, and research program of the centre, see Riccardo Petrella and Adam Schaff, *A European Experiment in Cooperation in the Social Sciences* (Vienna: European Coordination Centre for Research and Documentation in Social Sciences, 1974).

38. Arnold S. Tannenbaum, et al., *Hierarch in Organizations* (San Francisco: Jossey-Bass, 1974).

39. Petrella and Schaff, *European Experiment*, p. 41.

40. Information for this section was gathered on a three-month visit to IIASA, June-August, 1975, sponsored by the International Research and Exchanges Board.

41. "Sotrudnichestvo Uchenykh," *Pravda*, 5 August 1976.

42. This occurred in response to questions from the audience at a public lecture sponsored by the society "Znanie" at Moscow State University. Considerable interest was expressed in the functioning of the International Institute of Applied Systems Analysis as well as Soviet efforts in this field. D.M. Gvishiani, "Problemy Organizatsii i Upravleniia v Svete Reshenii XXV S"ezda KPSS," public lecture given at MGU, 2 June 1976.

43. This was the cause of some tension between Soviet and non-Soviet participants. Indeed, the former appeared more interested in copying materials, rather than in conducting research. Moreover, the possibility for senior research personnel to take extended leaves from their institutions in the USSR may be seriously limited. If such leaves are difficult to arrange, then IIASA would have problems in securing the most capable Soviet scientists.

44. These publications, unfortunately, have been slow to materialize. In fact, by 1976, the only material that found its way into print was "Systems Analysis: An

Outline for the State-of-the-Art Survey Publications." This was little more than a review of general aspirations for the project and various categories for analysis.

45. This examination of the TVA experience has been published. See H. Knop, ed., *The Tennessee Valley Experience* (Laxenburg: IIASA, 1976).

7. Organized Anarchies in the United States and "Americanizers" in the Soviet Union

1. John Steinbrunner, *The Cybernetic Theory of Decision* (Princeton, N.J.: Princeton Univ. Press, 1974), p. 9.

2. Ibid.

3. Herbert A. Simon, *The Architecture of Complexity* (Cambridge, Mass.: MIT Press, 1968), pp. 84–118.

4. Steinbrunner, *Cybernetic Theory*, pp. 35–36.

5. See Irving Janis, *Victims of Groupthink* (Boston: Houghton-Miflin, 1972).

6. Steinbrunner, *Cybernetic Theory*, pp. 40–44.

7. Robert Coulam, *Illusions of Choice* (Princeton, N.J.: Princeton Univ. Press, 1977).

8. Franklin C. Spinney, *Defense Facts of Life* (Mimeograph, 1980).

9. Morton Halperin, *Bureaucratic Politics and Foreign Policy* (Washington, D.C.: Brookings Institution, 1974).

10. Coulam, *Illusions*, chap. 6.

11. Thomas S. Kuhn, *The Structure of Scientific Revolutions*, 2d ed. (Chicago: Univ. of Chicago Press, 1970).

12. See, for example, Clagett G. Smith, "A Comparative Analysis of Some Conditions and Consequences of Intraorganizational Conflict," *Administrative Science Quarterly*, 10, (1966): 504–29; and Eugene Litwak, "Models of Organization Which Permits Conflict," American Journal of Sociology, 67, (1961): 177–85.

13. Allison, *Essence of Decision*, p. 145.

14. Ibid.

15. James March and Johann P. Olsen, *Ambiguity and Choice In Organizations* (Bergen, Norway: Universitatforlaget, 1976), p. 85. For other writings on organized anarchies, see Michael P. Cohen, James G. March, and Johann P. Olsen, "A Garbage Can Model of Organization Choice," *Administrative Science Quarterly*, 17 (March 1972): 1–25; and Michael D. Cohen and James G. March, *Leadership and Ambiguity* (New York: McGraw-Hill, 1974), esp. chap. 5 and 9. For earlier insight, see Philip Selznick, *Leadership in Administration* (Evanston, Ill.: Ron, Peterson, 1957).

16. Ibid.

17. Todd R. LaPorte, "Organized Social Complexity" in Todd R. LaPorte, ed., *Organized Social Complexity* (Princeton, N.J.: Princeton Univ. Press, 1975), pp. 3–39).

18. John Gerard Ruggie, "Complexity, Planning and Public Order," in LaPorte, ed., *Organized Social Complexity*, pp. 119–150.

19. Ibid., p. 129.

20. See James Clay Thompson, *Rolling Thunder*, chap. 4, for an extended discussion of this problem.

21. Ibid., p. 133.

22. For an extended examination of Americanizers in Soviet administrative science, see Richard F. Vidmer, "Management Science in the USSR: The Role of Americanizers," *International Studies Quarterly*, 24 (September 1980): 392–414.

23. See Evenko, "Sistemnyi Analiz—Sushchnost' i Osnovy metodologii," in B.Z. Mil'ner, ed., *SShA: Sovermennye Metody Upravleniia* (Moscow: "Nauka," 1971).

24. It appears that the published studies of Mil'ner's research team regarding American methods of management have found expression, albeit to a limited degree, in *Organizatsionnye Struktury Upravleniia Proizvodstvom* (Moscow: "Ekonomika," 1975).

25. B.Z. Mil'ner, ed., *Organizatsionnye Formy i Metody Upravleniia Promyshlennymi Korporatsiiami* (Moscow: "Nauka," 1972), p. 238.

26. Ibid., p. 242.

27. Ibid., pp. 242.

28. Ibid., p. 244.

29. See in particular, pp. 68–74. Moreover, Evenko's responsibility and status in this publication is heightened by the fact that of the four authors (including Mil'ner), he is listed first.

30. Madis Khabakuk, interview held at the Tallinn Polytechnical Institute, 22 April 1976.

31. See George S. Ordiorne, *Management by Objectives* (New York: Pitman, 1970).

32. S.K. Chakraborty, *Management by Objectives: An Integrated Approach* (New Delhi: Macmillan Co., 1976), p. 4.

33. Madis Khabakuk, "Upravlenie na Osnove Tselei," in *Organizatsiia Upravleniia* (Moscow: "Ekonomika," 1975).

34. Ibid., p. 139.

35. The similarity of Khabakuk's recommendations with certain American approaches is instructive. In this regard, see Kenton Ross, "Implementing a Management by Objectives Philosophy," in *Management by Objectives* (Cleveland: Association for Systems Management, 1971), pp. 9–31.

36. Madis Khabakuk, *Sovershenstvovanie Sistemy Priniatiia Resheniia pri Pomoshchi Dereva Tselei* (System SEKOR) (Tallinn, 1973), p. 5. For a review of the military applications of such optimal decision-making techniques in the United States, see Gvishiani, *Organization and Management*, pp. 347–67.

37. See Derek Newman, *Organizational Design: An Analytical Approach to the Structuring of Organizations* (London: Edward Arnold, 1973).

38. For a good bibliography of Soviet works on organizational structure and design, see *Sovershenstvovanie Organizatsionnoi Struktury Upravleniia Sotsialisticheskim Proivodtvom Kratkii Spisor Literatury na Rukom Iazyke za 1970–1975* (Moscow, 1973).

39. Cocks, "Retooling the Directed Society," p. 70.

40. Thus, the 1971 and 1972 studies by the Mil'ner team found expression in *Organizatsionnye Struktury* (1975).

41. It is suggested that this sequence was "not accidental," i.e., the American referent was a "learning experience" for Soviet analysts.

42. Mil'ner, *SShA: Sovremennye Metody*, pp. 57–61.

43. Mil'ner, *Organizatsionnye Struktury*, pp. 147–73.

44. Mil'ner, *Organizatsionny Formy i Metody*, p. 32.

45. Mil'ner, *Organizatsionnye Struktury*, p. 84.

46. For a brief review of the "life cycle" concept, see Mil'ner, *Organizatsionnye Formy*, pp. 32, 243.

47. For instance, the apparent failure to fully implement the suggestions of scientists and specialists (presumably the Mil'ner team) led to a public critique of the *"Uralelektrotiazhmash"* project. See I. Riabov, "Sovershenstvovat' Strukturu Upravleniia," *Izvestia*, 18 January 1976, p. 3.

48. The analysis of structure per se, as opposed to decision making, data processing, research and design, or particular analytic schools, appears to be Mil'ner's specialty.

49. See Fremont A. Shull, *Matrix Structure and Project Authority for Optimizing Organizational Capacity* (Carbondale: Southern Illinois Univ., School of Business, October 1965), p. 65.

50. Cocks, "Retooling the Directed," p. 71.

51. The Mil'ner team's analysis of program-goal structures is contained in *SShA: Sovremennye Metody Upravleniia*.

52. Ibid., p. 56.

53. Mil'ner, *Organizatsionnye Struktury*, p. 109.

54. This is the designation for graduates from the Department of the Planning of Industrial Production at the Plekhanov Institute.

55. Vitaly Ozira, "How Teaching Is Done at a School of Business," Literaturnia Gazeta, 41 (October 1968): 11; partially translated in Current Digest of the Soviet Press, 1 (November 1968): 15.

56. For example, see V. I. Ozira, "Obuchenie pri Pomoshchi Analiz Khoziaistvennykh Situatsii," Vestnik Moskovskogo Universiteta ser. (Economik), 5 (1968).

57. See V. I. Ozira, *Ob Opyte Shveinogo Ob" edineniia 'Bol'shevichka na Novuiu Sistemu Khoziaistvovaniia* (Moscow: MGU, 1969).

58. See V. I. Ozira and A.E. Luzin, *Konsul'tatsionnye Firmy 'Kapitalisticheskikh Stran po Upravleniiu* (Moscow: "Ekonomika," 1975).

59. V. I. Ozira, interview held at the Moscow Institute of the National Economy, 26, May 1976.

60. B.M. Mochalov, "The Application of Active Educational Methods in the USSR" National Science Foundation, 1975), p. 2.

61. V.I. Ozira, "Concrete Cases in Management Education" (Washington, D.C.: National Science Foundation, 1975).

62. Shorin's assessment was noted by D.D. Aufenkamp during his 1975 trip to the Soviet Union for the exchange agreement.

63. John Austin, personal communication, 21 June 1977.

64. Robert Graham and Clifford Grey, *Business Games Handbook* (Washington, D.C.: American Management Association, 1969), p. 17. Our commentary on business gaming draw heavily from this account.

65. "Gaming involves case studies because many games can be traced to individual or collective analysis of particular cases and because the nature of the post game analysis takes on many of the qualities of a case study." Ibid., p. 18.

66. V.I. Marshev and A.K. Popov, "Upravlencheskie Igry kak Metod Sovershen-

stvovaniia Upravleniia: Analiz Zarubezhnogo Opyta i Metodologicheskie Problemy," in G.K. Popov, ed, *Problemy Organizatsii Sovershenstvovaniia Upravleniia Sotsialisticheskim Proizvodstvom* (Moscow: Moskovskogo Universiteta, 1975), p. 172.

67. Our analysis of the Syroezhin system borrows heavily from this translation. Certain American observers, including John Lubin, characterize this approach as "collective decision games."

68. I.M. Syroezhin, I.I. Kurochkin, and S.R. Gidrovich, *Simulated Game Models as a Means of Management Training and a Form of Collective Decision-Making* (Leningrad, 1975), p. 14.

69. Ibid., pp. 1–2.

70. Ibid., p. 31. The attention to positive results is consistent with the normative-prescriptive purposes of the Soviet administrative paradigm. Indeed, the theory of the socialist enterprises is a prescriptive *(predpisyvaiushchaia)* notion.

71. Ibid., pp. 32–33.

72. Ibid., pp. 34–35.

73. Ibid., p. 42. These conclusions permits an "enlightened" approach to conflict in socialist systems, which, in turn, might weaken the dominant paradigm in Soviet administrative science.

74. These conditions are remarkably similar to those reviewed by Graham and Grey in *Business Games Handbook*.

75. This was noted in D.D. Aufenkamp, "Trip Report of US Delegation on 'Computer-Aided Refinement of Decision-Making," National Science Foundation, Washington, D.C., 1975, p. 17.

76. For a description of EPOS, see S.R. Givrovich and I.M. Syroezhin, *Igrovoe Modelirovanie Ekonomicheskikh Protsessov* (Moscow: "Ekonomika," 1976).

77. These games were briefly described by Aufenkamp in "Trip Report of U.S. Delegation," pp.15–17.

78. The differences (and competition) between the Moscow and Leningrad (i.e., Syroezhin) approaches to business gaming were suggested by G.K. Popov, interview held at MGU Management Center, 7 June 1976.

79. Despite the general similarities with American conceptions, substantial differences remain, e.g., the number of functioning games in the Soviet Union is quite modest and the availability of computing facilities is restricted, at least for purposes of teaching/training managerial personnel. Myron Uretsky, personal communication, 21 June 1977.

80. The similarity to Shubik's work was pointed out by Marshev, interview held at the MGU Management Center, 28 June 1976.

81. See V.I. Marshev, "Khoziaistvennye Situatsii i Upravlencheskie Igry v Obuchenii Ekonomistov i Rukovodiashchikh Kadrov," *Vestnik Moskovskogo Universiteta* ser. 7 (ekonomika), 2 (1975).

82. According to Marshev, this text has been translated as *Rukovodstvo po Delovym Igram* and is used at the MGU Center.

83. Some of these publications include the following: A. Galos and V. Sokolov, "The Business Game: A Method for Studying Complex Systems," *Active Systems*, Institute of Management Problems, Moscow, 1973; V. Burkov et al., *The Organization and Construction of Business Games* (Methodological Instructions), Moscow, IPU, 1975).

84. For a description of relevant activities, see "Delovye Igry i ikh Programmnoe Obespechenie," *Ekonomika i Matematicheskis Metody*, 3 (1976):602.

8. The Current "Jungle" in Soviet Management Theory

1. This chapter draws inspiration as well as specific questions from Harold Koontz's seminal article on the "jungle" in U.S. management science. See Harold Koontz, "The Management Theory Jungle," *Journal of the Academy of Management*, 4 (December 1961). Koontz uncovered more than simply academic disputes in the field. Theorists and would-be cult leaders were intent on carving out a distinct, if not original, approach to management. And to defend their position, they are willing and able to downgrade and/or misrepresent what others had said, thought, or done. Koontz's analysis of the American jungle also sheds light on the current situation in the USSR.

2. The emergence of this stage has been explicitly connected to the *possibility* and *necessity* of developing a socialist science of management. See G.K. Popov, *Problemy Teorii Upravleniia*, 2d ed., rev. & enl. (Moscow: "Ekonomika," 1974), p. 206.

3. Paul Cocks, "Retooling the Directed Society: Administrative Modernization and Developed Socialism," in Jan Triska and Paul Cocks, eds., *Political Development in Eastern Europe* (New York: Praeger, 1977), p. 84.

4. The *voluntaristic* element in economic development is stressed by certain theorists, notably administrative lawyers. Nevertheless, others pay more attention to deterministic concepts like *planomernost'* and emphasize that objective laws or *zakonomernosti* play a predominant role in economic affairs.

5. For an interesting examination of the organizational constraints on planned administrative change, see Karl Ryavec, *Implementation of Soviet Economic Reforms: Political, Organizational, and Social Processes* (New York: Praeger, 1975).

6. D.M. Gvishiani, "The Scientific and Technological Revolution and Social Progress," *Pravda*, 2 March 1974, pp. 3–4; partially translated in *Current Digest Of The Soviet Press*, 26, 27 March 1974, pp. 8–9.

7. For a good analysis of the Soviet literature, see Erik Hoffmann, "Soviet Views of the 'Scientific-Technological Revolution,' " *World Politics*, 4 (July 1978).

8. Cocks, "Retooling the Directed Society," p. 84.

9. This is consistent with Holloway's characterization of cybernetics in the USSR. David Holloway, *Technology, Management, and the Soviet Military Establishment* (London: ISS, 1971). But cybernetics may be but one of a multiplicity of competing definitions of *upravlenie*.

10. V. Afanasyev, "Further Improvement of the Management of Soviet Society," *Social Science*, 3 (September 1972):71.

11. For a good examination of that literature, see Robert F. Miller, "The Scientific-Technical Revolution and the Soviet Administrative Debate," in Paul Cocks, Robert Daniels, and Nancy W. Heer, eds., *The Dynamics of Soviet Politics* (Cambridge, Mass.: Harvard Univ. Press, 1976); Robert F. Miller, "The New Science of Administration in the USSR," *Administrative Science Quarterly*, 3 (1971); Alfred Zauberman, *The Mathematical Revolution in Soviet Economics* (London: Oxford, 1975); Michael Ellman, *Planning Problems in the USSR* (Cambridge: University

Press, 1973); Loren Graham, "Cybernetics," in George Fisher, ed., *Science and Ideology in Soviet Society* (New York: Atherton, 1967); Donald Schwartz, "Recent Soviet Adaptations of Systems Theory to Administrative Theory," *Journal Of Comparative Administration*, 2 (1973); Erik Hoffmann, "The 'Scientific Management' of Soviet Society," *Problems of Communism* (May-June 1977); Richard F. Vidmer, "The Emergence of Administrative Science in the USSR: Toward a Theory of Organizational Emulation," *Policy Sciences*, 1 (August 1979); idem, "Administrative Science in the USSR: Doctrinal Constraints on Inquiry," *Administration and Society*, 12 (May 1980); idem, "Management Science in the USSR: The Role of 'Americanizers,' " *International Studies Quarterly*, 24 (September 1980); Paul Cocks, "The Rationalization of Party Control," in Chalmers Johnson, ed., *Change in Communist Systems* (Stanford, Cal.: Stanford Univ. Press, 1970); Paul Cocks, "Rethinking the Organizational Weapon: The Soviet System in a Systems Age," *World Politics*, 32 (January 1980).

12. I. Kasitskii, "Problemy Izucheniia Nauchnoi Organizatsii Upravlencheskogo Truda," *Sotsialisticheskii Trud*, 8 (August 1964): 51.

13. I.A. Tikhomirov, *Vlast' I Upravlenie V Sotsialisticheskom Obshechestve* (Moscow: "Iuridicheskaia Literatura," 1968).

14. This chapter deals with Soviet *perspectives* on management theory, rather than with specific behaviors associated with administrative reform. Indeed, there are great differences between theory and practice, and even sophisticated developments in management science do not mean that the economy's performance will improve. But nevertheless, significant organizational changes have already occurred in the USSR because of the political leadership's increasing attention to management science. See Erik Hoffmann, Soviet Information Processing: Recent Theory and Experience," *Soviet Union*, 2 (1975).

15. Hoffmann arrives at a similar conclusion, only with respect to Soviet writings on the STR. See Erik Hoffmann, "Soviet Views on the Scientific-Technological Revolution.' "

16. This task was initially set forth by Brezhnev at the 1971 CPSU Congress and strongly reiterated at the 25th Party Congress held in 1976.

17. Marxists envisioned bureaucracy as largely a technical problem. Once stripped of its bourgeois character, the conditions would exist for the eventual withering away of state agencies. But production organizations would undergo quantitative, not qualitative, changes under proletarian rule, despite the expectation that workers would occupy key managerial roles in the new order. See Jeremy Azrael, *Managerial Power and Soviet Politics* (Cambridge: Harvard Univ. Press, 1966), pp. 12–27.

18. O.A. Pozdniakov, *O Problemakh Nauchnoi Organizatsii Truda I Upravleniia* (Moscow: "Lenizdat," 1969), p. 19.

19. *Referativnyi Ukazatel' Teknicheskoi Literatury* was widely distributed in the Soviet Union.

20. Vigilant examination of every major approach or school of thought in the 1920s could expose ideological and/or political deviance. For example, A.K. Gastev's micro-analysis *(rubka zubilom)* and preoccupation with separate work operations and the individual worker simply ignored the broader social context. And it proved difficult, if not impossible, to clearly separate this view from pure Taylorism. Soviet Fayolists were criticized for overemphasizing the subjective factor (human will) and

were charged with philosophical idealism. E.F. Rozmirovich's "production treatment" reputedly generalized Taylorism to analysis of the USSR's production and state apparatus as a whole. Macro-level theorizing, especially that done by mathematical economists, had too many advocates of balanced growth and equilibrium to suit those dedicated to overtaking the advanced countries of the West. Finally, A.A. Bogdanov ignored dialectical materialism and instead argued that tektology—reputedly an integrative "science of sciences"—had a *universal* character. Not surprisingly, Bogdanov was denounced as a heretic and buffoon, charged with idealism, and forbidden to play any further role in social and political life.

21. M.G. Babin, 'Problema Nauchnoi Organizatsii Truda v Sovetskoi Ekonomicheskoi Literature Dvadtsatykh Godov," Ph.D. diss., Moscow State University, 1966), p. 5.

22. For obvious doctrinal reasons, there would be little talk in the Soviet administrative literature about "intelligent gorillas," the Taylorist conception of the worker. And to their credit, many Soviet theorists felt more comfortable dealing with technical rationalization, rather than raising labor intensification.

23. At the Second Conference on *NOT* (March 1924), V.V. Kuibyshev emphasized that the scientific organization of labor was not a general system, but rather a technique to improve labor productivity.

24. For an excellent review of the rationalization movement, see Paul Cocks, "The Rationalization of Party Control," in Chalmers Johnson, ed., *Change In Communist Systems* (Standard, Cal.: Stanford Univ. Press, 1970).

25. See O.A. Deineko, "Izuchat' i Obobshchat' Organizatsionnyi Opyt Proshlogo," in A.I. Berg, ed., *Organizatsiia I Upravlenie: Voprosy Teorii I Praktiki* (Moscow: "Nauka," 1968).

26. Cocks, "The Rationalization of Party Control," p. 161.

27. The works of analytical economists like V.A. Bazarov and V.G. Groman were also cut off before they reached maturity. Both were Mensheviks, worked in Gosplan, and disappeared from public life in the early 1930s. See Richard Judy, "The Economists," in Gordon Skilling and Franklyn Griffiths, eds., *Interest Groups in Soviet Politics* (Princeton, N.J.: Princeton Univ. Press, 1971).

28. For a good review of administrative science in this period, see D. Kruk, *Razvitie Teorii I Praktiki Upravleniia Proizvodstvom V SSSR* (Moscow: Vsesoiuznyi Zaochnyi Finansovo-Ekonomicheskii Institut, 1974).

29. J. Stalin, *Economic Problems of Socialism in the USSR* (New York, 1952), p. 72.

30. Robert Miller has noted the administrative law sanctuary for the scattered remnants of theoretical inquiry. "The New Science of Administration in the USSR," *Administrative Science Quarterly*, 18 (September 1971): 248–50.

31. This is Alfred Zauberman's depiction. *The Mathematical Revolution in Soviet Economics* (London: Oxford Univ. Press, 1975). However, it should be pointed out that capitalist managers have traditionally made decisions on a similar trial-and-error basis.

32. See Judy, "Economists," p. 225.

33. Some of these ideas had been openly discussed by Soviet theorists in the 1920s. And their attraction to contemporary management specialists supports Cocks's trenchant observation that every search for something new in the USSR is in certain

respects a search for something lost. Thus, to solve pressing problems, the Soviet leadership has consciously looked to its own past for relevant examples and experience. See Cocks, "Rationalization of Party Control," p. 184.

34. L.V. Kantorovich not only made important contributions to mathematics in the mid-1930s, but published the first application of linear programing in 1939. However, this innovative work lay inert in the USSR until the late 1950s, i.e., until *after* the parallel work of U.S. theorists had been widely circulated.

35. For a good review of the emergence of cybernetics in the Soviet Union, see Loren Graham, "Cybernetics," in George Fisher, ed., *Science and Ideology in Soviet Society* (New York: Atherton Press, 1967).

36. Babin, "Problema Nauchnoi Organizatsii Truda v Sovetskoi Ekonomicheskoi Literature Dvadtsatykh Godov," p. 2.

37. Researchers have been unable to agree on whether *NOT* should deal primarily with scientific methods in the workplace (technical rationalization), the optimal arrangement of equipment and space (organizational rationalization), or the creative development of workers themselves (social rationalization).

38. Gvishiani spoke *authoritatively* to specialists in the field because of personal credentials: he is Kosygin's son-in-law.

39. Despite the devastating impact of cybernetics and EMM on political economy, that field continues to exert substantial political as well as institutional muscle in the field.

40. This movement is perhaps best symbolized by Soviet participation in the International Institute of Applied Systems Analysis in Vienna. Along with the United States, the USSR bears the greatest financial burden in this multi-national venture.

41. For a good illustration of such a defense, see I. Solovyev's article in *Pravda*, 4 June 1973, p. 2.

42. See Richard F. Vidmer, "Management Science in the USSR: The Role of 'Americanizers,' " *International Studies Quarterly*, 24 (September 1980).

43. The possibility and necessity of developing socialist theory can be attributed to changes occurring after the October 1964 plenum, i.e., *after* the political demise of Khrushchev. See Popov, *Problemy Teorii Upravleniia*, p. 206.

44. A.M. Erëmin, *Otnosheniia Sotsialisticheskoi Sobstvennosti I Ekonomicheskoe Upravlenie* (Moscow: "Ekonomika," 1973), p. 51.

45. Hoffmann correctly points out that such dichotomies serve an important ideological function, namely, to deny undue Western influence in Soviet society. See Hoffman, "Soviet Views of 'the Scientific-Technological Revolution,' " p. 626.

46. I.M. Syroezhin, a prominent Leningrad game theorist, pointed out these four schools during a research visit by Vidmer to the USSR in 1976.

47. This classification scheme avoids various micro-analytical approaches, such as *NOT*, the sociology of labor, and social planning in the collective. Although these fields can provide important data for managers and consultants, administrative theorists (mainly economists) regard them as excessively narrow, capable of dealing only with certain "aspects" of management. Of course, sociologists disagree with such conclusions.

48. This came to light after numerous interviews had been conducted by Vidmer with Soviet management specialists in Moscow, Leningrad, and Tallinn.

49. Ironically, there has been no review of Soviet approaches to match Gvishiani's trenchant analysis of management science in the United States. See D.M. Gvishiani, *Organization and Management: A Sociological Analysis of Western Theories* (Moscow: Progress, 1972).

50. For an attempt to order the field's terminological chaos, see I.S. Mangutov and L.I. Umanskii, *Organizator I Organizatorskaia Deiatel 'Nost'* (Leningrad: Leningradskogo Universiteta, 1975).

51. G. Anisimov, "O Predmete Politicheskoi Ekonomii," *Kommunist*, 18 (1966): 90.

52. I.M. Syroezhin, *Ekonomicheskaia Kibernetika: Chast' I, Osnovy Teorii Khoziaistvennyky Sistem* (Leningrad: Leningradskogo Universiteta, 1974), p. 30. And Syroezhin also believes that economic phenomena cannot be examined in a special theory, apart from the apparatus of political economy.

53. F. Binshtok, *Nauka Upravliat'* (Moscow: "Moskovskii Rabochii," 1967), p. 20.

54. D. Kruk, *Nekotorye Problemy Teorii Upravleniia Sotsialisticheskim Proizvodstvom* (Alma-Ata, 1970), p. 13.

55. Political economists have been challenged by theorists, mainly administrative lawyers, who regard *upravlenie* as primarily a voluntaristic phenomena, i.e., purposive human leadership. And whereas many acknowledge a complex intermingling of elements, they nevertheless emphasize its economic essence.

56. V.N. Volovich, *Mesto I Rol' Upravlencheskikh Otnoshenii Proizvokstva V Ekonomicheskoi Strukture Sotsialisticheskogo Obshchestva* (Leningrad, 1975), p. 5.

57. A.M. Erëmin, *O Sisteme Ekonomicheskikh Nauk* (Moscow: "Znanie," 1968).

58. This conclusion was suggested to Vidmer by certain management specialists in Leningrad, April 1976.

59. V.I. Oligin-Nesterov, *Ispol'Zovanie Ekonomicheskikh Zakonov Sotsializma I Upravlenie Proizvodstvom* (Moscow:"Mysl'," 1973), p. 48.

60. N.A. Moiseenko and M.V. Popov, *Demokraticheskii Tsentralizm—Osnovnoi Printsip Upravleniia Sotsialisticheskoi Ekonomikoi* (Moscow: "Lenizdat," 1975), p. 144.

61. V. Shcherbitskii, "Partiinye Organizatsii i Sovershenstvovanie Upravleniia Ekonomikoi," *Kommunist*, 6 (April 1973):19–33; excerpted in *Current Digest of the Soviet Press*, 25 3, October 1973):6.

62. This designation was suggested to Vidmer by I.M. Syroezhin in 1976. The term "empirical" does not refer to the micro-accumulation of data with the explicit purpose of describing and/or explaining organizational behavior. On the contrary, Soviet theorists focus on prescriptive recipes to improve managerial performance. And the approach that concentrates on training managerial cadres constitutes an empirical view to them.

63. Dale's contribution to the empirical approach in the West has been noted by Koontz, *Management Theory Jungle*, p. 177.

64. For a good illustration, see N. Adfel'dt, "Management Personnel and the Science of Administration," *Ekonomicheskaia Gazeta*, 40 (29 Sept. 1962): trans. in *Current Digest of the Soviet Press*, 14 (31 Oct. 1962):3.

65. For a detailed examination of this bias in Soviet administrative theorizing, see Richard F. Vidmer, "Administrative Science in the USSR: Doctrinal Constraints on Inquiry," *Administration and Society*, 12 (May 1980): 69–80.

66. For example, see B.Z. Mil'ner, ed., *Organizatsionnye Formy I Metody Upravleniia Promyshlennymi Korporatsiiami* (Moscow: "Nauka," 1972).

67. Madis Khabakuk, "Professional Loyalty and Its Influence on Managerial Decision Making," *International Studies of Management and Organization*, 2 (Summer 1972):197–212.

68. O.A. Deineko finds 21 disciplines relevant for management, *Metodologicheskie Problemy Nauki Upravleniia Proizvodstvom* (Moscow: "Nauka," 1970).

69. Gavriil Popov has said that "if *planirovanie* constitutes the heart of the Soviet economy, then *upravlenie* makes up its body." Interview, Moscow, June 1976.

70. In Popov's theory, *rukovodstvo* involves deductive principles generated at various levels of abstraction. By contrast, *isskustvo* deals with inductive principles based on generalizing managerial experience. They combine, in synthesis, to adumbrate the subject matter of socialist management science. See Popov, *Problemy Teorii Upravleniia*.

71. Popov, *Problemy Teorii Upravleniia*, p. 174.

72. In 1976 Moscow State University's Management Center had over $150,000 in consulting contracts with various agencies, including Gosplan RSFSR. Gavriil Popov, interview, Moscow, June 1976.

73. N.E. Drogichinskii, ed., *Sovershenstvovanie Mekhanizma Khoziaistvovaniia V Usloviiakh Razvitogo Sotsializma* (Moscow: "Ekonomika," 1975), p. 24. Drogichinskii has been head of a department in Gosplan for the introduction of innovative planning techniques.

74. A.P. Malkov, *Ekonomika, Upravlenie I Planirovanie Promyshlennogo Proizvodstva* (Kazan: Kazanskogo Universiteta, 1974), p. 196.

75. Ellman, *Planning Problems in the USSR*, esp. chap. 3.

76. To this check list might be added another factor, namely, the apparently successful work done in the United States by specialists like T.C. Koopmans and George Dantzig.

77. Ellman, *Planning Problems in the USSR*, p. 57.

78. For example, a biting criticism of the growing gap between theory and policy-relevant studies was included among the editorial commentary on the tenth anniversary (1975) of *TsEMI's* journal. Thereupon, in the next issue, a major shakeup of the editorial board was announced.

79. Aganbegian heads the prestigious *Institute Of Economics and Organization of Industrial Production* in Novosibirsk. The institute was originally staffed largely with former specialists from *TsEMI*, but there has been a recent migration of theorists back to Moscow.

80. For a good illustration of this trend, see V.S. Dadaian and R.L. Raiatskas, "Integrirovannye Makromodel'nnye Kompleksy," *Ekonomika I Matematicheskie Metody*, 12 (1976): 256–67.

81. For example, in 1976 a research group was integrated into *Gosplan* in Lithuania. Although the research group had no operational responsibilities at that time, researchers shared the same building and facilities with *Gosplan's* line personnel.

82. Some of the greatest semantic entanglements in Soviet management science

concern the relative importance of the concepts *upravlenie, planirovanie,* or *rukovodstvo.*

83. Such definitions, it should be noted, permit these specialists to carve out a meaty subject matter for themselves.

84. Ellman, *Planning Problems in the USSR,* p. 65.

85. Ibid., p. 141.

86. Graham, *Cybernetics,"* p. 86.

87. For an insightful view on how Soviet theorists have adapted cybernetic to administrative theory, see Donald V. Schwartz, "Recent Soviet Adaptations of Systems Theory to Administrative Theory," *Journal of Comparative Administration,* 2 (August 1973).

88. V.I. Ikonnikov, *Osnovnye Aspekty Formirovaniia Nauki Upravleniia Obshchestvennym Proizvodstvom* (Moscow, 1969), p. 3.

89. A.N. Kolmogorov, *Kibernetika* (Moscow, 1958), p. 149.

90. A.I. Berg, *Kibernetika Na Sluzhbu Konnumizmu* (Moscow, 1961), p. 29.

91. For a good illustration, see A.A. Godunov, *Sotsial'Noekonomicheskie Problemy Upraveleniia Sotsialisticheskim Proizvodstvom* (Moscow: "Ekonomika," 1975).

92. V.G. Shorin, ed., *Aktual'Nye Problemy Upravleniia* (Moscow: "Znanie," 1972).

93. A.S. Petrov, *Chto Takoe Organizatsiia Upravleniia* (Moscow: "Znanie," 1967), p. 40.

94. For a review of some of these arguments, see Erik Hoffman, "Soviet Information Processing: Recent Theory and Experience," *Soviet Union II,* 1 (1975): 22–49.

95. I.M. Syroezhin, ed., *Ekonomicheskaia Kebernetika: Chast' I, Osnovy Teorii Khoziaistvennykh Sistem* Leningradskogo Universiteta, 1974).

96. I.M. Syroezhin, I.I. Kurochkin, S.R. Gidrovich, *Simulated Game Models as a Means of Management Training and a Form of Collective Decision-Making (Leningrad, 1976). This monograph was presented as part of the U.S.-USSR cultural exchange in management science.*

97. *For a Soviet view of where ASU has been most successfully utilized,see V.G. Afanas'ev et al., Upravlenie Sotsialisticheskim Proizvodstvom: Voprosy Teorii I Praktiki* (Moscow: "Ekonimika," 1975), pp. 510–516.

98. For an examination of this Institute as well as the role of D.G. Zhimerin in its formation, see Wade Holland, "A Tsar for Soviet Computing," *Soviet Cybernetic Review,* 6 (November 1972).

99. The major elements of this approach have been described by Syroezhin, "Man-Machine Systems in the USSR," *Management Science,* 2 (October 1968): b-6.

100. Trapeznikov is often identified with a distinctive trend in Soviet cybernetics which, inter alia, is considerably more complex than the views promoted by the Institute of Cybernetics.

101. Moreover, some have argued that systems theory is a *concretization* of dialectical materialism. See A.S. Petrov, *Ekonomicheskie Osnovy Upravleniia Proizvodstvom* (Moscow: "Mysl'," 1966), p. 4.

102. I.M. Kozlov, *Upravlenie Narodnym Khoziaistvom SSR, Chast' I* (Moscow: Moskovskogo Universiteta, 1969), p. 4.

103. Even within a given institute, however, the diversity of competing views can be striking. For example, at the Voznesenskii Finance-Economics Institute in Leningrad, Ivan Syroezhin is a game theorist who has borrowed liberally from U.S. concepts and methods; I. Lavrikov, Rector of the Institute, is a traditional political economist; and V. Andreev is a management empiricist.

104. Koontz, "Management Theory Jungle."

105. For example, G.K. Popov recommends that a "special mechanism" be formed, perhaps modeled on *RABKRIN*, to help rationalize the economic mechanism. This would unite the knowledge and experience of scholars with that of managers in order to help formulate and then evaluate relevant policies. See Popov, *Problemy Teorii Upravleniia*, p. 150.

106. Zimmerman would characterize the interplay of conflicting forces in administrative science as a regulative policy process. See William Zimmerman, "Issue Area and Foreign-Policy Process: A Research Note in Search of a General Theory," *The American Political Science Review*, 67 (1973).

107. This is Paul Cocks's terminology. For a trenchant analysis of contemporary Soviet politics, see Paul Cocks, "Rethinking the Organizational Weapon: The Soviet System in a Systems Age," *World Politics*, 32 (January 1980): pp. 228–57.

108. Of course, only the CPSU has the strategic position in the Soviet establishment and the *political* authority to process demands, i.e., to pick and choose among competing claims. And it has shown *purposiveness* in pressing for innovative (and largely Western) techniques, much to the chagrin of many political economists as well as conservative party hacks.

109. For an interpretation of Soviet administrative theory as a repressive political ideology, see Michael E. Urban, "Bureaucracy, Contradiction and Ideology in Two Societies," *Administration and Society* (May 1978).

Epilogue

1. Michael Ellman, *Planning Problems in the USSR: The Contribution of Mathematical Economics to Their Solution 1960–1971* (Cambridge: University Press, 1973), p. 12.

2. For a brief review of the history and structure of this center, see Popov, Problemy Teorii Upravmeniia, rev. 2d ed., pp. 277–296.

3. The fact that the 1974 edition of *Problemy Teorii Upravleniia*, in distinction from the first edition, had a modest array of Western referents and citations was surely not accidental.

4. These include the following: (1) G.K. Popov and V. Lisitsyn, "Krugozor Khoziaistvennika," *Pravda*, 19 Jan. 1968, p. 2; (2) G.K. Popov and V. Lisitsyn, "Khoziaistvovanie: Problemy i Suzhdeniia," *Pravda*, 2 Dec. 1968, p. 2; (3) G.K. Popov, "Nauka Upravliat'," *Pravda*, 28 Feb. 1970, p. 2; (4) G.K. Popov and V. Poshataev, "Strategiia Upravleniia," *Pravda*, 15 Dec. 1971, p. 2.

5. G.K. Popov and V. Lisitsyn, "Krugozor Khoziaistvennika," *Pravda*, 19 Jan. 1968, p. 2.

6. Ibid., p. 2.

7. Popov, *Problemy Teorii Upravleniia*, p. 4.

8. Ibid., p. 48.

9. Ibid., p. 57.

10. Barry Richman, *Soviet Management: With Significant American Comparisons* (Englewood Cliffs, N.J.: Prentice-Hall, 1965).

11. Popov defines the management of socialist production in the following manner:

The management of socialist social production—is a ceratin type of laboring *activity, necessary* and *possible* owing to a definite level of the development of production forces and the socialization of a decisive part of the means of production; *which is based on* the creative utilization of the objective laws (most importantly, economic, but also natural-technical, organizational, social psychological) which are peculiar to the object of management—to socialist production and *directed* to the realization of the demands of these laws; *carried out* by the system of management, which includes the organs of the socialist state, social organizations and every worker, united and led by the Communist Party, which correspond to the laws, peculiar to the process, general for various types of management in the socialist formation and, finally, the laws which emerge under the synthesis of general and specific features which attain the character of art, of creativity. [Popov, *Problemy Teorii Upravleniia,* p. 89—emphasis in the original.]

12. Ibid., p. 90.

13. Ibid., p. 103.

14. Ibid., pp. 103–4.

15. Ibid., p. 129.

16. Although Popov feels that the process of management is an integral part of socialist theory, his subsequent treatment (1975) revelas the normative, rational bias in the Soviet administrative paradigm. The attention to how the system *should* function not only avoids descriptive analysis, but reveals little of how to implement this idealized imagery in practice. G.K. Popov, ed., *Organizatsiia Protsessov Upravleniia* (Moscow: "Ekonomika," 1975).

17. Popov, *Problemy Teorii Upravleniia,* p. 109.

18. Ibid., p. 140.

19. Ibid., p. 150.

20. Ibid., p. 187.

21. Ibid., p. 189.

22. Ibid., p. 173.

23. Ibid., p. 172.

24. Ibid., p. 174.

Selected Bibliography

Abernathy, William, and Robert Hayes. "Management Minus Invention." *New York Times*, 20 Aug. 1980, p. D2.

Adfel'dt, N.V. "Khoziaistvennye kodryi nauka upravleniia" ("Economic cadres and the science of management"). *Ekonomicheskaia gazeta*, 29 Sept. 1962.

———. "Management personnel and the science of administration." *Ekonomicheskaia gazeta*, no. 40 (29 Sept. 1962): 7; trans. in *Current Digest of the Soviet Press*, 14 (31 Oct. 1962): 3.

———. "Problemy organizatsiia upravleniia nauchnynov khoziaistvom" ("Problems of organizing management by scientific administration"). *Voprosy filosofii*, no. 3 (1965): 15.

Afanasyev, V. "Further Improvement of the Management of Soviet Society." *Social Science, 3* (September 1972):71.

———, et al. *Upravlenie sotsialisticheskim proizvodstvom: voprosy teorii i praktiki (Management of Socialist Production: Questions of Theory and Practice)*. Moscow: "Ekonomika," 1975.

Allison, Graham T. *Essence of Decision: Explaining the Cuban Missile Crisis*. Boston: Little, Brown, 1971.

Anisimov, G. "O Predmete politicheskoi ekonomii" ("On the Subject Matter of Political Economy"). *Kommunist*, 18 (1966):90.

Anonymous. "Delovye igry i ikh programmnoe obespechenie." *Ekonomika i matematicheskie metody*, 3 (1976):602–4.

———. "Systems Analysis: An Outline for the State-of-Art Survey Publications." Laxenburg, Austria: International Institute of Applied Systems Analysis," 1976.

Arakelian, A. *Upravlenie sotsialisticheskoi promiphlennast'iw (The management of Soviet Industry.)* Moscow: "Moskovskii Ravochii," 1947.

Argyris, Chris, and Donald Schon. *Organizational Learning: A Theory of Action Perspective*. Reading, Mass. Addison-Wesley, 1978.

Asch, Solomon. *Social Psychology*. Boston: Little, Brown, 1951.

Aufenkamp, D.D. "Trip Report of the U.S. Delegation on Computer-Aided Refinement of Decision-Making and Education of High-Level Executives to the USSR, September 18–30, 1975." National Science Foundation, 1976.

Azrael, Jeremy. *Managerial Power and Soviet Politics*. Cambridge, Mass.: Harvard Univ. Press, 1966.

Babin, M.G. "Problema nauchnoi organizatsii truda v sovetskoi ekonomicheskoi literature dvadtsatykh godov" ("The Problem of the Scientific Organization of Labor in the Soviet Economic Literature of the 1920s"). Ph.D. diss., Moscow State University, 1966.

Barnard, Chester. *The Functions of the Executive.* Cambridge, Mass.: Harvard Univ. Press, 1938.

Bauman, Zygmunt. "Eastern European and Soviet Social Science: A Case Study in Stimulus Diffusion." In *The Influence of East Europe and the Soviet West on the USSR,* ed. R. Szporluk. New York: Praeger, 1976.

Bendix, Reinhard. *Max Weber: An Intellectual Portrait.* Berkeley: Univ. of California Press, 1978.

Berg, A.I. *Kibernetika na sluzhbu konnumizmu (Cybernetics in the Service of Communism).* Moscow: 1961.

Berkovich, D.M. *Formirovanie nauki upravleniia proizvodst'vom (Formation of the Science of Production Management).* Moscow: "Nauka," 1973.

Binshtok, F. *Nauka upravliat.* Moscow: "Moskovskii rabochii," 1967.

Birman, A.M. *Nekotorye problemy nauki o sotsialisticheskom khoziaistivovanii (Certain Problems on the Science of Socialism).* Moscow: "Eknomicheskoi Literatury," 1963.

Bogdanov, A.A. *Ykazatel' proizvedeniia (An Index of Works).* Moscow: 1925. Quoted in David Kruk, *Razvitie teorii i praktiki upravleniia proizvodstvom v USSR (The Development of Theory and the Practice of Production Management in the USSR).* Moscow: 1974.

Bogolepov, V.P. "O Sostoianii i zadachakh razvitiia obshchei teorii organizatsii" ("On the Status and Tasks of Developing a General Theory of Organization"). In *Organizasiia i upravlenie: voprosy teorii i praktiki,* ed. A.I. Berg. Moscow: "Nauka," 1968.

Brezezinski, Zbigniew, and Samuel Huntington. *Political Power: U.S.A./U.S.S.R.* New York: Viking, 1963.

Brinkehoff, Merlin B., and Phillip R. Kunz, eds. *Complex Organizations and Their Environments.* Dubuque, Ia.: W.C. Brown, 1972.

Bronfenbrenner, Urie. *Two Worlds of Childhood: U.S. and U.S.S.R.* New York: Russell Sage Foundation, 1970.

Bronowski, Jacob. *The Ascent of Man.* Boston: Little, Brown, 1974.

Brown, Harold. *Department of Defense Annual Report: Fiscal Year 1982.* Washington, D.C.: Defense Printing Office, 1981.

Burkov, V., et al. *The Organization and Construction of Business Games (Methodological Instructions).* Moscow: IPU, 1975.

Carey, Alex. "The Hawthorne Studies: A Radial Criticism." *American Sociological Review,* 33 (1968):403–16.

Caro, Robert. *The Power Broker: Robert Morse and the Fall of New York City.* New York: Random House, 1975.

Chakraborty, S.K. *Management by Objectives: An Integrated Approach.* New Delhi: Macmillan Co., 1976.

Charnovskii, N.F. *Tekhniko-ekonomicheskie printsipy v metallo-promyshlennosti (Technical Economic Principles in the Metal Industry).* Moscow: "Orgmetall," 1927.

Cherniak, I., and I. Bitukov. "Noveishie naprovleniia razvitiia nauki upravleniia v kapitalisticheskikh stranakh" ("Latest Trends in the Development of Management Science in Capitalist Countries"). In *Itogi nauki: seriia organizatsiia upravleniia*, ed. D.M. Gvishiani. Moscow: VINITI, 1971.

Cincinnatus. *Self Destruction: The Disintegration and Decay of the U.S. Army during the Vietnam Era*. New York: Norton, 1981

Cocks, Paul. "The Rationalization of Party Control." In *Change in Communist Systems*, ed. Chalmers Johnson. Stanford, Cal.: Stanford Univ. Press, 1970.

――. "Rethinking the Organizational Weapon: The Soviet System in a Systems Age." *World Politics*, (22 January 1980): 228–57.

――. "Retooling the Directed Society: Administrative Modernization and Developed Socialism." In *Political Development in Eastern Europe*, ed. Jan Triska and Paul Cocks. New York: Praeger, 1977.

Cohen, Michael D., and James G. March. *Leadership and Ambiguity*. New York: McGraw-Hill, 1974.

Conquest, Robert. *Power and Policy in the USSR: The Struggle for Stalin's Succession, 1945–1960*. New York: Harper & Row, 1961.

Coulam, Robert. *Illusions of Choice*. Princeton, N.J.: Princeton Univ. Press, 1977.

Cray, Ed. *Chrome Colossus: General Motors and Its Times*. San Francisco: McGraw-Hill, 1979.

Crozier, Michel. *The Bureaucratic Phenomenon*. Chicago: Univ. of Chicago, 1964.

Cyert, Richard, and James March. *A Behavioral Theory of the Firm*. Englewood Cliffs, N.J.: Prentice-Hall, 1963.

Dadaian, V.S., and R.L. Raiatskas. "Integrirovannye makromodel 'nye kompleksy" (Integrated Macromodel Complexes"). *Ekonomika i matematicheskie metody*, 2 (1976). 256–267

Dallin, Alexander, and George Breslauer. "Political Terror in the Post-Mobilization Stage." In *Change in Communist Systems*, ed. Chalmers Johnson. Stanford, Cal.: Stanford Univ. Press, 1970.

Dalton, Melville. *Men Who Manage*. New York: Wiley, 1959.

Daughen, Joseph, and Penter Binzen. *The Wreck of the Penn Central*. Boston: Little, Brown, 1971.

Deineko, O.A. "Izuchat' i obobshchat' organizatsionnyi opty proshlogo" ("Study and Generalize from the Organizational Experience of the Past"). In *Organizatsiia i upravlenie voprosy teorii i praktike*, ed. A.I. Berg. Moscow: "Nauka," 1968.

――. *Metodologicheskie problemy nauki upravleniia proizvodstvom (Methodological Problems of The Science of Production Management)*. Moscow: "Nauka," 1970.

Deutsch, Karl. *The Nerves of Government*. New York: Free Press, 1966.

Downs, Anthony. *Inside Bureaucracy*. Boston: Little, Brown, 1967.

Drezin, E. *Rukovodstvo po organizatsii upravlenscheskogo apparata sovetskikh uchrezhdenii (Leadership of Organizations in the Administrative Apparatus of Soviet Institutions)*. Moscow: "NKRKI," 1927.

Drogichinskii, N.E., ed. *Sovershenstvovanie mekhanizma khoziaistvovaniia v usloviiakh rozvitogo sotslalizma*. Moscow: "Ekonomika," 1975.

Dubrovskii, I.N. "Problemy teorii i praktiki nauchnoi organizatsii truda" ("Problems of the Theory and Practice of the Scientific Organization of Labor"). *Vestnik moskovskogo universiteta*, ser. 7 (Ekonomika), no. 6 (November–December 1970):51.

Dunaev, E.P. "Mesto i rol' upravleniia proizvodstvom v sistem obshchestvennykh otnoshenii" ("The Place and Role of Production Management in the System of Social Relations"). *Vestnik moskavskogo universiteta*, ser. 8 (Ekonomika, Filosofia), no. 6 (1960):5.

Ellman, Michael. *Planning Problems in the USSR: The Contribution of Mathematical Economics to their Solution 1960–1971*. Cambridge: University Press, 1973.

Erëmin, A.M. *O sisteme ekonomicheskikh nauk*. Moscow: "Znanie," 1968.

_____. *Otnosheniia sotsialisticheskoi sobtvennosti i ekonomicheskoe upravlenie*. Moscow: "Ekonomika," 1973.

Ermanskii, O.A. *Nauchnaia organizatsiia truda dvadtsatykh godov. Sbornik Documentov i materialov (The Scientific Organization of Labor in the 1920s)*. Kazan: Economic Literature, 1965.

Eulan, Heinz. *Micro-Macro Political Analysis*. Chicago: Aldine, 1969.

Evenko. "Sistemnyi analiz—sushchnost' i osnovy metodologii." In *SShA: Sovermennye metody upravleniia*, ed. B.Z. Mil'ner. Moscow: "Nauka," 1971.

Fallows, James. *National Defense*. New York: Random House, 1981.

Farnsworth, Clyde, Agis Salpukas, Peter Schuyten, Henry Scott Stokes, and Edward Cowan. "Reviving Industry: The Search for a Policy." *New York Times*, 18–22 Aug. 1980, pp. 1, 1, 1, D1, D1.

Ford, Henry. *My Life and Work*. Garden City, N.Y.: Doubleday, 1922; reprint ed. New York: Arno, 1976.

Franke, Richard, and James Kaub. "The Hawthorne Experiments: First Statistical Interpretation." *American Sociological Review*,43 (1978): 623–43.

Friedrich, Carl J., and Zbigniew K. Brezezinski. *Totalitarian Dictatorship and Autocracy*. New York: Praeger, 1966.

Galos, A., and Sokolov, V. "The Business Game: A Method for Studying Complex Systems." *Active Systems*. Moscow: IPU, 1973.

Gal'perin, I.N., and E.L. Lartikian. *Khoziaistvennoe rukovodstvo i planirovanie sotsialistichoskoi ekonomikoi (Managerial Leadership and Planning in the Socialist Economy)*. Kharkov: 1963.

Gardner, Burleigh B. "The Factory as a Social System." In *Industry and Society*, ed. W.F. Whyte. New York: McGraw-Hill, 1946.

Gastev, Aleksei Kapitonovich. *How One Should Work*. Moscow: "Ekonomika," 1966.

Godunov, A.A. *Sotsial 'noekonomicheskie problemy upravleniia sotsialisticheskim proizvodstvom*. Moscow: "Ekonomika," 1975.

Gouldner, Alvin. "Organizational Analysis." In *Sociology Today*, ed. Robert K. Merton, Leonard Broom, and Leonard S. Cottrell, Jr. New York: Basic Books, 1959.

Graham, Loren. "Cybernetics." In *Science and Ideology in Soviet Society*, ed. George Fisher. New York: Atherton Press, 1967.

Graham, Robert, and Clifford Grey. *Business Games Handbook*. New York: American Management Ass'n, 1969.

Gredeskul, N.A. *Trudy i vserossiiskoi initsiativnsi konferentsii po nauchnoi organizatsii truda i proizvodstva (Works of the First All-Russian Conference on the Scientific Organization of Labor and Production)*. Moscow, 1921.

Gullick, Luther, and Lyndall Urwick eds. *Papers on the Science of Administration*. New York: Institute of Public Administration of Columbia University, 1937.

Gvishiani, D.M. *Organization and Management: a Sociological Analysis of Western Theories*. Moscow: Progress, 1972.

———. "The Organization of Management." *Izvestia*, 7 June 1966:3; excerpted in SDSP18, no. 23 (29 July 1966).

———. "Problemy organizatsii i upravleniia v sveti reshenii XXV s'ezda KPSS." Public lecture given at Moscow State University, 2 June 1976.

———. "Problemy upravleniia sotsialisticheskoi promyshlennost 'iiu" ("Problems of Managing Socialists Industry"). *Voprosy pilosofii*, no. 11 (1966):10.

———. "Razvivat' nauki upravleniia" ("Develop the Science of Management"). *Ekonomicheskaia gazeta*, 16 Mar. 1963.

———. "The Scientific and Technological Revolution and Social Progress." *Pravda*, 2 Mar. 1974:3–4; excerpted and trans. in *Current Digest of the Soviet Press*, 26 (27 Mar. 1974):8–9.

———. *Sotsiologiia biznesa (Sociology of Business)*. Moscow: Sotsial'no-ekonomicheskia literatury, 1962.

———, et al., eds. *Materialy k vsesoiuznoi naucho-tekhnicheskoi konferentsii (Materials on the All-Union Scientific-Technical Conference)*. Moscow: 1966.

Gvishiani, Jerman, and Gavrill Popov. "Developments in the Theory of Management within the Planned Socialist Economy." In *European Contributions to Organization Theory*, ed. Gurt Hofstede and M. Sami Kassem. Amsterdam: Van Gorcum, 1976.

Halperin, Morton. *Bureaucratic Politics and Foreign Policy*. Washington, D.C.: Brookings Institution, 1974.

Hoffman, Erik. "The Scientific Management of Soviet Society." *Problems of Communism* (May–June 1977).

———. "Soviet Information Processing: Recent Theory and Experience." *Soviet Union II*, 1 (1975).

———. "Soviet Views of the Scientific-Technological Revolution." *World Politics*, 4 (July 1978).

Holland, Wade. "A Tsar for Soviet Computing." *Soviet Cybernetic Review*, 6 (November 1972).

Holloway, David. *Technology, Management, and the Soviet Military Establishment*. London: ISS, 1971.

Holsti, Ole R. "Individual Differences in Definition of the Situation." *Journal of Conflict Resolution*, 13 (1970):303–311.

Huntington, Samuel. *The Common Defense*. New York: Columbia Univ. Press, 1961.

Ikonnikov, V.I. *Osnovnye aspekty formirovaniia nauki upravleniia obshchestvennym*. Moscow: 1969.

International Institute of Applied Systems Analysis. "Information Gathered during a Three Month Visit Sponsored by the International Research and Exchange Board." June–August 1975.

Iuksviarav, R.K. "Nekotorye vazheishie voprosy upravleniia promyshlennost' iu i ikh razrabotka" ("Certain Very Important Questions on the Management of Industry and Their Elaboration"). In *Materialy k vsesouiznoi nauchno-tekhnicheskoi*, ed. D.M. Gvishiani, et al.

Janis, Irving. *Victims of Groupthink*. Boston: Houghton-Mifflin, 1972.

Judy, Richard. "The Economists." In *Interest Groups in Soviet Politics*, ed. H. Gordon Skilling and Franklin Griffiths. Princeton: Princeton Univ. Press, 1971.

Kanter, Arnold. *Defense Politics: A Budgetary Perspective*. Chicago: Univ. of Chicago, 1980.

Kasitskii, I.I. "O Nauke upravleniia proizvodstvom" ("On the Science of Production Management"). *Kommunist*, no. 15 (1962).

————. "Problemy izucheniia nauchnoi organizatsii upravlenchskogo truda" ("Problems of Studying the Scientific Organization of Managerial Labor"). *Sotsialisticheskii trud*, no. 8 (August 1964):50.

Katsenbogen, B.I. "K Voprosy o teorii sotsialisticheskoi organizatsii proizvodstva" ("On the Question of a Theory of Socialist Production Organization"). *Organizatsiia upravleniia*, 3 (1936):6.

Katsenelinboigen, Aron. *Soviet Economic Thought and Political Power in the USSR*. New York: Pergamon, 1980.

Katz, Daniel, and Robert Kahn. *The Social Psychology of Organizations*. New York: Wiley, 1966; 2d ed. New York: Wiley, 1978.

Kerzhentsev, P.M. *Prinstsipy organizatsii (Principles of Organization)*. Ekatepuhhoyprl: Ypatkhura, 1923.

Kachalina, L. "Problemy nauchnoi organizatsii upravlencheskogo truda" ("Problem of the Scientific Organization of Managerial Labor"). *Kommunist*, no. 15 (October 1964):45.

Kamenitser, S. "Upravleniiu promyshlennym proizvodstvom. Nauchnuiu osnovu" ("Managing Industrial Production: The Scientific Bases"). *Sotsialisticheski TTUD*, no. 11 (1965): 48.

Khabakuk, Madis. "Professional Loyalty and Its Influence on Managerial Decision-Making." *International Studies of Management and Organization*, 2 (Summer 1972):197–212.

————. *Sovershenstvovanie sistemy priniatiia resheniia pri pomoshci dereva tselei (System SEKOR)*. Tallinn: 1973.

————. "Upravlenie na osnove tselei." In *Organizatsiia upravleniia*. Moscow: "Ekonomika," 1975.

Khrushchev, Nikita S. "Razvitie eknomiki SSSR i partiinci rukovodstvo narodnym knoziaistvom" ("Development of the Economy in the USSR and Party Leadership of the National Economy"). *Pravda*, 20 (November 1962):3.

Knop, H., ed. *The Tennessee Valley Experience*. Laxenburg: IIASA, 1976.

Kolmogorov, A.N. *Kibernetika (Cybernetics)*. Moscow: 1958.

Koontz, Harold. "The Management Theory Jungle." *Journal of the Academy of Management*, 4 (December 1961).

Kozlov, I.M. *Upravlenie narodnym khoziaistvom SSR, chast'i.* Moscow: Moskovskogo Universiteta, 1969.

Kruk, D. *Nekotorye problemy teorii upravleniia sotsialisticheskim proizvodstvom.* Alma-Ata: Ekoninomika, 1970.

————. *Razvitie teorii i praktiki upravleniia proizvodtvom v SSSR (Development of the Theory and Practice of Production Management in the USSR)*. Moscow: Vsesoiuznyi zaochnyi finansovo-ekonomicheskii institut, 1974.

Kuhn, Thomas S. *The Structure of Scientific Revolutions*. 2d ed. Chicago: Univ. of Chicago Press, 1970.

Landau, Martin, and Russell Stout, Jr. "To Manage Is Not To Control: Or the Folly of Type II Errors." *Public Administration Review*, 39 (March–April 1979): 148.

LaPorte, Todd R. "Organized Social Complexity." In *Organized Social Complexity*, ed. Todd R. LaPorte. Princeton: Princeton Univ. Press, 1975.

Leontief, Wassily, ed. *Essays in Economics: Theories and Theorizing*. New York: Oxford, 1966.

Levy, Frank, and Edwin Truman. "Toward a Rational Theory of Decentralization: Another View." *American Political Science Review*, 65 (June 1971):: 177.

Lindblom, Charles. "The Science of Muddling Through." *Public Administration Review*, 19 (Spring 1958):79–88.

Linden, Carl. *Khrushchev and the Soviet Leadership*. Baltimore: Johns Hopkins Univ. Press, 1966.

Lititsyn, V.N. "Otoglavleniia—k nauke" ("From the Table of Contents to Science"). *Ekonomicheskaia gazeta*, 26 Oct. 1963.

Litwak, Eugene. "Models of Organization Which Permit Conflict." *American Journal of Sociology*, 67 (1961):177–85.

Liubovich, I.O. *Metody khoziaistvennogo i teknichoskogo rukovodstva proizvodstvom (The Methods of Economic and Technical Production Leadership)*. Moscow: 1938.

——. *Organizatsiia proizvodstva v mashinostroenii Uchebnoe posobie* (Organizing Production in Machine Building: Educational Textbook). Moscow: 1973.

——. *Sotsialisticheskaia organizatsiia proizvodstva kak predmet prepodavaniia (Socialist Organization of Production as the Subject Matter of Teaching)*. Moscow: "Moskovskii Rakochnii," 1938.

Malkov, A.P. *Ekonomika upravlenie i planirovanie promyshlennogo proizvodstva*. Kazan: Kazanskogo universitera, 1974.

Mangutov, I.S., and Umanskii, L.I. *Organizator i organizatorskaia deiatel'nost*. Leningrad: Leningradskogo Universiteta, 1975.

March, James and Johann P. Olson. *Ambiguity and Choice In Organizations*. Bergen, Norway: Universitatforlaget, 1976.

——, March, James, and Herbert A. Simon. *Organizations*. New York: Wiley, 1958.

Marshev, V.I. "Khoziaistvennye situatsii i upravlencheskie igry v obuchenii ekonomistov i rukovodiashchikh kadrov." *Vestnik moskovskogo universiteta*, ser. 7 (Ekonomika), 2 (1975).

McClelland, David. *Personality*. New York: Holt, Rinehart & Winston, 1951.

McKean, Roland. "Criteria of Efficiency in Government Expenditures." In *Public Budgeting and Finance*, ed. Robert T. Golembiewski. Itasca, Ill.: F.E. Peacock, 1968.

Men'shikov, S.M., ed. *Noveishie tendentsii v organizatsii upravleniia krupnymi firmami v SSha*. Moscow: "Nauka," 1966.

——, and N.E. Mnogolet. *SSha: ekonomicheskie rychagi v upravlenii firmami*. Moscow: "Nauka," 1971.

Merton, Robert. "Bureaucratic Structure and Personality." In *Reader in Bureaucracy*, ed. Robert Merton, Ailsa P. Gray, Barbara Hockey, and Hanon Selvin. Glencoe, Ill.: Free Press, 1952.

Miller, Robert F. "The New Science of Administration in the USSR." *Administrative Science Quarterly*, 18 (September 1971):248–50.

Mil'ner, B.Z., ed. *Organizatsionnye formy i metody upravleniia promyshlennymi korporatsiiami.* Moscow: "Nauka," 1972.

_____, ed. *Organizatsionnye struktury upravleniia proizvodstvom.* Moscow: "Ekonomika," 1975.

Mochalov, B.M. "The Application of Active Educational Methods in the USSR." Washington, D.C.: National Science Foundation, 1975:2.

Mohr, Lawrence. "The Concept of Organizational Goal." *American Political Science Review,* 67 (June 1973): 470–81.

Moiseenko, N.A., and M.V. Popov. *Demokraticheskii tsentralizm—osnovnoi printsip upravleniia sotsialisticheskoi ekonomikoi.* Moscow: "Lenizdat," 1975.

Mouzelis, Nicos. *Organizations and Bureaucracy.* Chicago: Aldine, 1967.

Nette, J.P. *The Soviet Achievement.* New York: Harcourt, Brace & World, 1967.

Newman, Derek. *Organizational Design: An Analytical Approach to the Structuring of Organizations.* London: Edward Arnold, 1973.

Oligin–Nesterov, V.I. *Isod'zovanie ekonomicheskikh zakonov sotsializma i upravlenie proizvodstvom.* Moscow: "Mysl," 1973.

Ordiorne, George S. *Management by Objectives.* New York: Pitman, 1970.

Organizatsiia i upravlenie proizvodstvom v kapitalishicheskikh predpriiatiiakh anglii i SSHA (The Organization and Management of Product in Capitalist Factories in England and the USA). Moscow: 1957.

Ozira, V. "Concrete Cases in Management Education." Washington, D.C.: National Science Foundation, 1975.

_____. "How Teaching Is Done at a School of Business." *Literaturnaia gazeta,* 41 (October1968):11; partially trans. in *CDSP,* 1 (November 1968):15.

_____. "Obuchenie pri pomoshci analiz khoziaislvennykh situatsii." *Vestnik moskovskogo universiteta,* ser. 7 (Ekonomika), 5 (1968).

_____. *Ob opyte shveinogo ob "edineniia 'bol'shevickhka na novuiu sistemu khoziaistvovaniia.* Moscow: MGU, 1969.

_____, and A.E. Luzin. *Konsul'tatsionnye firmy kapitalisticheskikh stran po upravleniiu.* Moscow: "Ekonomika," 1975.

Parsons, Talcott. *Structure and Process in Modern Societies.* New York: Free Press, 1960.

Perrow, Charles. *Complex Organizations: A Critical Essay.* Glenview, Ill.: Scott, Foresman, 1972.

Petrella, Riccardo, and Adam Schaff. *A European Experiment in Cooperation in the Social Sciences.* Vienna: European Coordination Centre for Research and Documentation in Social Sciences, 1974.

Petrov, A.S. *Chto takoe organizatsiia upravleniia.* Moscow: "Znanie," 1967.

_____. *Ekonomicheskie osnovy upravleniia proizvodstvom.* Moscow: "Mysl," 1966.

Pine, Art. "Reagan's August Guns: Critics Shout Their Warning Cries." *Washington Post,* 7 June 1981, p. H1.

Popov, G.K. "Nauka upravliat," *Pravda,* 28 Feb. 1970, p2.

_____, ed. *Organizatsiia protsessov upravleniia.* Moscow: "Ekonomika," 1975.

_____. *Problemy teorii upravleniia,* 2d ed., rev. and enl. Moscow: "Ekonomika," 1974.

_____, and V. Lisitsyn. "Khoziaistovovanie: Problemy i suzhdeniia." *Pravda,* 2 December 1968, p. 2.

_____, and V. Lisitsyn. "Krugozor Khoziaistvennika." *Pravda*, 19 Jan. 1968, p. 2.

_____, and V. Poshataev. "Strategiia upravleniia." *Pravda*, 15 Dec. 1971, p. 2.

Popov, M.V., and N.A. Moiseenko. *Demokraticheskii tsentralizm: osnovnsi printsip upravlenii sotsialisticheskoi ekonomikoi.* (*Democratic Centralism: Basic Principle of Managing the Socialist Economy*). Leningrad: "Lenizdat," 1975.

Pozdniakov, O.A. *O Problemakh nauchnoi organizatsii truda i upravleniia.* Moscow: "Lenizdat," 1969.

Presthus, Robert. *The Organizational Society.* New York: Vantage, 1962.

Razumova, I.I. *SShA organizatsiia upravleniia zavodami. Referativnyi ukazatel'tekhnicheskoi literatury (Reference Guide to Technical Literature).* Moscow: "Nauka," 1975.

Reskim, V. "Chto takoe PERT?" ("What Is PERT?"). *Sotsialisticheskii trud.* no. 8 (August 1964).

Riabov, I. "Sovershenstvovat' strukturu upravleniia." *Izvestia*, 18 Jan. 1976, p. 3.

Richman, Barry. *Management Development and Education in the Soviet Union.* East Lansing, Mich.: Michigan State Univ. Press, 1967.

_____. *Soviet Management: With Significant American Comparisons.* Englewood Cliffs, N.J.: Prentice-Hall, 1965.

Roethlisberger, Fritz. *Management and Morale.* Cambridge, Mass.: Harvard Univ. Press, 1941.

_____, and William Dickson. *Management and the Worker: Technical vs. Social Organization in an Industrial Plant.* Boston: Harvard Univ. Graduate School of Business Administration, 1934.

Ross, Arthur. "The Data Game." *Washington Monthly*, 1 (February 1969):64.

Ross, Kenton. "Implementing a Management by Objectives Philosophy." In *Management by Objectives.* Cleveland: Association for Systems Management, 1971.

Rowe, James L., Jr. "Corporate American Wallowing in Debt," *Washington Post*, 18 Aug. 1980, p. D1.

Rozmirovich, E.F. *Metodologiia i praktika tekhnika upravleniia (Methodology and the Practice of Administrative Techniques).* Moscow: "Teknika Upravleniia," 1927.

_____. "K itogam raboty tki po not" ("On the Results of RKI's Work on *NOT*") *Voprosy sovetskogo khoziaistva i upravleniia*, 45 (1924):277.

Ruggie, John Gerard. "Complexity, Planning, and Public Order." In *Organized Social Complexity*, ed. Todd R. LaPorte. Princeton: Princeton Univ. Press, 1975.

Ryavec, Karl. *Implementation of Soviet Economic Reforms: Political, Organizational, and Social Processes.* New York: Praeger, 1975.

Schapiro, Leonard. *The Communist Party of the Soviet Union.* New York: 1959. Quoted in Abraham Katz, *The Politics of Economic Reform in the Soviet Union* New York: Random House, 1968.

Schwartz, Donald. "Recent Soviet Adaptations of Systems Theory to Administrative Theory." *Journal of Comparative Administration*, 2 (August 1973):233–63.

Selznick, Phillip. *Leadership in Administration.* Evanston, Ill.: Ron, Peterson, 1957.

_____. *The Organizational Weapon.* Glencoe, Ill.: Free Press, 1960.

Serb, P. "Nauchnaia organizatsiia truda na rabochem meste" ("The Scientific Organization of Labor in the Workplace). *Sotsialisticheskii trud.*, no. 8 (August 1964):33.

Shcherban', A.N., ed. *Nauchnaia organizatsiia truda i upravleniia (The Scientific Organization of Labor and Management)*, 2d ed. Moscow: 1966.

Shcherbitskii, V. "Partiinye organizatsii i sovershenstvovanie upravleniia ekonomikoi." *Kommunist*, 6 (April 1973):19–33; excerpted in *Current Digest of the Soviet Press*, 25, no. 36 (3 Oct. 1973):6.

Sherif, Muzafer. *The Psychology of Social Norms*. New York: Harper & Bros., 1936.

Shorin, V.G., ed. *Aktual'nye problemy upravleniia*. Moscow: "Znanie," 1972.

Shull, Fremont A. *Matrix Structure and Project Authority for Optimizing Organizational Capacity*. Carbondale: Southern Illinois Univ. School of Business, 1965.

Simon, Herbert A. *Administrative Behavior*. New York: Macmillan, 1961.

——. *The Architecture of Complexity*. Cambridge, Mass.: MIT, 1968.

——. *Models of Man*. New York: Wiley, 1957.

——. "The Proverbs of Administration." *Public Administration Review*, 6 (Winter 1946):53–67.

——. *The Sciences of the Artificial*. Cambridge, Mass.: MIT, 1969.

——. *The Shape of Automation for Men and Management*, New York: Harper & Row, 1965.

Sloan, Alfred P., Jr. *My Years with General Motors*. Garden City, N.Y.: Doubleday, 1972.

Smith, Clagett G. "A Comparative Analysis of Some Conditions and Consequences of Intraorganizational Conflict." *Administrative Science Quarterly*, 10 (1966):504–29.

Society of Machine-Building (*Vintomash*). *Organizatsiia i ekonomika mashinostroitei' nogo proizvokstva (The Organization and Economics of Machine-Building Production)*. Moscow: "Mashgiz," 1951.

"Sotrudnichestvo uchenykh." *Pravda*, 5 Aug. 1976.

Sovershenstvovanie organizatsionnoi struktury upravleniia sotsialistecheskim proizvodstvom: kratkii spisor literatury na russkom iazyke za 1970–1975 gg. Moscow: 1973.

Spinney, Franklin C. "Defense Facts of Life." (Mimeograph, 1980.)

Spulber, Nicolas, ed. *Foundations of Soviet Strategy for Economic Growth: Selected Soviet Essays, 1924–1930*. Bloomington: Indiana Univ. Press, 1964.

Stalin, Joseph. *Economic Problems of Socialism in the USSR*. New York: International, 1952.

Steinbrunner, John. *The Cybernetic Theory of Decision*. Princeton, N.J.: Princeton Univ. Press, 1974.

Suppes Patrick, and M. Schlag-Rey. "Analysis of Social Conformity in Terms of Generalized Conditioning Models." In *Mathematical Models in Small Group Processes*, ed. Joan Criswell, Herbert Solomon, and Patrick Suppes. Palo Alto, Cal.: Stanford Univ. Press, 1962.

Syroezhin, I.M. *Ekonomicheskaia kibernetika: chast'i, osnovy teorii khoziaistvennyky sistem*. Leningrad: Leiningradskogo Universiteta, 1974.

——. "Man-Machine Systems in the USSR." *Management Science*, 2 (October 1968):b4–b7.

——. I.I. Kurochkin, and S.R. Gidrovich. *Simulated Game Models as a Means of*

Management Training and a Form of Collective Decision-Making. Leningrad: 1975.

Tannenbaum, Arnold S., et al., *Hierarchy in Organizations.* San Francisco: Jossey-Bass, 1974.

Taylor, Frederick Winslow. *The Principles of Scientific Management.* New York and London: Harper & Bros., 1911; paperback ed. New York: W.W. Norton, 1967.

Thompson, James Clay. *Rolling Thunder.* Chapel Hill: Univ. of North Carolina Press, 1980.

Thompson James D. *Organizations in Action.* New York: McGraw-Hill, 1967.

Thompson, Victor. *Modern Organizations.* New York: Knopf, 1961.

Tikhomirov, I.A. *Vlast' i upravlenie v sotsialisticheskom obshechestve.* Moscow: "Iuridichekaia Literatura," 1968.

———, et al. "O nauke upravleniia" ("On the Science of Management"). *Sovetskoe gosudarstva i pravo,* no. 9 (1964):112–22.

Ulrich, Robert A., and George F. Wieland. *Organization Theory and Design,* rev. ed. Georgetown, Ont.: Irwin-Dorsey, 1980.

Urban, Michael E. "Bureaucracy, Contradiction, and Ideology in Two Societies." *Administration and Society,* May 1978.

Vasil'ev, I.P. *Novaia tekhnika v sisteme upravleniia proizvodstvom za rubezhom.* Moscow: Progress, 1972.

Vidmer, Richard F. "Administrative Science in the USSR: Doctrinal Constraints on Inquiry." *Administration and Society,* May 1980.

———. "The Emergence of Administrative Science in the USSR: Toward a Theory of Organizational Emulation." *Policy Sciences,* 11 (1979).

———. "Management Science in the USSR: The Role of Americanizers." *International Studies Quarterly,* 24 (September 1980):392–414.

Volovich, V.N. *Mesto i rol' upravlencheskikh otnoshenii proizvokstva v ekonomicheskoi strukture sotsialischeskogo obshchestva (The Place and Role of Administrative Relations of Production in the Economic Structure of Socialist Society).* Leningrad: 1975.

Von Laue, Theodore H. *Why Lenin? Why Stalin?* New York: J.B. Lippincott, 1964.

Voznesinsky, Nicholai Aleksievich. *The Economy of the USSR during World War II.* Washington: Public Affairs Press, 1948.

Wahba, Muhmaud, and Lawrence Bridwell. "Maslow Reconsidered: A Review of Research on the Need Hierarchy Theory." In *Organizational Behavior and Human Performance,* 15 (1976):212–40.

———. "A Review of Research on the Need Hierarchy Theory." In *Organizational Behavior and Industrial Psychology: Readings with Commentary,* ed. Kenneth Wexley and Gard Yukl. New York: Oxford Univ. Press, 1975.

White, Robert. "Motivation Reconsidered: The Concept of Competence." *Psychological Review,* 66 (1969):297–333.

Wilensky, Harold. *Organizational Intelligence.* New York: Basic Books, 1967.

Wilson, Woodrow. "The Study of Administration." *Political Science Quarterly,* June 1887; reprinted in *Classics of Public Administration,* ed. Jay M. Shafritz and Albert C. Hyde. Oak Park, Ill.: Moore, 1978.

Wright, J. Patrick. *On a Clear Day You Can See General Motors*. New York: Avon, 1979.

Yenyutim, Lyudmila. "Management: Exchange of Views." *Soviet Life*, April 1975:54–56.

Zajonc, Robert. *Social Psychology: An Experimental Approach*. Belmont, Cal.: Wadsworth, 1966; Brooks-Cole, 1967.

Zaltman, Gerald, Robert Duncan, and Jonny Holbek. *Innovations and Organizations*. New York: Wiley-Interscience, 1973.

Zauberman, Alfred. *The Mathematical Revolution in Soviet Economics*. London: Oxford Univ. Press, 1975.

Zimmerman, William. "Issue Area and Foreign-Policy Process: A Research Note in Search of a General Theory." *American Political Science Review*, 67 (1973).

——. *Soviet Perspective on International Relations, 1956-1967*. Princeton: Princeton Univ. Press, 1969.

——. "The Soviet Union." In *Conflict in World Politics*, ed. Stephen Spiegel and Kenneth Waltz. Cambridge, Mass.: Winthrop, 1971.

Index

Academy of Sciences Soviet, 75–76, 94, 95, 99, 100, 102
Adfel'dt, N. V., 92
Administrative Science
  as rooted in assumption of rationality, 106–8
  definition of, 2
  diffusion into Soviet Union, 3–6
  emergence of, 8–30
  flaws in early, 3
  interdisciplinary nature of the field, 6–7
  similarities between US and USSR, 4
Afghanistan, Soviet invasion of, 1, 6, 99
Aganbegyan, Abel, 77, 102, 146
Allison, Graham T., 1, 50, 56
All-Union conference, 46, 75
All-Union Institute for Scientific and Technical Information (VINITI), 93–94
All-Union Scientific Research Institute for Problems of Organization and Management, 148
American Council of Learned Societies, 99
American Management Association, 123
Ansoff, Igor, 118
Arapov, M., 33
Asch, Solomon, 61
Ashby, W. Ross, 79
ASTRA (gaming model in the Soviet Union), 127
Austin, John, 123

Automotive industry in US
  early years, 19–21, 52
  government intervention in, 52, 54
Averchevyi, V. P., 117

Babin, M. G., 81, 137
Ball, George, 62
Barnard, Chester, 97
Beer, Stafford, 79
Berg, A. I., 79, 147
Beria, Laurenti, 73
Bermant, Mikhail, 99
Binzen, L., 56
Birman, A. M., 84
Birshtein, M. M., 128
Bogdanov, A. A., as related to Tektogy, 42–43, 88
Bogodarov, P., 33
Bohr, Neils, 15
Bratsk-Ilimsk Territorial Production Complex (BITPC), 104
Brezhnev, Leonid, 90, 92, 133, 137, 139, 150, 152
Bukharin, 74
Bukov, V. N., 128
Bulganin, 74
Bureau of Foreign Science and Technology (BINT), 40, 134
Business games
  as influencing Soviet administrative science, 114
  as a training device in the Soviet Union, 126–28
  in the Soviet Union, 121, 123–26